tomorrow's naked lawyer

NewTech, NewHuman, NewLaw

How to be successful, 2015 to 2045

entrepreneurlawyer®
LAWYERS OF TOMORROW, TODAY

Author
Chrissie Lightfoot

Published by
Globe Law and Business Ltd
3 Mylor Close
Horsell
Woking
Surrey GU21 4DD
United Kingdom
Tel: +44 20 3745 4770
www.globelawandbusiness.com

ISBN: 978-1-78358-174-0
A catalogue record for this book is available from the British Library

Contents

preface

AND SO it began... Exactly four years since *the naked lawyer* hip hopped and jazzed onto law law land's stage, after much soul searching, deliberation, and dogged determination, I sat down to bring the sequel to you. Here it is – *tomorrow's naked lawyer* – my second book in the cheeky naked lawyer series. WooHoo! Prrrrrrrrrrrrr.

It's not the book I intended to write, for writing a sequel is darn difficult, you see. The pressure and expectation I put on myself to produce a book to follow on from my (well-received) first effort was exacerbated and amplified by our world continually moving along at an accelerating speed, in so many fields, that I found it difficult to bring together a coherent manuscript that wouldn't be out of date by the time you came to read it! And, no doubt, it may already be so!!! Harrumph! Hey-ho, onward we go...

There's just so much really good stuff I wanted to try this time around, so much I wanted to talk about and share with you that, inevitably, I had to be rather ruthless with the final material to make sure that it met the quality standard of the *naked lawyer* series. I came to the realisation during the research stage that I had way too much material, too many topics I was bursting to explore, and an abundance of ideas to pursue so that, to remain focused on producing a manuscript about the innovation of the ROAR model to benefit the lawyer of today, tomorrow, I had to remind myself that 'if it doesn't fit in, then it doesn't fit in'. Focus pussycat, focus. Prrrrrrrrrrrrrrrrr.

The positive way to look at this, of course, is to realise that there is definite scope for a third book in the *naked lawyer* series! But let's chat about *tomorrow's naked lawyer*, shall we?

I hope you will agree, once you've turned the final page, that this book met (or exceeded) your expectations. It's rather different to what's out there already. Similar in mischievous theme and naughty style to *the naked lawyer*, naturally, but that's where the similarity ends. This book picks up where the previous one ended with a quick recap and reflection on the themes and lessons of the first book, and then moves swiftly on to cover the evolution of the ROAR model (in theory and practice) in this Digital, Technological, and Robotic Age.

tomorrow's naked lawyer is VERY futuristic (future focused), as well as being practical today (present focused), proffering insights, ideas, and examples which can be put into practice today to help you, the individual lawyer, and your business to grow toward, and be prepared for, the future.

I'm going to share with you some of the stuff I've shared with clients, delegates at conferences and private gatherings I've spoken at since *the naked lawyer* was published back in November 2010 to present day (i.e. over the past four years, 2010 to 2014). I'm also going to share with you case studies, interviews with, and comments from leading people in the law, and (to some degree, more importantly) those outside of the profession, some of whom have practised the ROAR model these past four years and achieved outstanding results. And, I'm going to be sharing with you my experience (positive and negative) during this period along with my insights into our likely future.

As you may suspect and expect, I build on the current thinking of a variety of subjects and explore, debate, and challenge conventional thinking and wisdom, particularly with regard to marketing, branding, technology, and the future of law for the period 2015 to 2045.

No, I don't have a crystal ball! No, I don't profess to be a soothsayer and don cape and pointy hat!! No, I don't have the talent, audacity, or balls (I'm a naked lady lawyer) to predict what our exact future is going to be!!! But YES, I do have the courage to attempt to predict what our future is likely to be, based on compelling research and thought leadership from a wide spectrum of resources and fields, and through speaking with a variety of authoritative, respected, admired, and credible people.

As ever, I don't anticipate that all (or presume that any) of you will simply accept and/or agree with all (or any) of what I say. In fact, I positively encourage you to question, reflect on, and debate the content with your colleagues, your friends, and most of all, yourself. For it may well be that while reading *tomorrow's naked lawyer* you experience a 'eureka moment' and need to prance off and give yourself a good talking to in search of the answers to questions you may be asking yourself as a direct outcome of what you read.

Please note: I don't have all the answers. I believe my job is to comfort those of you who have questions. In true NAKED LAWYER style I reckon my role is also to provoke those of you who are meandering along, and to entice you at the very least to begin to be curious, and at best to be stimulated to enquire about the possibilities for your future. Period. And, by the end of the read, if I have achieved this for you, then my job is done. If you are dissatisfied, then go ROAR in the mirror!

why write tomorrow's naked lawyer?

I've written *tomorrow's naked lawyer* because of readers' demands, publisher's expectations, my personal desire to help, and love of the law and justice. Bottom line: I was egged on to do it from numerous quarters, and no persuasion was necessary. *tomorrow's naked lawyer* exists now because those who read the first book want more goodies, more dancing, more ROARing, and updated prrrrrrrrrrrrrrrrrrrrrrrrrring.

the naked lawyer has been a best-seller, read feverishly around the globe and in every corner. It's enjoyed a 'long-run'. It has helped countless lawyers, law firms, and businesses of law – and I wish to continue helping wherever possible! Accordingly, questions, answers, and insights in relation to the legal world need to be explored and shared further. It's timely.

Since the dawn of mankind, we have evolved to survive many challenges, radical changes, disruptions, and 'ages'. In the legal world and beyond, we are now experiencing a new 'Artificially Intelligent' and 'Robotic Age', and those who want to survive it and be a part of it will need to evolve too. Today's lawyers, legal leaders, entrepreneurs, you and I, face an uncertain future. With changes already underway to everything from training culture, the competitive environment, to different modes of service delivery, we need to equip ourselves for the road ahead.

To quote the futurist Dr Peter Bishop: 'There will be significant change within our tenure within any position within our lifetime for sure, that we will have to learn to live in a new world… It will be new enough that we will be uncomfortable, we will be unprepared, and that we will have to learn new skills and new techniques in order to be successful in that future compared to how we are being successful today, or indeed how we were prepared to be successful when we were in school or training.'

We all know about all the change that's already affecting us within the legal profession and industry, including changing regulation, legal aid cuts, increased competition, and ever more pressure on the bottom line. But the pace of change will only pick up, and in ways we may not expect.

The problem – or blessing, depending how you wish to view and/or feel about the Robotic Age – is that tomorrow, everything will be connected. Today, there's actually a load of stuff that is already connected. (Anybody who has recently uploaded IOS8 no doubt shared my frustration re the darn thing connecting all of my digital devices and deciding to automatically share everything, everywhere!)

Stating the obvious, technology is rapidly transforming how we communicate, shop, play, live, love, and work. Having witnessed cupcakes served by a machine 'hole-in-the-wall' recently, I reckon the writing (err, robot) is on the wall…

the robots have taken all the jobs

The transition is already underway. Cities will be run by robots and machines could potentially wipe out a significant proportion of the workforce, globally. And that means (potentially) you and me too. So, we can either deal with this potential evolution in a positive way and adapt for the good of the (global) legal and justice systems, the consumer/customer/client, the business, and ultimately for ourselves, or we can fight the machines. The latter, I reckon, may not even be an option…

The global internet, artificial intelligence/machine intelligence, and robotic engineering has already bolted from the R&D labs and been embraced in a multitude of fields, industries, and services, commercially. The money-go-round is already spinning. Fight the machines? Pah! The luddites didn't succeed and nor will the 'robodites' (IMHO). And so to my thoughts about the implications and opportunities with regard to artificial intelligence and robotics in the legal world. Let's look at dealing with all this stuff positively…

The problem with the legal and justice system and legal service delivery, not just in the UK but across the globe, is that it is usually expensive, slow, inefficient, outcomes are uncertain, and increasingly legal issues cross geographic and language boundaries.

The lawyers/law firms are, in truth, not always TRULY client-focused, TRULY customer-centric – i.e. are not TRULY interested in challenging some of the problems I highlight because of pure self-interest. So, consider this, if a) we lawyers (or, maybe, it is our company leaders/power-monger/equity-fat lawyers/shareholders at the top of the tree) were not so egotistical, arrogant, ignorant, complacent, self-interested, self-absorbed, greedy, risk-averse, unadventurous, unimaginative, and lacking in innovative oomph; and b) technology was not a constraint… what are the kind of things we could see improved and automated with regard to lawyering, for the client/customer good, the public good, the business good (to build a viable/sustainable/feasible legal business) and the good of the legal justice system? I suggest the following:

1. THINKING – The quality and level of advocacy/reasoning and judgment could

be improved, and arguably automated, in due course.

We could, for example, introduce/discern truth telling and lie detecting into the legal process – that is, we could be able to deal with uncertainty better, which would assist lawyering whether by the human or the machine. Is this not the crux of the legal matter for many clients: a positive, quick outcome without having to pay exorbitant legal fees? (Aka a focus on prevention, rather than cure?) Surely, it is in the client's interest for a business of law to offer a legal service (even if machine-aided/enhanced) with the best mix of human and machine and technical support to achieve a win?

2. COLLABORATION – The enabling of multiple parties to come together 24/7/365 across multiple geographic boundaries.

   Improvement and automation may only be a stone's throw away where all parties could collaborate on the same document at the same time, virtually, and be aided by machine/artificial intelligence. For example, we could have multiple lawyers and their respective clients from all around the world gathered around the virtual table. We wouldn't need to meet face to face. Imagine the HUGE amount of time and expense that could be saved, and how the speed of the legal matter could be accelerated, if we could eliminate the requirement to travel, and come together anytime, anyplace, anywhere 'on the line' or 'in the cloud'?

3. LANGUAGE TRANSLATION – The improvement and automation of language translation in legal documents.

   For example, the IBM Watson machine technology (artificial intelligence) understands English language and metaphors. It is inevitable, therefore, that machines/robots can/will speak, in due course, no doubt supporting/assisting both contentious and non-contentious lawyering.

   Currently, the computerised (AI) document systems 'out there' deal with the grunt-work, 'doing' aspect usually attributed and associated with junior lawyering. As the DOING aspect become more prevalent and acceptable in law law land, the real value going forward for the client, the lawyer, and the business of law will be in the THINKING element, I believe. Accordingly, if a machine/robot can think and do better than a human lawyer, then could this be the holy grail/USP/POD/competitive edge for the savvy lawyer, the business of law, and ultimately the client? Can robots think now? Sort of. (I will share this with you in Chapters 3 and 6.)

   Without sounding defeatist or pessimistic, for you know I am forever the pragmatist and optimist, I envisage that the usual problems in law law land will remain, for we seem to see the recurring issues and problems perpetuating year after year, decade after decade, with marginal progress. No doubt we will continue to stick plasters on the same issues whether they land on skin or silicone. So, if you want to make sure you, the company, the legal system, we/mankind, evolve and change for the better, we'd all better sit up, get AIG, and do something. NOW!

I propose we begin by:

- Embracing the new breed of consumer/customer/client;

- Embracing our humanness;
- Embrace additional/new lawyerly skills such as relationship building, rainmaking, commercial savvy, intrapreneurial and entrepreneurial skills;
- Embrace the role technology plays for the lawyer, the business, and the client, for example CRM – it's an aid/tool to assist humanness/relationship-building, maintenance, and growth;
- Embrace the full spectrum of choice and opportunity to provide low-cost commoditised services juxtaposed with high-cost, high-end, IC, EI, intelligent provision;
- Being smarter about relationships, marketing, business development, communication;
- Being smarter about being social; and
- Being smarter about pricing and profit', ergo:
    - Ensuring the work we do is valued as well as of value;
    - Respecting the lean start-ups and behemoth international players – every lawyer, and business of law, has its place and value;
    - Watching and learning from the new sexy players in law law land that have a blank sheet, that can start from scratch with a new sexy business model, new sexy investors, and with the latest sexy technology – usually cloud-based vfm tech rather than expensive legacy systems.

And so, if you hadn't already figured it out, this book follows on from the content in *the naked lawyer* and covers the practice, evolution, and future use of the ROAR model in this Robotic Age. Unlike *the naked lawyer* in which each volume/chapter knits together as a step-by-step sales model, this book is different; it attempts to deal with a variety of problems which still plague law law land and proffers solutions based on theory and practice from both the legal world and business world of the present and (likely) future.

As the title suggests, *tomorrow's naked lawyer: NewTech, NewHuman, NewLaw – How to be successful, 2015 to 2045*, is VERY futuristic as well as practical for today, proffering insights, ideas, and examples which can be put into practice now to help you and your business grow toward, and be prepared for, the future.

I look at what's happened since I wrote *the naked lawyer* back in 2010 (the past four years), where we are now (questioning, have we truly progressed?), and crystal ball gaze at where 'law law land' is likely headed in the context of helping to prepare you, the individual lawyer and business person, for our likely future.

I particularly look at the burgeoning tension between the liberalisation and exploitation of artificial intelligence and robotics and the requirement to balance the human and technological aspect of lawyering for the benefit of the lawyer, the business, and the client, keeping ROAR as the central model and the need to 'get naked' as the central theme throughout.

It is my belief that placing the client at the centre of everything, the continual striving toward extraordinary customer service and reaching out and relating ('R-O-A-R-ing'), whether by human touch, machine intelligence, or robotic interaction, will continue to be THE differentiator between those lawyers who (and businesses which) survive, grow, and excel and those who simply walk slowly toward an inevitable demise (or splat horrendously). In short, I attempt to reduce the complex to the simple.

how is the book organised?

Throughout *tomorrow's naked lawyer*, I share

my experiences and escapades over these past few years, along with insights into our likely future together and ideas for the way forward in the guise of an imaginary prancing, private dancing, prrrrrrrrring 'naked lawyer' in law law land (again). After all, it would be rude not to.

The information I share is presented in a variety of ways and styles. For example, there are chapters and sections where I indulge in storytelling, cheekiness, and sexiness, and others that are (perhaps alien to those of you who read *the naked lawyer*) written in a more typically journalistic and lawyerly prose.

I have done this for a reason. I wish this book, not unlike *the naked lawyer*, to reflect and practise what it preaches, and I'd like you to enjoy 'an experience' as you read. We are in a world of contrast, uncertainty, and in some respects, no rules. I reckon it would be beneficial for you to actually feel this as you turn the pages and enjoy this book as an adventure, not knowing where it is going or what is going to happen next. This is, after all, the nature of business, law, and life!

Unlike *the naked lawyer*, in this sequel you're not just going to be hearing from me. There are a handful of eminent professionals who have contributed a variety of quotes from my interviews with them, or paragraphs, and even sections. Their contributions add a great deal of value to what you are about to read and learn. I promise.

Chapter 1 sets the scene (the context in which I am writing the book) and provides you with my personal views on the kind of world we live and work in, the past, present, and future legal landscape, and I compare and contrast the old and new legal way and the problems and opportunities each of these creates.

In Chapter 2, I switch up a gear and begin to stick my dancing legal beagle bootie in. I share with you past, present, and future trends along with a number of pertinent reports and research material from prominent and credible individuals and companies to enlighten you as to what to watch out for. I then proffer a variety of insights, guidance, and tips as to how to embrace this knowledge and prepare yourself for your likely future.

In Chapter 3 we go 'far out' – I'm talking about our robotic life, 2015 to 2045, the era of avatars, artificial intelligence, icyborg lawyers, and robot lawyers in a Robotic Age. Exciting times. Exhilarating chapter!

Chapter 4 is all about you, 'tomorrow's naked lawyer' – that is preparing yourself for your transition and likely lawyerly role in the years to come. I proffer ideas in relation to improving your education, training, and skill sets, highlighting gamification, psycho-lawyernetics, rainmaking, storytelling, intrapreneurism, and entrepreneurism, to name a few.

Throughout Chapter 5 we look in detail at our imminent future – that is the next few years, 2015 to 2020 – and I introduce you to a new concept – SocialHuman in online 'social land'. We're talking social savvy junkie re-invented, the magic of a brand trio, brand piggy-backing, smart words, smart behaviour, and smart pricing of the brand message. I then tease you with what is likely to be the next big thing in social (with the help of a scientist) – namely, resonance, vibe tribes, and social vibe intelligence, sharing a description of the latest technology together with '3D diagrams'. I conclude the chapter with a number of case studies documenting what is likely to be the successful way forward for you in social land in the near future.

In the penultimate chapter (6), I'm talking about the NewTech, NewHuman, and NewLaw referred to in the title. Yep, we are prancing, dancing, and prrrrrrrrrrrrring into the really futuristic stuff, but not without first addressing the legal technology available today to support you in your transitioning hybrid lawyer role. Perhaps some of you may think I'm going a little too far by talking 'robot wife', 'robot hooker', and 'law on Mars' in the Robotic Age. Nevertheless, you'll be able to say that 'you read it first here'!

Chapter 7 brings everything together. It's a wrap-up chapter of all that has come before in Chapters 1–6 in terms of key messages, theories, concepts, practicalities, and future thinking and action. I pose to you the question: 'Are you ready to change your world, or change the world?' For in this 'age of magic and miracles', nothing is certain – but anything is possible. And, of course, I couldn't leave you without injecting some more humour, so you can expect it here.

who is the book written for?

If it is not already obvious, I am writing the book to be appealing, globally, and to be of benefit to, in particular:

- Lawyers and 'non-lawyers' (I hate that term) – All of you, from student to the board in the businesses of law and GCs in corporate behemoths;
- All personnel in professional service firms – The content is as relevant for you as it is for lawyers;
- All support personnel in professional service firms – E.g. business development, marketing, sales, CRM, relationship managers, learning and development, knowledge managers, social media managers/executives, etc., etc., etc.;
- All suppliers to the professions;
- Consumers and businesses – You, the buyer of professional services and products;
- Investors interested in funding a start-up businesses of law, or getting involved with an existing company providing legal services and products;
- Entrepreneurs, intrapreneous, and innovators; and
- Anyone who is curious as to their future and how to skill-up and prepare for it.

do you need to read *the naked lawyer*?

No. You don't need to have read *the naked lawyer* to enjoy and learn from *tomorrow's naked lawyer*, that's why I've provided a handy recap of that report's key takeaways at the front of this book. But those of you who have read it will, perhaps, gain just that little bit more from this title. (No, this is not a ruse to get you to line my pockets with golden doubloons or cryptocurrency bitcoins. I simply respectfully draw your attention to the fact that the concepts, teachings, and substance of the ROAR model I wrote about in *the naked lawyer* cannot possibly be regurgitated in their entirety here – understandably.)

the mischievous Prof

You may recognise the title of the final volume of *the naked lawyer*, 'XXX rated – tomorrow's lawyer', in the title of Professor Richard Susskind's latest book *tomorrow's lawyers* (published three years later, in 2013), which he no doubt nicked (oops, I mean he was 'inspired') as we continue to challenge and, dare I presume, inspire one another in our work and shared passion. Respect, dear Prof. Prrrrrrrrrrrrrrrrrrrr.

Accordingly, I felt that the title of the sequel to *the naked lawyer* ought to reflect the ongoing friendly duel and mutual respect between two professionals who approach our respective topics in completely different styles, yet share the same dance in continually innovating, pushing the boundaries, and breaking down the walls in law law land.

warning – naked adult content

While I deal with serious matters by providing serious information, messages, solutions, material, and ideas throughout *tomorrow's naked lawyer*, I take an idiosyncratic approach, yet again. It is, after all, the *naked lawyer* series' indomitable style. But it may or may not be to your taste.

In the chapters which follow you will note that there is an 'adult' element and theme throughout. But that's OK, I reckon. We're all adults. And, of course, you have the choice as to whether you wish to read any further. I dare you to read on...

Most writers are reserved in their writing style, tone, and approach for fear of causing offence, being rebuffed, receiving negative feedback, and being vilified. Sorry, not me. If you don't like what I'm saying or don't want to hear what I'm saying, then that's okay. Ignore me. It's your choice. If you don't wish to have a laugh, either at me or yourself, then *tomorrow's naked lawyer* is probably not your cup of cocoa. Go and work through a hum-drum professional or academic marketing/branding/social media/technology/futurist book instead, perhaps?

Only those of you who wish to give yourself the best possible chance of succeeding in the challenging years ahead, those of you who wish to take control of your future by preparing and acting now for it, and ultimately those of you who wish to create your future and embrace it with a sense of humour and with an appreciation for sex will truly enjoy it. I am confident that we are many.

In case you hadn't got the picture by now, I'm not going to beat around the bush. I'm just going to say it as it is... No nonsense. No sugar-coating. Just pure gut-wrenching thought, feeling, and action. This book is NOT going to be like the usual boring, dry-rot, scholastic clap trap tomes. There's a place for that – it's called the traditional law firm. For this book is written purely for you, the aspirant lawyer, existing lawyer, and non-lawyer who:

- Wishes to excel in the business of law; and/or
- Proudly serves in a truly customer-centric business of law; and/or
- Will bring about positive change in legal provision throughout the world; and/or
- Will truly be the difference; and/or
- Wishes to change your world; and/or
- Wishes to change THE world.

And with this in mind, we're going to have some fun, because when we have fun, we learn best. If I can help even just a handful of you, again, then the potential vilification will be worth it... and most of all, I'd be honoured. For those of you who choose to read on, I promise you this: *tomorrow's naked lawyer* will certainly be an informative, fun, and sexy way of my pouring and prrrrrrring (teaching) and you sponging (absorbing).

do you need to read *tomorrow's naked lawyer*?

No. If you prefer to stick your head in the sand and arse in the air in the hope that the Technological Age and all this digital, artificial intelligence, and robot gubbins is going to go away, then don't bother.

Yes, absolutely. If you're curious, intrigued, and want to be prepared for the inevitable robotic (legal) world of our future. Whatever you perceive and/or envisage that to be and whatever evolves and transpires. One thing is for certain...

the robots are coming

They're already here! I am, therefore, unwaveringly confident that the stuff I share with you throughout this book will be of some value. As the idiom states: 'forewarned is forearmed'. I have every confidence that when you work through *tomorrow's naked lawyer*, you will understand and appreciate precisely why it is an apt title.

why listen to me?

Because I give a damn. I genuinely care about you (the lawyer) and your future, and you, the entrepreneur who aspires to agitate, disrupt and make changes for the better with regard to legal services and provision, and most of all for YOU, the reader, who may at some point in your personal or professional life need legal help.

What's more, I draw constant inspiration and the ear of the leading lawyers, professors, thinkers, innovators, scientists, futurists, and consultants in various fields around the world who share their insights with me (and now you) and who continually devote their lives to theorising (thinking) and preparing in practice (doing) for the short, medium, and long term in law law land.

To give you confidence, this is what delegates have said about what I have shared with them in my speeches, writing, and counsel these past few years – and it's what I will be sharing with you (and more) throughout this book:

- '...eloquent description of the past, the present and the future'
- '...you go a lot further into the future than Professor Richard Susskind in his talks. It is a scary thought but hopefully one that we can capitalise on'
- '...delivered a fascinating talk which really gave our delegates a real jolt. Chrissie reminded them that embracing change need not be a step in the dark, but rather a chance to revitalise their businesses. Chrissie is a pro who is very knowledgeable and above all, good fun to work with!'
- '...technological developments at a high level... potential impact on professional services... you took that awareness to a very new level. Your talk was fascinating and it's given me an opportunity to consider application of technologies in a way that I hadn't contemplated before'
- '...if you want to conquer Social Media then you must listen to this lady!'
- '...a very worthwhile investment!!'

for more rave reviews... please check out:

- the naked lawyer eBook: http://entrepreneurlawyer.co.uk/products-services/ebook/reviews
- Speaker testimonials: http://entrepreneurlawyer.co.uk/products-services/seminars-events
- Advisory/consultancy work: http://entrepreneurlawyer.co.uk/about/testimonials

I am confident you will find *tomorrow's naked lawyer* a worthy investment too. All that remains is for you to pour yourself a glass of wine, curl up in a comfy chair, click on your reading light, and turn the page... Enjoy!

about the author

HI! WELCOME to *tomorrow's naked lawyer*, the most recent book in the *naked lawyer* series! I'm Chrissie Lightfoot, a 'prominent international legal figure', an entrepreneur turned solicitor and back again as CEO of EntrepreneurLawyer Ltd, a global consulting business specialising in relationship 'SocialHuman' sales and based in the UK. It is an absolute delight and honour to be your host and to have this opportunity again to entertain you.

bit of background

I am a solicitor (non-practising), consultant, regular international keynote speaker, legal futurist, legal and business commentator, a writer, and 'an inspirational woman entrepreneur'. In 2013 I was nominated and honoured as 'Legal Professional of the Year 2013', and a 'Top 100 International Executive' – as published in the *International Top 100 Business Magazine*.

I love advising you – individual lawyers, entrepreneurs, and your companies – globally on the future of legal services, products and provision, smart legal buying, personal branding, social media, social networking, marketing, business development, innovation, technology, artificial intelligence, and robotics in the law.

As a legal and business commentator I am quoted periodically in *The Times* (London), and the newspaper reported that I was 'one of the Top Ten Best Legal Tweeters'. So, you're in safe hands.

as an author...

I write for Lexis Nexis, *The Global Legal Post* e-zine, *Managing Partner* magazine, *TheRouse* e-zine, *The Law Society Gazette* ('In Business' blog), *Trinity Mirror* ('Totally Legal' blog), *ALPMA* (practice management blog), *Brand Yorkshire* (Marketing features/blog), *EnCountry* ('Entrepreneur Country' blog), and *Fresh Business Thinking* (blog).

As a UK national award and prize winning researcher I am honoured to be sought after to write many articles in both the legal and business press and am blessed to be a contributing author of a number of legal and business books.

I am best noted for my first solo book – the pioneering and groundbreaking best-seller *the naked lawyer: RIP to XXX – How to Market, Brand and Sell YOU!* – together with my consultancy and training in The ROAR Experience Social Media Programme. *the naked lawyer* is recommended and mentioned in Professor Richard Susskind's recent book, *Tomorrow's Lawyers* (2013), along with only a handful of select books as the go-to literature on the future of legal services.

In the past, I have held the positions of vice-chairman of the Federation of Small Businesses, (Teesside Branch – UK), women's enterprise ambassador (Yorkshire, UK), and a mentor on behalf of The Prince's Trust Million Makers Corporate Challenge (Yorkshire, UK). For 25 years I have been involved in various entrepreneurial, innovative, and commercial ventures and enjoyed successes throughout my exciting career to date, primarily in the legal, new media, management consultancy, and sport and leisure (including health and fitness) sectors.

as a lawyer and serial entrepreneur...

Sales and innovation have been my forte and passion. While training as a solicitor I was interested in the future of legal services, providing extraordinary client service, and increasing sales. Accordingly, I was proactive in innovating the quality and delivery of legal advice and was the brainchild of the firm's business start-up legal package, e-commerce proposition, in-house corporate knowledge hub, and entrepreneur and employee share scheme niche focus.

I was the first trainee solicitor in the UK and globally in the digital age to devise a unique personal brand – *Chrissie Lightfoot, The Entrepreneur Lawyer* – which achieved impressive sales and marketing results. I qualified as a solicitor in 2009 at a mid-tier law firm in Leeds, UK.

as an academic...

I achieved Bachelor of Arts (Honours) degree, 1st Class, in Leisure & Business Studies (1996), Masters in Law degree (2006), and Legal Practice Certificate (2008) at Nottingham Law School.

as an innovator and futurist...

I remain a passionate, vibrant, and determined woman on a mission dedicated to innovating in the legal industry to benefit you – the lawyer, entrepreneur and layman. My legal innovation involvement throughout the period 2010 to 2015 has included:

- 2015 – LawWithoutWalls project and initiative (Miami University School of Law, Florida, USA) – Entrepreneur Mentor for the project 'Harnessing The Power of Watson: Utilizing Cognitive Technology to Help the Law Firm Make Better Decisions and Build a Stronger Relationship with Clients'.
- 2014 – LawWithoutWalls Entrepreneur Mentor for the project 'Robot Lawyers: The Future of Online Chat Attorneys'.
- 2013/14 – Thought leader and contributor in ILTA's and *FastFuture*'s 2014 report 'Legal Technology Future Horizons: Strategic Imperatives for the Law Firm of the Future'.
- 2011/12 – Law Firm Marketing course (Fordham University School of Law, New York, USA).
- 2011/12 – College of Law (London, UK) LNTV Core Programme 5650 – Practice Management & Compliance: Branding, Social Media and Networking (co-contributor with Eversheds Managing Partner).

as a speaker and consultant...

I continue to be a speaker and consultant throughout the world to businesses of law and corporate enterprises beyond law law land with turnovers ranging from six figures to multi-billions.

Clients include(d): Top 20 law firms in the UK (including magic circle), Europe, USA, Australia and New Zealand, Law Society of England & Wales, Law Society of Scotland, International Bar Association (IBA), SIFA (UK), Fordham University School of Law (New York, USA), Harvard Law School (USA), Oxford University (UK), The University of Law (UK), UK National Associations, LawTech Europe, International Legal Technology Association (ILTA, USA & UK), Association of European Lawyers (AEL), Geneva Bar Association, Australian Legal Practice Management Association (ALPMA – Australia), Future Firm Forum (New Zealand), The Lawlink Group Ltd (New Zealand), Simpson & Western (Auckland, New Zealand); Jackson Russell (Auckland, New Zealand), McCullough Robertson Lawyers (Queensland, Australia), Schjodt Law Firm (Norway), Berwin Leighton Paisner LLP, Eversheds LLP, DLA LLP, Shoosmiths LLP, Nabarro LLP, Herbert Smith Freehills, King & Wood Mallesons, Pannone LLP, Connect2Law, X-Press Legal Services Ltd, Law Plain And Simple Ltd, St Paul's Chambers, Arcobalenomedia, Barker Brooks Publishing, Wilmington Publishing & Information Ltd, Easyjet, Baker Tilly, Grant Thornton, PwC Legal, Winscribe, Peppermint Technology, Deltek, Thomson Reuters, LexisNexis, Clio, *The Guardian*, *The Times*, Barclays Bank, Clydesdale Bank, and more...

Client achievement example: One partner in an Australian law firm, after reading the naked lawyer eBook, hearing me speak, consulting with me on the ROAR model, and putting into practice what I advocated (from a standing start and as a direct result) achieved £1 million ($1.6 million Aussie) in new client instruction fees financial year May 2011/2012, £2 million in 2012/13, and £4 million in 2013/14.

how can I help you and what do I actually do?

Well, I:

- Write, speak, advise, and consult on the topic 'How To Market, Brand & Sell YOU!' – throughout the UK & Internationally;
- Deliver The ROAR Social Media Experience – A groundbreaking sales programme which unlocks intrapreneur, rainmaker, and commercial potential;
- Advise on sales and marketing and innovation of the same, particularly in relation to the development of personal brands and use of the same in social media and social networks to attract and retain prospects and clients;
- Present/speak (20–90 minute sessions) and run sessions/workshops/roundtables – part planned, part ad-hoc – to meet individual and/or group objectives on the subjects of:
  - The future of law;
  - Smart legal buying;
  - Role of the lawyer;
  - SocialHuman – Personal brand and niching;
  - Social media, social networking, social brand, social business, and social technology;
  - Implications of artificial intelligence and robotics in the legal ecosystem;
  - Effective use of technology, artificial intelligence, and robotics in legal service and provision;
- Get involved in marketing and sales strategy, planning, creation, development, implementation, and execution of the same (including personal brands, and social media/networking) to build the sales pipeline and increase sales/instructions;
- Support the development of the internal business development/marketing/sales/social media/training/learning and development/IT function;

- Act as a high-level business introducer – Professional network (12,000+ globally) comprising leaders in industry, politicians, academics, entrepreneurs, and those in the professions of law, accountancy, banking and finance, health/medicine, insurance etc.;
- Author provocative content (for clients and press/media) to help educate and raise awareness for legal service providers and buyers of legal products as to the options and possibilities available;
- Challenge conventional thinking and practice and proffer solutions, insights, and ideas for innovative alternatives;
- Author provocative best-seller books, such as *the naked lawyer: RIP to XXX – How to Market, Brand and Sell You!*

Please do feel free to check out my track-record and profile by Googling me.

I'd welcome the opportunity to connect, so here's a few ways in which we can:

- Website: http://entrepreneurlawyer.co.uk
- Blog: http://entrepreneurlawyer.co.uk/blog
- Speaking: http://entrepreneurlawyer.co.uk/products-services/seminars-events
- LinkedIn: www.linkedin.com/in/chrissielightfoot
- Twitter1: @TheNakedLawyer
- Twitter 2: @EntrepreneurLaw
- Facebook: www.facebook.com/EntrepreneurLawyer
- YouTube1: www.youtube.com/TheNakedLawyer
- YouTube2: www.youtube.com/EntrepreneurLawyer

author's note

tomorrow's naked lawyer would never have been written without the encouragement and support of so many fabulous people. There are far too many wonderful people to thank individually, so please forgive me for this blanket message when I say a 'MASSIVE THANK-YOU' to all of you for inspiring and challenging me during the period it has taken to roll-out the sequel to the naked lawyer.

This book has been greatly improved as a result of your sharing, caring, and daring. Furthermore, just like *the naked lawyer*, I feel that it has been significantly enhanced by both the life and business experiences of you, my fellow friends, family, mentors, entrepreneurs, and lawyers in 'law law land', 'social land', and the business world, to whom I am hugely grateful.

To each and every one of you: a hug, my appreciation, and a prrrrrrrrrr.

Warmest regards

Chrissie Lightfoot

The Entrepreneur Lawyer (of the naked kind)

dedication

I DEDICATE this book to the pioneers, present and future, in law law land and beyond. You know who you are.

*

Oh, and my lover… for being so patient and understanding when I growled at you in exasperation and frustration: 'Will you please shut up?! I'm trying to write!'

*

Prrrrrrrrrrrrrrr

legal notices and disclaimer

I'D LOVE to believe that you (and every reader of *tomorrow's naked lawyer* for that matter) will follow the suggestions within and become wonderfully successful as a result. The truth is that I can't promise that will happen for you and/or your company.

As the information in *tomorrow's naked lawyer* is of a general nature I simply can't guarantee that it will suit every individual and/or business and/or every situation. One size does not fit all – truly!

So, here's the legal gubbins...

copyright acknowledgements

Grateful acknowledgement is made to each of Jazz Rasool, Andy Bounds, Matthew Scott, Bob Burg, Andrew Aitkin, David Lister, Wendy Reece, Rosalyn Lemieux, Carolyn Mumby, Richard Burcher, Mitch Jackson, and George Beaton for their contributions and granting me permission to reprint their respective (substantial) excerpts from each of their copyrighted works, which I believe have contributed powerfully and significantly in support of the messages that I have conveyed throughout *tomorrow's naked lawyer.*

I would also like to say a special thank you to Professor Stephen Mayson for his very thought-provoking foreword, which captures exactly what *tomorrow's naked lawyer* is all about, and for being so generous with his time in encapsulating so concisely how this book is of real benefit to you. I am hugely grateful and continue to be inspired by you all! Thank you again.

legal disclaimer:

This book has been prepared with reasonable efforts, but the information provided herein is provided 'as is'. To the fullest extent permitted by law – but without excluding or limiting any liability for fraud, death, or personal injury caused by negligence or any other matter for which liability cannot be excluded and/or limited under the law:

1) the Author, Owner and Publisher each makes no representation, statement, warranty, undertaking, guarantee, assurance, or promise whatsoever with respect to the accuracy or completeness or usefulness of the contents of this book, whether or not in any particular circumstances or context;
2) any and all implied warranties and/or other terms whatsoever are excluded and disclaimed;
3) there shall be no liability for any loss of profit, loss of anticipated savings, loss of business, loss of opportunity, or loss or corruption of data in each case of a direct or indirect nature;
4) there shall be no liability for any indirect or consequential losses or damages whatsoever; and
5) there shall be no liability for any downloader, transferor, transferee, recipient, reader or user of the digital book version of *tomorrow's naked lawyer* doing such an action negligently, improperly, illegally and in any other way whatsoever.

Consumer statutory rights are not affected

This book identifies product names and services known to be trademarks, registered trademarks, or service marks of their respective holders. They are used throughout this book in an editorial and nominative fashion only. In addition, terms suspected of being trademarks, registered trademarks, or service marks have been appropriately capitalised, although the Author, Owner, and Publisher cannot attest to the accuracy, completeness, or usefulness of this information.

Use of any term or wording in this book should not be regarded as affecting the validity of any trademark, registered trademark, or service mark. The Author, Owner, and Publisher are not responsible for any third party product, service, or vendor mentioned in this book.

The laws of England and Wales apply to the above, and the courts of England and Wales have exclusive jurisdiction.

foreword

By Stephen Mayson

IT'S HERE at last! Four long years of waiting are over. Chrissie Lightfoot's sequel to *the naked lawyer* has arrived…

the naked lawyer blazed a trail. Its innovative style, approach, and language went where no-one else had quite been before. It looked at the psychology and processes of winning new business and providing stand-out service. Chrissie offered a template for navigating the modern world of law with obvious passion and success.

The core idea of the first book was about *relating* to others – hence so many metaphors and images of intensely personal and private relationships that might have been unsettling for those of a prudish or more traditional disposition. Whatever the sensitivities, the notion of ROAR (reach out and relate) was – and remains – a key platform for Chrissie's ideas.

tomorrow's naked lawyer takes off from where *the naked lawyer* left us. We have ventured through the self-discovery and personal brand foundations offered by *the naked lawyer.* We now have the ability to demonstrate value and empathy in winning and retaining business. In that personal journey, we were stripped bare, we looked deep into ourselves, and we were prepared well for the new, hyper-competitive, 'law law land' that was about to emerge from the global financial crisis and the reforms of the Legal Services Act 2007.

But that world has now arrived, and has not stood still either. Arguably, we have only felt the first fluttering of the butterfly wings of climatic change that the legal ecosystem is about to experience. *tomorrow's naked lawyer* is about looking forward. After summarising in the recap and introduction the key messages of her first book, Chrissie treats us to three chapters describing the world that tomorrow's naked lawyer must face.

She draws on an impressive array of data, forecasts, and opinion. And she doesn't confine herself to national boundaries: here you will find material and case studies from around the world, building on her experience of working across Europe, North America, Asia, and Scandinavia. The picture she paints is a global one, because all markets are being affected by the forces she describes.

Her brush strokes also have such compelling (and evidenced) force that they will frighten the pants off a lot of lawyers. It is a world that many will resist. It is also one for which no lawyer has been trained – and, more importantly, for which no lawyer is currently being trained.

Here lies one of the fundamental themes, and challenges, of *tomorrow's naked lawyer* – contrast. Tomorrow's world of law will be so different to yesterday's and today's that the contrast will be psychologically and organisationally disruptive. No-one has been prepared for it. That is why this latest book is so necessary: it will help anyone with a care about law's future and their role in it.

The drivers of competition, new entrants, and future technology will transform law law land. Digital and social media have developed exponentially in the past four years, bringing potential, momentum, and disruption to the world of law – and that's before we come to the idea of the robotic, automaton (not human) lawyer that is explored so convincingly in the following pages.

The certainties of the old legal world have gone: career for life, reasonable expectation of rising fee income and rewards, promotion to partnership, client loyalty, self-regulation, professional and organisational autonomy, legal aid, and so on.

Uncertainty, change, and constant challenge are now the order of the day. However, the end of the world as we currently know it is not in fact the end of the world, just the emergence of a new one. Contrast and transformation implies big change; and that, in turn, creates opportunities and excitement. If other people fear to tread in this new world, entrepreneurs don't.

But entrepreneurs also understand that business is about *people*. However much we create processes, commodities, and robots, we still need some people to produce and some people to buy (even if production methods and buying habits change over time). The world will remain human and social.

Nevertheless, the relentless march of industrialisation, wearable technology, and robotic artificial intelligence will push the boundaries of what it means to be human and social. Chrissie explores in depth the meaning and consequences of these developments for legal services – and then rightly poses some challenging and uncomfortable questions about where this all takes us in matters of ethics.

Through all its insights of change, uncertainty, technological development, market disruption, job and relationships transformations, and entrepreneurial response, *tomorrow's naked lawyer* encourages us to think about what it *really* means to be a lawyer (and what it will mean to be a *real* lawyer) in the twenty-first century.

It is blending all these things into a seamless vision of your own future and how you will live it that lies at the heart of *tomorrow's naked lawyer*. Those who understand the union of entrepreneurialism, future technology, and the nature of being human will have embraced the message of this book, and you can dance confidently into the future. Indeed, you can then go back to *the naked lawyer* and start all over again: the insights and techniques from that work will be even more necessary and valuable when you're pursuing the vision of the future from this one.

Stephen Mayson is professor of legal services regulation at the University of Law, and honorary professor in the Centre for Ethics and Law at University College London. He now spends most of his time as an independent non-executive director working with a number of law-related organisations (www.stephenmayson.com).

recap: *the naked lawyer*

FOR THOSE of you who need a refresher on the first book in *the naked lawyer* series or who haven't gotten around to reading it yet (shame!), this section should help you out.

let's ROAR!

ROAR (an acronym for 'reach out and relate') is the model toward self-reliance, fulfilment, extraordinary rainmaking potential (and potentially extraordinary sex), and ultimately a solution to how to get more clients, sales, referrals, income, value, growth, and success in this Digital Age – and imminent 'Robotic Age'. It is explored in detail in *the naked lawyer* and summarized here.

If 'a picture paints a thousand words', then I'm about to save us a lot of time...

Check out The ROAR Model diagram overleaf.

the naked lawyer Volumes 1–12	Element
1: RIP – announcing the roar model	* the present
2: wakey wakey rise and shine	* emotional intelligence
3: slowly slowly catch a nichey	* niche identification
4: getting under your skin	* personal brand creation
5: raving referral lobsters rule!	* referral network building
6: social savvy junkie	* social media & social networking
7: nurturing fuzz to get more buzz	* relationship marketing, unsales & fuzz
8: talking dirty to a saint when I'm a pure little devil	* communication and behaviour
9: touch, touch and touch me again	* extraordinary customer service
10: continual stimulation	* innovation
11: yes! yes!! yes!!!	* other really cool stuff
12: XXX rated – tomorrow's lawyer	* the future

the **roar** model

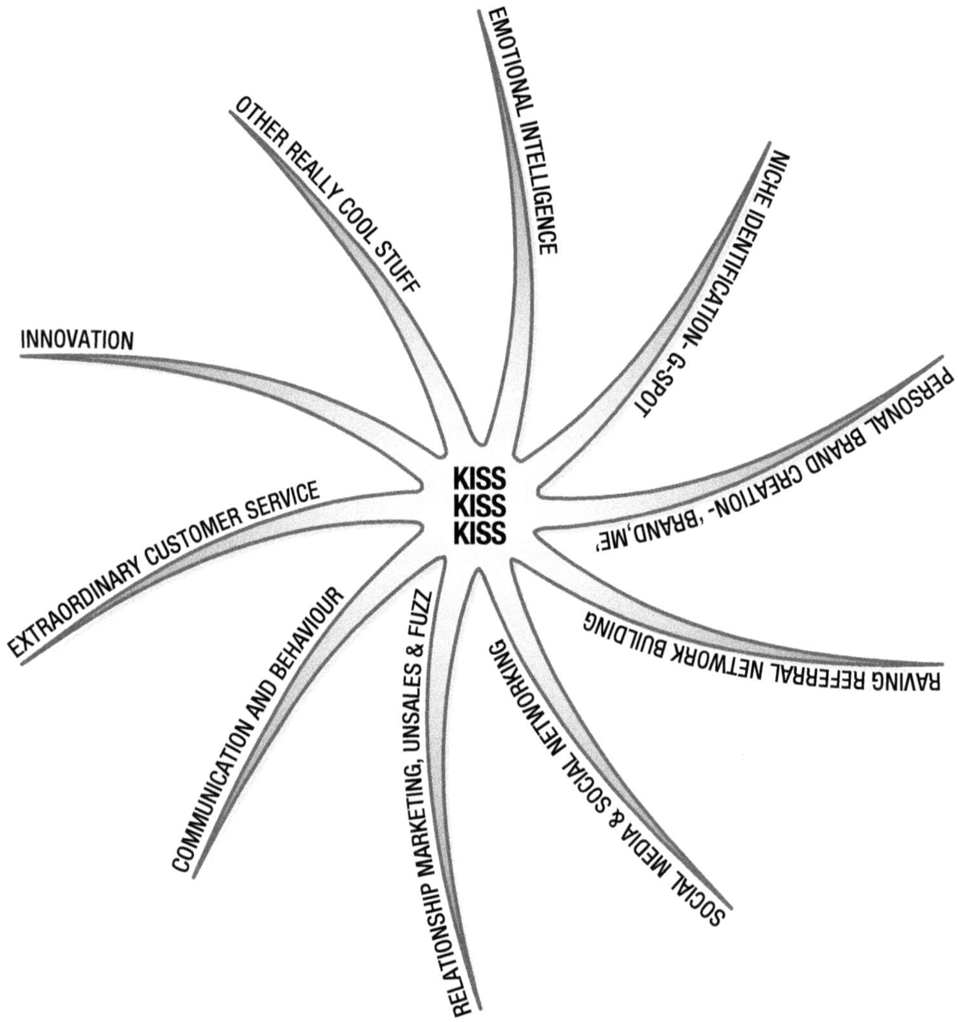

Figure 1: The ROAR model

xxx rated – after dark, before light

If you're up for making the transition from traditional lawyering to entrepreneurial lawyering, of the truly naked kind, then here is a summary of the key takeaways from Volumes 1–11 of *the naked lawyer* to assist you on your travels. To step out of the dark and into the light:

- Live your 'Big Rocks' (i.e. know your priorities and make them priorities);
- Develop and practise your EI (emotional intelligence);
- Be constantly SWOT aware (i.e. always consider what are your strengths, weakness, opportunities, and threats);
- Appreciate your 'ethicability conundrum'

(i.e. decide what you do (not) believe);
- Live your ME Code of Conduct (i.e. stick to what you do (not) believe);
- Have pride of epitaph (work out what YOU want it to be);
- Adopt the Rainmaker Mindset, Attitude, and Motivation ethos;
- Live your PEE Poor Work Ethic (i.e. with passion, energy, and enthusiasm);
- Continually work on your ideal niches;
- Work your positioning, differentiation, USPs, PODs, and g-spots (target market(s));
- Blow your horn every day as 'Brand,Me' (and 'Brand,Firm');
- Rave with your raving 'Referral Lobster Net-Kingdom', offline and online (i.e. build up a network of top quality referrers you can depend on);
- Practise your SM (social media) savvy and SN (social networking) nous and netiquette daily;
- Make lots of FUZZ (network noise);
- Work up your unsales process 80:20/G:R (i.e. spend 80 per cent of your time giving and only 20 receiving);
- Practise devilish communication and behaviour techniques – SRO style;
- Have fun devising stunning straplines and talking DIRTY (direct, impact, rapport, them, yes);
- Continually establish rapport;
- Continually build enduring extraordinary relationships;
- Continually strive to achieve customer service excellence;
- Practise touch #1 (engagement), touch #2 (re-engagement), touch #3 (cross-sell and up-sell), with speedy follow-on;
- Live your 'Brand,Me' communication game programme;
- Work your CRM system;
- Continually innovate your business process;
- Continually develop, innovate, hone, and cherish your LIC (lawyerly intellectual capital);
- Have an open mind to paradigm shifts;
- Learn to apply commercial savvy and business nous to your legal work and dealings;
- Practise the seduction of persuasion;
- Draft in some external coaching/ consultancy/training help where necessary; and
- Continually update your sales spreadsheet and Formidable ME Strategy & Plan (FMSP).

smorgasbord of quick fix tips

I began our journey in *the naked lawyer* with the suggestion that 'sales begins by "buying" the salesperson – YOU'. So, once again, here's a summary of ALL the ROAR tips I shared with you in Volumes 1–11 as to what you need to think and do so that lobsters, prospects, and clients will buy YOU:

- Strive to be an extraordinary rainmaker by thinking 'extraordinary sex';
- Get a grip;
- Get personal;
- Get real;
- Speak up;
- Speak out;
- Find and be your true ME;
- Don't be afraid;
- Don't allow fear to interfere;
- Park ego firmly at the door;
- Give up waiting;
- Let go of resisting change;
- Be honest – with yourself and others;
- Be transparent;
- Just do it;
- Believe it's time;
- Respect everyone's uniqueness and individuality;
- Do not tolerate people who are

attempting to mould you into something you are not;

- Be confident;
- Don't be afraid to stand alone;
- Celebrate your uniqueness;
- Be thorough – Research deeply, slowly, methodically, systematically;
- Brainstorm! Think lots;
- Be creative;
- Be commercial;
- Be courageous;
- Don't wait;
- Don't stand still;
- Be sexy in your positioning;
- Be sexier in your differentiation;
- Be particular in pursuit of the g-spot (target market);
- Say 'NO' to kneeling on the job (i.e. begging the boss for work);
- Use your initiative;
- Engage in fourplay (i.e. find your niche);
- Get everything – brand stable;
- Be accommodating;
- Don't allow your role to define YOU;
- Get digging;
- Get surfing;
- Be authentic;
- Harmonise 'Brand,Me' and 'Brand,Firm';
- Be NUTS (now, unconventional, timing, social);
- Think domination!;
- Share your brand ideas;
- Think emotional benefits;
- Think BIG PERSONALITY;
- Think search engine optimisation;
- Think social search optimisation;
- Think brand reputation;
- Make 'Brand,Me' count!;
- Take the plunge;
- Exit 'The Comfort Zone';
- Exit 'The Ivory Tower';
- Build multiple bridges;
- Strive to be accomplished in the four traits:
  - Be GIVING;
  - Be a CONNECTOR;
  - Be a LISTENER;
  - Be EMPATHETIC;
- Live your brand;
- Get your name EVERYWHERE;
- Rave about THEM (remember 80:20/G:R);
- Work your 'Me,Tale' off;
- Make time – Devote 30 minutes each day to SM and SN activity and make it a habit;
- Lay out a designated time to carry out your SM and SN activity, morning, noon, or night perhaps?;
- Use Microsoft Outlook, calendar, contacts, and tasks (or an equivalent software package) to help organise, manage, and analyse your activity and effectiveness;
- Use your sales spreadsheet to highlight, monitor, benchmark, and analyse your SM and SN activity and results;
- Set yourself three to five priority activities each day;
- Share 'Brand,You';
- Blow your horn every day;
- Be a secret agent provocateur;
- Be a permissive Googler: go, ogle;
- Fumble around;
- Improve your LUST;
- Get fuzzy;
- Get bizzy;
- Get nurturing;
- Build equity;
- Think 'befores' and 'afters';
- 'Brand,You' fuzz focus;
- Market 'Brand,You' focus;
- Unsales focus;
- Be Receiver orientated;
- Think client-centric first, last, always;
- Create stunning straplines;
- Be mysterious;
- Talk DIRTY;

- Be chatty chatty;
- Think bonding;
- Be attentive;
- Think bang bang sexy legs (aka get chatting and build a rapport);
- Know your FORM;
- Pursue rapid traction;
- Record the highlights;
- Be speedy with follow-on;
- Think engagement, re-engagement to avoid disengagement;
- Don't be a scarlet pimpernel (i.e. elusive);
- Think up-sell and cross-sell;
- Think about bundling products;
- Think Va-Va-Voom VALYOU;
- Go the extra 10,000 miles;
- Never be 'too busy' to avoid touching;
- Be hot for the lot (i.e. be customer service focused);
- Like retain;
- Love maintain;
- Get jiggy with a CRM system;
- Have a communication game plan;
- Strive to be extraordinary;
- Be innovative;
- Be stimulating;
- Think LIC (lawyerly intellectual capital);
- Think niche;
- Think value;
- Re-think your business process;
- Re-think your way of working;
- Re-think your way of managing and/or leading;
- Be open to a paradigm shift;
- Take a few risks;
- Be bold;
- Embrace change;
- Get up early;
- Get organised;
- Prepare for the day ahead the night before;
- Work on commercial savvy and business nous;
- Get some real business experience;
- Get a grip on the seduction of persuasion;
- Star gaze;
- Smile, smile, smile;
- Think Yes! Yes!! Yes!!!;
- Be the change that you want to see in the yourself and the profession; and
- Be happy!

As the saying goes: 'The best makeup is a smile. The best jewellery is modesty. The best clothing is confidence.'

I am confident that, if you do all of the above, you will become tomorrow's naked lawyer. Building on the key messages from *the naked lawyer*, above, this sequel will show you just how it's done.

introduction: XXX rated – tomorrow's lawyer

'99 per cent of lawyers give the rest a bad name!' – Clive Anderson

FORGIVE ME reader for I have sinned. It's been four years since we last danced. Prrrrrrrrrrrrrr… A lot of stuff has happened since then in law law land. What strikes me, though, is that despite the profession's gallant attempts to up its game and improve its reputation, the following still rings true: '99 per cent of lawyers give the rest a bad name!' This perhaps explains why, back in 2010 and throughout *the naked lawyer*[1] book,I suggested that entrepreneurs are from Venus and lawyers are from Mars. Accordingly, I proposed that we lawyers needed to become more entrepreneurial and to 'get naked'. And we have. And we did. Respectively! Please note, however, that if you take this literally, you WILL get suspended. Which was the outcome for the 52-year-old French lawyer, earlier this year, who was suspended for 'naked advocacy'…

the law is an arse

Yes, you read it right. An un-named Strasbourg advocate was recently suspended for three months after appearing in court 'going commando' under his robes. He even admitted to appearing 'sans briefs' for a couple of years and was only caught, one hot day, when a sudden blast from the air conditioning unit caused his robes to billow up.[2] It sounds like the Strasbourg advocate has 'got his knickers in a twist' over the suspension. Oh, I forgot, he doesn't wear any. It used to be said that the law is an ass. I do believe it is now an arse…

So please, dear reader, for the sake of good order, when I speak about getting 'naked' throughout the naked lawyer and tomorrow's naked lawyer, it is a metaphor for being authentic and being naked until you clothe yourself with your unique personal brand. Getting naked may sound appealing, but in reality society is still not ready for lawyers baring all. So, keep your kit on underneath your robes you decent, lawful people! The world, and our courtroom, remains a far safer and more respectable place for it. But hey, it's not just the lawyers who are stripping off…

the naked rambler

Staying with the law and the theme of getting 'naked', I'd also like to share with you an edited version of Matthew Scott's excellent blog and post entitled 'Stop wasting public money prosecuting and gaoling The Naked Rambler',[3] which Matthew has kindly agreed to share here with you:

'[Stephen] Gough is a strange obsessive, whose determination never to wear clothes has apparently even alienated him from his own children. His obsessiveness is matched by the determination of Hampshire Police and Wessex CPS who have been relentless and very successful in their attempts to ensure that the sensitive residents of Winchester are not caused any distress by the sight of Mr Gough's private parts. They have persuaded a court to impose an indefinite anti-social behaviour order, or ASBO, on him, which means that he commits a criminal offence if he does not wear his clothes in public. The only exceptions are that he is allowed to go naked in a changing room, on a nudist beach or for a medical examination. Gough has spent most of the last eight years in prison. His latest crime was committed as soon as he was released from his last sentence.

It is not, in itself, unlawful to go naked in public. It is an offence under Section 66 of the Sexual Offences Act 2003 to expose ones genitals with intent that someone should thereby be caused "alarm or distress" but nobody has ever suggested that Mr Gough had such an intent. It can be an offence to cause a public nuisance and "harm the morals of the public or their comfort, or obstruct the public in the enjoyment of their rights" but as an earlier and more successful nudist, Vincent Bethell, showed in 2001 juries are reluctant to find that merely being naked in the street does anything of the sort.

Prosecutors are too canny to charge Mr Gough with these offences, not least because there are defences to them and they fear that he would be acquitted.

Mr Gough has in the past been charged under Section 5 of the Public Order Act 1986, which makes it an offence to use "threatening, abusive or insulting words or behaviour, or disorderly behaviour… within the hearing or sight of a person likely to be caused harassment, alarm or distress thereby". This offence however, is only triable in the Magistrates Court and cannot be punished by a sentence of imprisonment.

So the only way that Mr Gough can be reliably jugged is to tailor him, as it were, a bespoke ASBO. As far as I am aware nobody else is subject to a similar order. The result is that the only person in the country who actually wants to wander naked around the streets of Winchester is also the only man in the country who commits a crime by doing so.

It is extremely hard to come up with a defence to breaching an ASBO. In the past Mr Gough has been represented by very able counsel who have struggled, without much success, to persuade judges that it breaches his human rights. On this occasion, it sounds as though he was again defending himself, while the prosecution were represented by Simon Jones, a senior barrister.… untroubled by any defence arguments, the jury duly took less than 15 minutes to convict him.

Judge Jane Miller QC then sentenced him to two and a half years imprisonment, while expressing the wish that he could be found some sort of "closed community" where he could live a life of cloistered nakedness.

Anybody who knows Judge Miller would agree that a more humane and sensible judge would be impossible to find, but in this case I think she was wrong. An eccentric who poses no risk to anybody is being made to spend the rest of his life in gaol – incidentally, at huge public expense – because of a law that has been crafted to criminalise his chosen way of life.

He has already spent most of the last eight years in prison. When he is released (after serving half of his latest sentence), he will have served the equivalent of virtually a 20-year prison sentence. Had he defrauded an elderly lady of her life savings he could not have been sentenced to more than ten years. Had he raped a twelve year old child he might have received a sentence of about 16 years.

Judge Miller obviously recognised the undesirability of these repeated gaol sentences, hence her suggestion that he might be able to live in some "closed community". Obviously, a prison might qualify, but I think she had something rather more congenial in mind… somewhere like the Croft Country Club, a "friendly family orientated Naturist club located in the middle of the fens on the Norfolk Cambridgeshire border"…

[Or if] Mr Gough could be persuaded to go "glamping" in Ashwood our camping pod (bring your own bedding and towels or bedding bale for hire)… it would work out about half as expensive as accommodating Mr Gough in prison, even if he didn't bring his own bedding.

All this might provide a solution if the Naked Rambler was willing to eke out the rest of his life playing pétanque in Wisbech. Unfortunately, he would rather wander around Winchester, or, failing that, go to prison.

The solution is a very simple one. Stop prosecuting him for breaching his ASBO. If he does things that would constitute a crime if done by others by all means throw the book at him. Otherwise, please stop wasting our money on what has long since become the persecution of a harmless eccentric. He has chosen to look ridiculous. The law is making itself look ridiculous.'

Hmmm… the law is a ridiculous arse, perhaps? And musing on the ridiculous, I recall Professor Stephen Mayson's opinion that The Legal Services Act 'is heading for the regulatory equivalent of the knacker's yard,[4] while for new Legal Services Board chairman Sir Michael Pitt, it is a 'job half done'.'[5]

Oh dear. We haven't really progressed that much. Or have we? The point I am trying to make, before we dive into *tomorrow's naked lawyer*, is that we need to pause and take a good look at ourselves as a profession. We should perhaps ask ourselves: 'Are we doing enough? Do we need to go further? Should we push the boundaries? This is what *tomorrow's naked lawyer* is all about…

the future?

Given the aftermath of the global recession, the turmoil in the world of finance, the disruption in law law land, the increasing demand for customer service excellence and rising expectations from prospects and clients, coupled with the choice available to them as to WHO they wish to buy their legal products and services from (present and future), if the path you have chosen is to become 'tomorrow's naked lawyer', then you'd better be prepared for a rough, tough, and bumpy passage. It's NOT going to be plain sailing, anymore. PERIOD.

Just to stick the prancing, dancing, *tomorrow's naked lawyer*'s bootilicious bootie in a bit more, if we take on board Tom Peters's views (see Volume 2 of *the naked lawyer*) and Ray Kurzweil's predictions of a future in which we are moving toward 'singularity'[6] – where humans transcend biology as a result of the combined effect of the revolution in genetics, nanotechnology, and robotics (artificial intelligence) – things are likely to get even tougher.

Ray Kurzweil's main concept is that our technological knowledge has been snowballing, and that once strong artificial intelligence is achieved, it will become a runaway phenomenon of rapidly escalating super-intelligence. When we reach this point in time (predicted 2040 or around 25 years from now) we will no longer recognise the world as we know it, nor our place (and space) in it. (More about this in Chapters 3 and 6 of *tomorrow's naked lawyer.*)

Certainly, we're in for a lot more CHANGE! So much has changed since 2010, and I predict we will need to handle even more in the years and decades to come. Am I talking about fact or fiction? I reckon FACT.

Reality check: there remains an obvious over-supply of law students, an obvious under-supply of training contracts (and/or paralegal or apprentice positions) available, and a pool of highly qualified and skilled lawyers already in the market who were 'let go' in 2008–10, ever hopeful of reclaiming a rowing position on the 'good ship legal enterprise' (many have done so as the economy picked up post-2013). Combine the above with accelerating technological advancement, and what have we got? I shall leave you to pause and muse while I attend to my wine glass. Prrrrrrrrrrrrrrrrrr…

Hopefully, you've already reached the point, mindset, and realisation which Jim Rohn speaks of: 'Let others lead small lives, but not you. Let others argue over small things, but not you. Let others cry over small hurts, but not you. Let others leave their future in someone else's hands, but not you.'[7] You are the master of your own mutiny. You are, after all, the captain of your mother ship.

portfolio handbag – skills and careers

Fortunately, if you've been studious in reading and acting upon the activities suggested by *the naked lawyer* (if you need a refresher, see the 'Recap' in this book), you're likely to have some new and/or improved skills to act as armbands; you're acquiring a portfolio handbag of skills that will stand you in good stead for whatever future you decide to pursue and whatever lifestyle you intend to sculpt.

If you become and/or remain a lawyer, then my legal experience and business experience has led me to believe that, for you to stay ahead of the 'competition' and to attract the entrepreneurial and business owner/decision-maker clients of the past, present, and future, you're going to have to deliver outstanding client service and develop extraordinary relationships… You're going to have to ROAR to make your clients' grade. Building a portfolio of skills is a sure-fire way of achieving this.

I reckon that the combination of commercial savvy, business nous, soft skills, rainmaking skills, and technical law excellence will be a godsend when it comes to capturing the hearts and minds of 'lobsters' (mavens), prospects, clients, and colleagues. So… If you want to achieve bottom line results, then you're going to have to be prepared to be on the frontline with your 'Brand,Me'.

XXX – sexily serendipitous, salubriously serene, socially savvy

You're no doubt aware of the original acronym 'KISS', meaning 'Keep It Simple, Stupid'. Well, in true ROAR model style, I figured I would innovate 'KISS', and multiply it:

XXX = KISS KISS KISS

To be a successful 'tomorrow's lawyer' (and now 'tomorrow's naked lawyer') and/or successful in business and/or life, I reckon you need to:

- KISS: Keep it sexily serendipitous;
- KISS: Keep it salubriously serene; and
- KISS: Keep it socially savvy.

The future, as I see it, for a tomorrow's naked lawyer – an entrepreneurial lawyer of the naked kind (such as YOU perhaps) will be all about XXX in the present and the future YOU create. Although I believe that every day is a blank page just waiting to be scribbled on, I make every effort to plant a firm 'X' 'X' 'X' on it. Why? 'X' really does mark the spot… 'X' 'X' 'X' hits it and makes it count!

after dark activity

Okay now. Let's get active…

just do something!

The ROAR model holds the key to unlocking the power within YOU to:

- Take control of those things that seemed so elusive in the past;
- Make those difficult choices that have niggled away for so long; and
- Dig deep for the courage and confidence to help you make ALL of the required changes…

…in the quest to achieve YOUR dream life.

One of my key messages throughout *the naked lawyer*, and which lies at the heart of the ROAR model, is to GIVE, GIVE, GIVE – and then GIVE some more. Without expecting anything in return. I stand by it. (Or, perhaps I should say, I prance by it.) Accordingly, I would deem it a privilege and an honour to be your new friend while you're reading *tomorrow's naked lawyer*, whether it is for a reason, a season, or a lifetime. And so, my foreword wisdom (well, actually, it's Mark Twain's, but I subscribe to it): 'Whenever you find yourself on the side of the majority, it is time to pause and reflect.' Let's go star gaze, dream maker… It's time to 'eat chocolate, drink wine, sleep naked'. It's time to GET NAKED! Prrrrrrrrrrrrr…

References

1. Lightfoot, C., *The Naked Lawyer: RIP to XXX – How to Market, Brand and Sell YOU!*, Ark Group, London, 2010.
2. 'Exclusive: lawyer suspended for naked advocacy', *RollOnFriday*, 3 October 2014, see www.rollonfriday.com/TheNews/EuropeNews/tabid/58/Id/3567/fromTab/36/currentIndex/3/Default.aspx .
3. For the full post, see Scott, M., 'Stop wasting public money prosecuting and gaoling The Naked Rambler.', *barristerblogger*, see http://barristerblogger.com/2014/10/08/stop-wasting-public-money-prosecuting-gaoling-naked-rambler/#more-1013. October 8th 2014.
4. Hilborne, N., 'Mayson: Legal Services Act heading for "knacker's yard"', *Legal Futures*, 9 September 2014, see www.legalfutures.co.uk/latest-news/mayson-legal-services-act-heading-knackers-yard.
5. Rose, N., 'LSB chair: regulators need to help push down cost of legal services', *Legal Futures*, 10 September 2014, see www.legalfutures.co.uk/latest-news/lsb-chair-regulators-need-help-push-cost-legal-services.
6. Kurzweil, R., *The Singularity Is Near*, New York, Viking, 2005. Ray Kurzweil is one of the world's leading inventors, thinkers and futurists, with a twenty-year track record of accurate predictions. He has been called 'the ultimate thinking machine' by Forbes magazine, the 'rightful heir to Thomas Edison' by Inc. magazine (and selected as one of the top entrepreneurs) and 'the restless genius' by *The Wall Street Journal*.
7. Quote by Jim Rohn: personal development and motivational guru, www.jimrohn.com.

Chapter 1: new and sexy law law land

'We must accept finite disappointment,
but we must never lose infinite hope.'
Martin Luther King, Jr

begin with the future in mind

Whenever I begin a speech, presentation, piece of writing, or consultancy, I like to grab the person's attention and cultivate curiosity – immediately. What better way to start than with the statement: 'It's robotic times. It's time to get naked!' Prrrrrrrrrrrr...

the kind of world we live in

We live in a topsy-turvy world of contrasts. We operate in our working, leisure, family, and home lives in an economic environment which is volatile and difficult to read. We have to deal with crazy, weird, challenging stuff in these uncertain times. Here is a sporadic handful of the kind of things I'm talking about:

- The rich are getting richer and the poor are getting much poorer... But the 100 richest people in the world earned enough money this year to end global poverty four times over.[1]
- New banking and funding sources have evolved – crowd-sourcing, crowd-funding, and cryptocurrency (e.g. bitcoin) – no doubt triggered by the global banking/financial crisis and recession of 2008–2012/13.
- Two-thirds of Germany's web users now bank online.[2] Here in the UK, we still like to 'pop into our local branch'.
- In some parts of the world people without any money exchange sexual favours for food and shelter, just to survive.
- Slavery exists, today, in the western thriving economies as well as in other emerging economies across the globe. It may be happening in your own street and you wouldn't even know about it.
- The iPhone 6 CPU has 600 times the number of transistors to the 1995 Intel Pentium. That's a 1990s supercomputer in your pocket.
- Technological processing power is doubling every 18 months: by 2020 the desktop PC will have the same speed and multi-processing ability as the human brain; by 2050 it will have the computing power of the whole of humanity. In some parts of the world they still cultivate land using a horse-drawn plough.
- A Chinese city has created a footpath for the use of smartphone addicts only. We can't even organise cycling lanes here in the UK.
- People have started listing Google Glass, GoPro, and Xbox One as skills on their LinkedIn profiles.
- A huge percentage of the populations across many nations (including the UK) are unemployed... and will never work.
- The population of the UK currently sits at 64 million(ish); 17 per cent of these people are over 65 years of age.[3] 65 per cent of the population of India are less than 35 years old.[4]

- By 2038 the population of the UK is predicted to be 74 million and 25 per cent of these people will be over the age of 65.[5]
- The 'rise of the grey population' can be seen globally; by 2060 over 40 per cent of the Japanese population will be over the age of 65.[6]

If I was a cynic and a pessimist I would say that the large majority of the population in the UK (and globally) in our future are obviously not going to generate significant legal work, save for probate! But, as you know, I am a realist and an optimist. And in adversity, I see opportunity.

Currently 14 per cent of the working population in the UK are self-employed.[7] This figure, unsurprisingly, is predicted to increase, meaning, more entrepreneurs, meaning potentially more commercial related legal work. Again, there is a similar trend across the globe. Back in 2010, world-renowned futurist Rohit Talwar, through his research, predicted that, by 2020, 20 per cent of the population of the USA will be self-employed.

In simple terms, more (entrepreneurial) people means:

- More legal work needed by people;
- More legal work needed by business; and
- More legal work wrangling by business and lay people.

Keep reading…

Undoubtedly, the world (and not just the legal landscape which has been documented thoroughly in both the legal and business world media) has experienced a seismic shift in the past 20 years, and particularly in the last five. Our world – all of it – has become increasingly volatile, fragmented, disaggregated, price sensitive, dynamic, technological, digital, client driven, and data driven.

Old certainties have become new uncertainties. But I would argue that one thing remains constant: We remain in a world where we pay a high price (metaphorically as well as in reality) for law and justice…

high price for law and justice

It is widely documented that many lay people are priced out of the market to find recourse in the legal systems throughout the world. However, less commonly reported is that the same applies for businesses. If we look at the British legal market, a recently released report from Annecto Legal has found that SME wariness in legally challenging another company could be costing them a great deal of money. According to Mark Beaumont, co-founder of Annecto Legal:

'This research confirms our belief that all too often SMEs are put off pursuing justice because they feel bullied by big companies; are worried about the cost of court; and are unsure that they could win…The extent to which small and medium-sized businesses feel bullied by big companies is astounding, with more than a quarter saying they have felt this way. Despite this, almost a third haven't pursued a potential legal case in the last five years due to underlying fears.'[8]

The main reasons listed for not pursuing legal action was expense, time, and uncertainty fear over winning the case. Recall what I shared with you in the introduction earlier? Keep reading…

In contrast, in another area of the law, the start of the new legal year in 2014 witnessed unprecedented protests by the combined legal profession. I agree with

Catherine Baksi of the *Law Society Gazette* that the MoJ could learn something from the nursery rhyme – 'For want of a nail the shoe was lost' – as it continues slashing the criminal legal aid rates. I love her version of the rhyme:

'For want of a fee the advocate was lost.
For want of an advocate the case was lost.
For want of a case, justice was lost.
For want of justice, civilisation was lost.
And all for the want of a fee.'

'It appears a false economy to allow trials and the justice system to collapse for want of paying advocates an appropriate fee.'[9] Perhaps it is understandable that the fee cuts of up to 30 per cent on lawyers whose fees have already been reduced by more than 30 per cent over the past six years have pushed the disgruntled lawyers beyond their limit of professional quiet acceptance. Accordingly, it is the barristers, lawyers, and solicitors who cannot afford to represent clients, and it is our society which suffers with the whimpering cry 'for want of justice, civilisation is lost'. In contrast again, the stereotypical 'shark lawyer' remains, as always. Yes, there's good and bad in all professions, but I still cringe when I hear about (and personally witness) the lawyers who milk their client, with intent! It sickens me. I am ashamed and embarrassed to adorn the title of 'lawyer' when my colleagues behave in such an unscrupulous manner.

It happens in all areas of law, but it can be particularly prevalent in family/matrimonial law as heartless lawyers play on the emotions of their client, and do in fact fan the flames of the dispute rather than guiding their client to an amicable solution as quickly and cost-effectively as possible, consequently costing their client and the opposing side far more than is necessary or required.

(I shall not, of course, name the guilty individuals and firms here. You know who you are. Shame on you! For those '99 per cent of lawyers give the rest a bad name': you make the law an arse!)

the kind of law law land we live in...

If this is the kind of world we live in, it is understandable that the kind of legal market we operate in is and will continue to be volatile, highly competitive, price sensitive, technological, digital, dynamic, challenging, and uncertain. Which begs the question: what will the legal market look like in 2015 and beyond? Who will be the winners and who will be the losers – and why? How can firms and lawyers thrive in a turbulent, dynamic, and competitive market?

Many authors have written and spoken about the changing legal landscape. But let's be blunt, shall we? The old legal market is knackered. It's being torn apart. Or, perhaps, what's happening is best described as something on a par with the wicked witch in the Wizard of Oz gradually melting, to the point that all that remains is the crumpled cloak (aka corporate veil) festering in a stinking heap.

Only a few months after the publication of *the naked lawyer* (in late 2010), here in the UK, we witnessed the following revelations:

- Rocket Lawyer had been backed by Google Ventures with a whopping $18.5million treasure chest. Rocket Lawyer, founded by a lawyer, provides legal documents for consumers. It has a network of approximately 6,000 practising lawyers in the USA on hand to review forms created by Rocket Lawyer's documentation system. It's not a law firm and the lawyers involved are part of a referral network; they are not employees. It entered the UK legal market in 2012.

- LegalZoom, the best known legal brand in the USA, also founded by lawyers, had $66 million pumped into the business in Q1 and Q2 2011. Again, not a law firm, LegalZoom provides legal documents created via its documentation system and checks are made by its customer care team who amend errors such as spelling mistakes, capitalisation, and so on. It also entered the UK online legal market in 2012.
- Aderant acquired Client Services and CompuLaw for an undisclosed sum. Aderant, a software vendor used by law firms for billing, content management, and practice management is now the legal technology field's largest independent software provider and its newly expanded applications catalogue is similar to that of LexisNexis, but without content and research services.
- Hewlett-Packard purchased Autonomy, a leading e-discovery provider, for a staggering $10 billion.
- Slater & Gordon, a leading Australian law firm and the world's first to list on the Stock Exchange, was eyeing up the UK legal market opportunities. And again, Slater & Gordon nudged into the UK legal market.

Clearly, even as far back as early 2011 the transformation (and arguably re-invention) of legal service provision which I had envisioned in *the naked lawyer* was well and truly underway.

Businesses of law backed by venture capital companies and with the ability to raise funding though listing on stock exchanges in England and Australia is a global game changer for those operating within the legal world, and for society at large in years to come. IMHO, it was at this point in time that we began crossing over from the 'old' legal marketplace to the 'new' one.

In reading Jordan Furlong's thought-provoking 'Goodbye to all that' blog post[10] back in August 2011, three statements struck me:

1. 'The new providers and new technologies are not going to replace lawyers'... but they are going to *marginalize* us and 'render law firms mostly irrelevant';
2. 'Lawyers still have outstanding value to offer in certain quarters, but we need to concentrate our market offerings around that value, and we need better platforms for our services than traditional law firms provide'; and
3. 'Lawyers are smart, knowledgeable, creative and trustworthy professionals who, unfortunately, suffer from poor business acumen, terrible management skills, wildly disproportionate aversion to risk, outsized revenue expectations, and a business model about 25 years out of date. The market won't abandon them — they have unique and sometimes extraordinarily valuable skills and characteristics — but it will find the best use for them: expert specialists with limited influence over the larger process.'

I agree entirely, which is why I wrote *the naked lawyer* back in 2010 and proffered a 'survival model' – the ROAR model – for lawyers, documenting the kind of stuff you will need in the years ahead.

Subsequently, I would add that as we lawyers become marginalized, our role and value will be in extolling our expert niche specialism with exceptional emotional intelligence while delivering extraordinary customer service – something artificial intelligence (AI) and computers, with its forte in large process, will never be able to provide… Or will they? More about this in Chapters 3 and 6.

Throughout 2011, 2012, 2013, and 2014 the 'traditional law firm' wicked-witch meltdown began, globally. Copious reports flooded law law land and mainstream media during 2012, 2013, and 2014 about the implosion of many law firms, the most prolific being Dewey & LeBoeuf LLP, the global law firm, headquartered in New York City, that is now in bankruptcy. Closer to home I witnessed the demise of Cobbetts and Halliwells, which was a true 'wake-up call' for many law firms and their rulers here in England.

And then, back in March 2013, when the legal services market was being battered by the wicked west winds of change driven by the Legal Services Act and Legal Aid, Sentencing and Punishment of Offenders Act 2012 (LASPO), and tidal forces of insurance and compliance, I wrote a piece in *The Global Legal Post* stating that I'd been bombarded with RSS feeds full of reports from copious legal journals about personal injury practices facing financial meltdown as a result of all of this.

It looked like the demise of Blakemores (Lawyers2You) was only the tip of the iceberg as the SRA painted a miserable picture of financial instability among law firms in general, and the Law Society revealed that the number of private practice solicitors had fallen for the first time.

The society warning of the threat of ABSs reshaping the high street coincided with an article in *The Times* entitled 'Farewell tweedy high street, hello online' suggesting that 'the mix of internet, reforming legislation and the demise of legal aid is creating an evolutionary jolt in the legal high street, consigning traditional practice to a museum of professional history.'

1 in 3 law firms face financial meltdown

Fast forward to 2014 when I read a piece by Jack Flanagan in *Real Business* in which he reported: '…the UK economy is estimated to grow by 2.4 per cent in 2015 – well below the 3.1% growth expected this year.

Weaker global growth, low wage growth and financial and political risks, such as the situation in the Middle East and Ukraine, have contributed to financial uncertainty, according to forecasting group EY Item Club…'[11]

In October this year, inflation in the Eurozone fell from 0.4 to 0.3 – depicting a slow and uneven recovery on the continent, whose effects might also reach the UK.[12] Accordingly, I then read somewhere that a climate of financial instability is still the backdrop from which UK legal firms are operating, with the disturbing prediction that one in three could face bankruptcy in 2014.[13]

These are scary statistics. We might think they apply only to small UK firms, squeezed by new government regulations in areas such as legal aid and personal injury practice, but it is a much wider problem. For example, even firms with global offices face financial challenges – that is, those like Dewey & LeBoeuf LLP. These types could be at greater risk.

In a difficult global economic climate, individual firms might be tempted to believe that there is little they can do to minimise the risks. I disagree. For starters, all legal firms/businesses of law, whatever their size, can look to future proof their businesses. How do you do this? All future-proofed companies work on three horizons:

- Horizon 1: Year 1 (months 1–12) – Focus working on operational excellence;
- Horizon 2: Years 1–3 – Focus and work

on the drive for innovation and efficiency; and

- Horizon 3: Years 4–10 – Focus and work on creating growth and the future.

You need different people in your company and/or together with external consultants working on these three horizons in tandem – that is, you need to be running all three tracks at the same time. The businesses which provide legal products and services that are doing well, and will continue to survive and thrive, are covering all three horizons, now, daily. So:

- *Question*: Are you working on all three horizons?
- *Question*: WHY the focus on three horizons?
- *Answer*: Because clients are asking 'will you be around in ten years' time?'

Accordingly, CEOs and managing partners are now asking themselves the same questions:

- 'Will we?'
- 'How?'

CEOs are now talking about what is feasible, viable and sustainable. Are you?

Traditional practices, and those who use them, are being challenged and in some cases swept away, and replaced by new types of businesses of law. Make sure you are not one of them. Keep reading…

new sexy models and players

I read a fascinating, brilliant, and entertaining blog post by Professor Stephen Mayson entitled 'Breaking News: Humpty Dumpty Falls Off Wall'[14] in which Stephen suggests that the traditional law firm model is well and truly scrambled. I reckon it's fried. Sadly, it's taken a global economic nose-dive off a cliff, smart liberalisation in the form of legal reforms (Legal Services Act 2007 and alternative business structures), and switched-on entrepreneurial global venture competitors to prompt traditional law firms and their lawyers to start writing new messages on Humpty's wall.

As Stephen shares with the reader his expertise on the subject, it is apparent that there can be a sunny side for those firms and individuals who are prepared to re-invent their model and strategies – which, in essence (IMHO) is what the strong firms and individuals have done and will continue to do.

Since 2011 there has been a swathe of new legal start-ups, and more are still to come. Consequently, there has been a plethora of articles written about 'Tesco law', 'big law', 'tiny law', 'micro law', 'boutique law', 'virtual law', 'BT law', 'Google law', 'Virgin law', and 'robot law' in an attempt to capture the diverse range (and threats) of the new sexy business models and new sexy players.

Not only have the Yanky traditional law firms, the Yanky new sexy players (LegalForce, ClearSpire, Legal Zoom, Rocket Lawyer), the Chinese, the Kiwis (LegalVision), the Aussies (Slater & Gordon), and the entrepreneurs (James Caan with Knights Solicitors, Ajaz Ahmed with Legal365, LawBite, Axiom, Keystone Law, Riverview Law) etc., swept into the UK legal market like Mary Poppins with her nannying umbrella on the east wind, but so too have the BIG BOYS. I refer now to the mighty global accountancy, insurance, banking, wealth behemoths, the blue chips, and more. For example, the AA, the CoOperative, PricewaterhouseCoopers, Ernst & Young, KPMG, Capita, Paragon, Das, Maitland Group, and BT – to name a few.

Riverview Law is worth a special mention, for it can proudly boast about the kind of new sexy business model that has been lacking in law law land for far too long. I believe it has a fabulous business model wherein it applies simple business sense to the legal market. In short, Riverview Law, often described under the umbrella term of 'new model law firm' is a legal services firm run like a business rather than a traditional law firm.

There is a recent Harvard Business School case study[15] by Dr Sylvia Hodges entitled 'Riverview Law: Applying Business Sense to the Legal Market'. The case study guides you through Riverview Law wanting to expand its unconventional concept from the UK to the US. It's a fun and informative read as you follow Heather Larson, a (fictional) US lawyer Riverview is trying to recruit, and learn about the firm's unusual approach:

- Performing legal work for annual fixed-price contracts;
- Using data and analytics to advise clients' on ways to reduce their legal problems (and spend); and
- Evaluating lawyers' performance based on client satisfaction surveys rather than traditional metrics like billed revenues.

With detailed information on the firm's financial performance, service teams, pricing, culture, and business model, you can make up your mind about how big of a threat Riverview Law and similar new model firms pose to traditional law firms and, in contrast, how welcome it is for GCs and other business and lay legal buyers. My mind is already made up.

While some have described the new model law firms as flexible, adaptable, and better for clients, I believe that there is scope for all types of businesses of law, business models, and sexy (or non-sexy) players to service the diverse range of sexy (and non-sexy) legal buyer. Moreover, lawyers aren't limited to Big Law or solo practice anymore; there are many options available to the aspirant, the existing 'traditional lawyer', and the ambitious and entrepreneurial lawyer.[16] This is a good thing. Choice is good.

However, I wholeheartedly subscribe to the view that success lies in internationalisation and that only global firms and 'super niche' will prosper in the long term. Echoing William Gibson (possibly) in noting that 'The future is already here. It's just not evenly distributed yet?', in a collaborative, digital, data-rich, carbon, and silicon world, it's a no-brainer that small/boutique/niche is (and will be) a better way to go. For internationalisation and niching brings greater opportunity, IMHO, in existing and new markets, in existing and new industries, and in existing and new sectors, coupled with either their existing or new sexy business models…

new sexy markets

There was a saying and an understanding not so long ago in the marketing and sales world that you don't ignore the custom and clients that are on your doorstep. That is, target your immediate, local buyer before you reach out further afield in your quest for new clients and greater market share. This still rings true, to some extent, where niching is concerned.

Know your market, know your client, be aware of your competition, has and always will be the foundation of your marketing, sales, and client drive, strategy, and plan.

- *Question*: 'Where are my clients of the present and future?'
- *Answer*: 'Potentially everywhere.'

Yes, you can niche of a niche of a niche of a niche local to global, for free and quickly. Fast, free, and globally frisky is the way to go in 2015 and beyond, I reckon. Why? Because the world is now about global lawyering to/and for global clients by global businesses of law. Accordingly, it would be foolish to ignore the top ten emerging markets which proffer a ripe opportunity for your individual and company growth. It's no surprise that we read, almost daily, about the movers and shakers strategic antics with regard to the emerging markets of:

1. Russia;
2. India;
3. South Africa;
4. Turkey;
5. Brazil;
6. Argentina;
7. Mexico;
8. China;
9. Vietnam; and
10. Indonesia.

Significantly, the Asia-Pacific region represents the world's fastest growing legal market and is set to double by 2017. That's a whole lot of opportunity, in my book.

Good news: not all economic predictions are doom and gloom, either. If you choose to believe Andrew Aitken of UBS, he is of the opinion that the UK economy is predicted to be strong throughout the end of 2014 and into 2015. Similarly, the US economy is looking positive along with China, predicted to grow over 7 per cent, meaning global growth of 3.5 per cent overall. Andrew was happy to share his personal view and experience that for his clients: 'it's been a great five years to invest. Still some positive returns ahead but not as substantial as the past five years.' And let's face it, UBS isn't too shabby a business and Andrew hasn't got to where he has today (or his clients) by not knowing his stuff.[17]

And so, with opportunity, such as:

- The opening up of the UK legal market through LSA 2007 and ABS;
- Increasing numbers of self-employed and entrepreneur ventures in the digital field;
- Globalisation, the internet, world wide web, digital communication and the take-up of digital devices etc.; and
- Economies picking up...

...the entire world is now your doorstep. And with that comes increasing competition; notably, the competition and comprrrrrrrrrrrrrrrrrtition is now rattling your wind chimes from east and west, banging on your door and then curling up on your doorstep. And let's face it, when leading law firms (aka you, the lawyer) fail to move with the times, the predictions for many years and depressing potential outcomes related to the changes and challenges for 'traditional practice' in a crowded marketplace from many respected legal strategists and consultants now appear to be the reality.[18]

In the UK we're now experiencing the 'new legal market', the 'new normal', the 'new business of law', where the Americans, Aussies, Kiwis, Chinese, and entrepreneurs have arrived in the legal market space. Similarly, UK law firms have extended their footprints to attract local footfall from new markets in a variety of continents and nations around the globe.

We cannot ignore the recent new entrants, the competitive uprising, and the burgeoning opportunities. Heck, when Richard Branson's Virgin Galactic eventually launches into space successfully in 2015/16/17 who knows, the Martians may even arrive too with a new Virgin law world order furthering the legal space frontier.

Maybe when Sir Richard Branson hears of *the naked lawyer* and this sequel (and, dare I suggest, reads them), with your help, he won't mind reading my POV, which is: I think you're missing a HUGE opportunity by not launching Virgin Law. It's got to be easier than hurling a spaceship and its trusting star-gazer guinea pigs safely beyond our law ravaged planet!

Little green men aside, the rest are here to stay, compete, and quite possibly help in this new and sexy law law land.

In summary, let's look at the context and drivers that have contributed to the shift and changes so far:

- Topsy-turvy economic times, globally – The global recession of 2008 to 2012/13 was not just another recession; it was the result of a catastrophic financial meltdown which gave the evolution of mankind a real jolt. It ushered in the desire to seek a 'new way', a *better* way for society to deal with:
  - ☐ Struggling economies,
  - ☐ Struggling societies,
  - ☐ Struggling clients,
  - ☐ Struggling law firms, and
  - ☐ Struggling lawyers;
- A new consumer attitude – 'I don't want a lawyer to tell me what I cannot do. I hire him to tell me how to do what I want to do';[19]
- The Legal Services Act 2007 (LSA) and alternative business structures (ABSs) in England and Wales – The traditional way of lawyering is being questioned, superseded, and/or supported by other ways of operating and delivering legal advice, products, and services;
- The evolution of the internet (worldwide), and the technological revolution – Legal service provision has become increasingly entrepreneurial (and even run by entrepreneurs!); and
- The new players – Newcomers are moving into existing and new markets, to camp, to stay, to agitate, and to disrupt, internationally and globally.

Let's have a look at some interesting marketing, networking, social media, branding, digital, and technology trends, shall we? But before we do, let's indulge in some…

after dark activity

With the advancement of web 2.0 to 4.0; the 'social phenomenon'/'social movement' of social media, social networking, social brand, and social business; the accelerating movement toward 'singularity' with the combined discovery and advancements in nanotechnology, robotics, and genetics; with the evolution of artificial intelligence; global economic effects; emerging economies and markets; consumer sovereignty, and the inevitable population time-bomb; the employment time bomb; working patterns and lifestyle shakeup…

- *Question*: What has been the impact on law law land?
- *Answer*: Uncertainty and fear – juxtaposed with opportunity.

We are now experiencing the 'new normal', a new legal world order where the contrast, choice, change, and competition is set to accelerate. Clients do business with those they know, like, trust, really 'get', understand, and share common interests with. Accordingly, how will prospects and/or clients get to know you if they don't know you exist? If you're not 'digitally present' and/or 'digitally positioned' in our digital world?

just do something!

Sit quietly now with your glass of water/juice/wine/beer/coffee/cocoa and *think*. Really think, and ask yourself, in this digital age and globally ripe legal market:

- Do I *really* know myself?
- Do I *really* know my market?
- Do I *really* know my client?
- Do I truly understand the trends and drivers that will affect and shape my prospects, clients, and will shape me, currently and in the months and years to come?

If you're struggling, let me help you… Turn the page. Let's dance…

References

1. According to an Oxfam report, see: http://rt.com/news/oxfam-report-global-inequality-357/.
2. According to a BITKOM survey, conducted by ARRIS, as cited in press release on 23 September 2014.
3. According to the Office for National Statistics (ONS). See: www.ons.gov.uk/ons/dcp171778_363912.pdf.
4. See: www.linkedin.com/pulse/article/20141006151256-337113487-11-must-know-marketing-trends-for-2015?trk=nus-cha-roll-art-title
5. Ibid.
6. Ibid.
7. According to ONS, see: www.ons.gov.uk/ons/dcp171776_298533.pdf.
8. See: www.annectolegal.co.uk/latest-news-events/sme-litigation-research.
9. Baksi , C., 'For want of a fee, justice was lost', *The Law Society Gazette*, see: www.lawgazette.co.uk/5039565.article?utm_source=dispatch&utm_medium=email&utm_campaign=GAZ290114.
10. Jordan Furlong is a legal commentator, lawyer and futurist. See: www.law21.ca/2011/08/goodbye-to-all-that.
11. Flanagan, J., 'UK economic growth will slow next year', *Real Business*, 20 October 2014, see: http://realbusiness.co.uk/article/28055-uk-economic-growth-will-slow-next-year-.
12. Hesse, J., 'Eurozone inflation falls, along with hopes of recover, 17 October 2014, see: http://realbusiness.co.uk/article/28046-eurozone-inflation-falls-along-with-recovery-hopes.
13. Based on research carried out by The Association of Business Recovery Professionals.
14. Mayson, S., Breaking News: Humpty Dumpty Falls Off Wall', 16 August 2011, see: http://stephenmayson.com/2011/08/16/breaking-news-humpty-dumpty-falls-off-wall/.
15. Gardner, H.K., and Silverstein, S. H., 'Riverview Law: Applying Business Sense to the Legal Market, 4 June 2014, see: http://hbr.org/product/riverview-law-applying-business-sense-to-the-legal-market/an/414079-PDF-ENG.
16. See the white paper 'Flexible Practice Models for Flexible Law Firms, available at: http://landing.goclio.com/Flexible-Practice-Models-for-Flexible-Law-Firms.html?utm_source=Twitter&utm_medium=Social_Organic&utm_campaign=Twitter_Flexible_Practice_Models.
17. UBS is the largest wealth management company in the world. It is a business which operates locally and internationally. Andrew Aitken heads up the Leeds, Yorkshire office and he personally looks after High Net Worth individuals in Yorkshire, England. Interview conducted 4 September 2014.
18. For more on this, see Beaton, G., *NewLaw: New Rules – A conversation about the future of the legal services industry*, Beaton Capital Pty Ltd, Melbourne, 2013; Kowalski, M., *Avoiding Extinction: Reimagining Legal Services for the 21st Century*, American Bar Association, 2012.
19. Attributed to J. Pierpont Morgan.

Chapter 2: trends, tips, and robot hits

'What's changed is that competitive advantage is no longer the sum of all efficiencies, but the sum of all connections.'[1]
Greg Satell

time to get naked

I recently came across *LexisNexis's Bellwether Report* (2014), *Brave New World*,[2] which focuses on sole practitioners, independent lawyers, and small law firms, and the extent to which they are rising to meet the industry, economic, and business challenges in the present and future. The report identifies new working practices, increased optimism, and the emergence of a new breed of entrepreneurial lawyers:

'Practitioners are emerging business-savvy, resilient and fiercely independent, with more confidence in the future of their practice than ever before. Rising above the pack, a new breed of entrepreneurial lawyers are embracing the emerging opportunities – and achieving impressive results.'

In relation to performance, growth is higher (55 per cent) amongst the 'emerging breed of dynamic entrepreneurial lawyers with top tier pedigree' (13 per cent more than the average respondent). Nevertheless, it looks like the dynamic independent lawyers who are really shaking things up are focusing on building their business through the smart use of marketing, networking, and technology:

'These entrepreneurs are networked, dynamic and ambitious. Often niche specialists with superb credentials, they've set up their businesses to compete directly with the major industry players, and they're frequently winning due to their agility and top-class customer service. Always thinking at least one step ahead, they're utilising every tool at their disposal to hone their competitive edge – from strategic partnerships and gaining ABS status, to outsourcing for increased efficiency, to harnessing the latest technologies to run their firm and connect with new clients.'

In contrast to the doom and gloom I described in the previous chapter, it certainly appears to be a positively 'brave new world', according to this report.[3]

Focusing on building their business through the smart use of marketing, networking, and technology, eh? No-brainer. It's yet another report about the outcome of what happens when you GET NAKED and ROAR. It took five years and a heap of legal research time and green notes to prove what my gut and intuition told me five years ago: that the ROAR model IS the solution for success and growth, no matter whether you are a solo lawyer, an ABS UK legal purebred, or an ABS international conglomerate mongrel providing a full range of legal, accountancy, tax, insurance, wealth, and/or business services.

It has now been proven, through a great deal of research in the legal world and beyond,[4] via a plethora of reports and case studies relating to the bold activities of entrepreneurial lawyers and their businesses of law, and epitomised in their bountiful financial results.

Bottom line: if you don't market, brand and sell yourself (aka get marketing, networking, and using technology and the internet) you won't experience the growth your peers are enjoying. Please take note:

- If you don't have a voice on the internet, you won't have a place in the future of law; and
- In an increasingly technological, digital, artificially intelligent, silicon, and robotic legal world, if you don't embrace technology, you will indeed be committing professional suicide.

Was it Shakespeare who wrote 'Let's kill all the lawyers?' I predict if he were alive today he wouldn't need to. If you don't get a grip with marketing, (social) networking, and technology per se, you might as well dig your own grave. I can see the epitaph now: 'I wish I'd gotten NAKED.'

Marketing, networking, and technical skills are paramount for a lawyer, both currently and undoubtedly in the near and distant future. Very soon, saying NO to technology[5] won't even be an option for you.[6] Before long, I reckon for firms that say NO to social media, social networking, and technology, and/or do not encourage all of their lawyers to get a grip with it, they will soon experience a client exodus or a career meltdown, respectively.

Here is why I can confidently predict this… According to research by Hubspot on trends as recently as 2013, marketing will be more accountable for revenue generation, more focused on mobile applications, and more 'human', with companies developing a personality through storytelling. People from across the business will need to become 'inbound marketers', promoting the business's products and services, and investment will increasingly focus on online marketing.

Take a peek at these 2013 online marketing trends:[7]

- Campaigns fade out, real-time marketing is in;
- Inbound marketing grows enterprise-wide;
- Know thy customer – beyond CRM systems;
- Marketing becomes more accountable for revenue generation;
- Social media gets integrated;
- Be mobile or fall behind;
- Social and content impact SEO even more;
- Marketing speaks like a human;
- Inbound, not automation, becomes priority; and
- Outbound marketing loses traction.

social media, social networking trends, and statistics

Social media has transformed the way we communicate and distribute information beyond all recognition, locally and globally. You cannot have failed to read or hear that a greater percentage of the world's population are registered with a social networking site than have a toothbrush! If this is the first time you've heard this, you need to get out more. Actually, you need to be reading and networking more, offline and online!

Regardless of consumers' preferred social networking site (there's so many of them now I can't possibly cover them all, let alone discuss them), the use of social media continues to grow and is definitely here to stay. Whether, as a business of law or as a lawyer, you choose to join in or not, social media conversations will continue to happen with or without you.

If your customers are on social networks you should be there too. Because one thing is for sure: your competitors are. What's more:

- 52 per cent of all marketers found a customer via Facebook in 2013 (Hubspot);
- 22 per cent of UK internet users' time is spent on social media (Experian);
- Approximately 46 per cent of online users count on social media when making a purchase decision (Nielsen); and
- 25 per cent of consumers who complain about products on Facebook or Twitter expect a response within one hour (American Express).[8]

Whether you are one of the 85 per cent of businesses that have already recognised that social media is important,[9] or you are completely new to social media, there is an army of self-professed 'social media experts' out there to help you evaluate, integrate, and maximise social media to increase marketing return on investment and customer engagement.

I help lawyers and law firms with social media and social networking, but I only do so insofar as it is integrated within the entire ROAR model and the entire organisation I am working with. Social media and social networking as a standalone activity will not bring you the results you crave. It is a tool. And a tool needs a master. And the master must wield his tool sculpted by his behaviour. Accordingly, like an artist (as in all things), to be truly successful the 'beginning of every activity should have a plan for the end'. This is why the ROAR Model works because it is a complete behaviour model.

However, I am not an expert, or a guru, for I am a great believer that NOBODY is an expert in the social media and social networking realm. Why do I believe this? Well, there are a number of reasons:

- The 'social movement' and its social tools and gizmos move too darn fast!
- There are new social players entering the digital marketplace at ten-a-penny, meaning there are far too many social thingies to handle and become expert in all at the same time.
- Those of us who are regularly active 'on social' have varying degrees of knowledge and experience in its use, and tend to gravitate toward favoured media and networks for a particular purpose: business, leisure, family etc.
- It's just not possible to be on 'social everything' for a significant enough period of time to become a guru.

It's fair to say that social media and social networking is still viewed with suspicion by many lawyers and law firms, and/or it's not used effectively by the vast majority in achieving sales and building professional relationships. But here's the thing: Social media is not just a place for people to share their holiday snaps or keep up with celebrity gossip. We lawyers need to get chatting and tweeting or risk extinction.

I'm guilty. Guilty beyond reasonable doubt of having an addiction – guilty of being a social media, social networking, social savvy junkie. And I'm here to defend my case against the cynics who continually persecute and ridicule me and my fellow junkies in the misguided belief that social media is a fad, a trend – a charade even.

How many times have I and my fellow travellers had to listen politely to the smug bluster of middle-aged know-it-alls pompously promulgating the argument that those benefitting from social media are limited to dysfunctional teenagers who have lost the ability to communicate by traditional human means, or fading 'celebrities' who are trying to generate some temporary public interest in their near-forgotten careers? Countless times.

But I submit that we lawyers – and all those working in our businesses of law – mustn't be prejudiced by the blinkered views of the frightened or lazy. Instead, we should embrace the extraordinary benefits of social media. Why? Because of the simple and practical business phenomenon of the 'survival of the savviest'.[10]

In 2010, Facebook wunderkind Mark Zuckerberg said 'over the next five years or so, social networking will make it possible to pick any industry and rethink it'. So let's consider the legal profession. Because of the ubiquity of the worldwide internet and the internet in business, not even the traditionally conservative legal sector has been able to ignore it. Social media has become an integral part of that environment: it is evolving into our 21st-century playground and office space; there are some 1.2 billion active users on Facebook, LinkedIn, Twitter, and Google+, totalling one sixth of the world's population.

Law firm clients, prospective clients, competitors, friends, and family all use social media. If you, the individual lawyer, do not engage you are going to be excluded from the globally networked society and collaborative[11] community. You will feel ostracised because you will be ignorant of the context in which the seven vices – wrath, greed, sloth, pride, lust, envy, and gluttony – are now played out online, in business as well as with family and for leisure.

As lawyers, if we hope to represent clients – whether in contentious or non-contentious matters – we're going to have to understand and empathise[12] with them in the space they frequent. Social media is a medium through which we can interact on a more personal level with contacts, show-case our professional accomplishments, expand our knowledge, amplify our core messages, start and monitor conversations, find potential customers, carry out public relations, manage our (brand)[13] reputations, and provide extraordinary client service[14] by satisfying the expectations of our customers in 'real-time'. With social media, a little effort can produce a return of a four, five, or even six-figure instruction, reaching a potential annual seven-figure revenue from social networking activity alone.[15] With potential numbers like those, why wouldn't we use social media?

The bottom line is that being a successful lawyer in the 21st century requires being sociable in 21st-century media. Lawyers who use the free social media streams will have a higher survival rate. And that's why, all things considered, I'm happy confessing my guilt as a social savvy junkie. The defence rests.

Oh, and here's a stack of statistics just to stick *the naked lawyer* dancing bootie in:

- More online exposure means more customers[16];
- 22 per cent of consumers use social media to find a lawyer[17];
- Twitter and Facebook are the new golf course[18];
- In 2013, 60 per cent of companies had adopted some element of inbound marketing;
- Yet 40 per cent of marketers are 'not prepared' for the digital future – are you?;
- 85.2 per cent of people do not read (print-based) newspapers/magazines any more;
- 50 per cent of internet sales to occur via social media by 2015;
- The future is digital;
- 20 per cent of bricks and mortar shops will be gone by 2018;

- The move from internal emails to social media will increase productivity;
- Social networking is in wide use around the world;
- Saucy apps can keep lawyers up-to-date;
- Social media and social networking is causing lots of juicy legal work, for example, Facebook being sued by a Dutch patent-holding company over the 'like' feature[19];
- Consumers and businesses rely on the internet and social networks to find a lawyer.[20]

Social media and social networking helps you compete against existing players and newcomers – even against the non-lawyers who are aiming to rule the world. For example, the latest legal start-up kiddies in law law land that I mention in the previous chapter. Notably they haven't got any results from it, yet. It may well be because of this:

- More than 50 per cent of clients consider law firms to be ineffective in their use of social media and over one third of clients say firms' use of intranets, extranets, and digital media is ineffective;[21]
- They're not using the ROAR model – for example, in contrast to the above point, Shoosmiths throughout the UK (Gary Assim), McCullogh Robertson Lawyers in Australia (Jeremy Kennedy), and Mitch Jackson in the USA all use the ROAR model with great success (more about this in Chapter 5); and
- They're not using smart technology systems (properly) to capitalise on how they can truly succeed in the new normal – for example, in Scandinavia, Knut Magnar of Schjodt law firm (Oslo, Norway) uses Deltek technology (more about this in Chapters 5 and 6 too).

Simply put, those businesses of law and lawyers who are not succeeding in their online 'SOCIAL' activities are likely to be using SOCIAL as a 'tool' rather than a ROAR 'behaviour': embracing the ROAR model in its entirety. It is only in the past year that I have actually begun to see a gentle shift by law firms to invest in their individual lawyers to embrace social media and social networking. (More about this later in Chapter 5.)

So, how do you succeed as a lawyer in this digital age and pending robotic age?

1) develop business

You have to become a better business developer (a rainmaker, even) using your EQ/EI. Then, you must 'rock 'n' roll' from bland to brand.

2) devise 'Brand,You'

You have to create, devise, manage, and control your personal brand, your 'Brand,You'. That includes your offline and online reputation/identity/profile (R/I/P).

You are NAKED, vulnerable, until you clothe yourself with your unique personal brand, and this is why the prospect and client will choose you instead of a competitor. Why? Because, as I said before (in *the naked lawyer*), prospects/clients do business with those they know, like, trust, really 'get', understand and share common interests with.

Let's look at some recent research carried out by Microsoft, Peppermint Technology, *Legal IT Insider*, and *LegalFutures*, which proves my statement, experience, and achievement – along with the achievement of my clients who use the ROAR model.

Here are a few snippets from the research:

- *Question*: Businesses – if you were purchasing legal advice, how important would you consider the following six factors?[22]

Answer:

- ☐ Know and trust a lawyer (53 per cent);
- ☐ Recommended by someone (19 per cent);
- ☐ Quality and promptness of service (17 per cent);
- ☐ Price (6 per cent);
- ☐ Office location (3 per cent);
- ☐ Trusted brand name (firm brand last) (2 per cent).

- *Question*: How would you go about finding a legal service provider? *Answer*: 24 per cent of consumers and businesses would search the internet first.

Roll on to 2014 and the latest research by Microsoft, Peppermint Technology, *Legal IT Insider*, and *LegalFutures* reveals[23]:

- A dramatic increase and appetite by customers for online legal services and interaction;
- Clients want control;
- Clients want to package up legal services; and
- Clients want a personalised service.

Strikingly:

- 51 per cent of law firms have no plans to introduce online legal services and interaction;
- 60 per cent of firms spend less than 5 per cent of their marketing budget on social media and social networking; and
- Less than 25 per cent had integrated a social media and social networking strategy into wider marketing plans.

How can you be known, let alone trusted, and give a personal personalised service if you (the individual lawyer) are not even present online in the social streams?

Social media and social networking is very much akin to the lottery, you see... If you're not in it, you can't win it. And what clients and prospects find of real value is 'Val,You': 'Brand,You'.

3) communication & care

A human and technology mix – the use of CRM systems and truly KNOWING and understanding your market, prospect, client, and yourself. To be truly successful (to be *tomorrow's naked lawyer*) you need not only be a better business developer/rainmaker with a personal brand, you will need to be an extraordinary communicator who genuinely cares.

Accordingly, the new trends in effective client relationship and business development that reap rewards and results are:

- Unbrand (NOT brand firm) – It's all about 'Brand,You';
- Unmarketing (positioning) – Pulling not pushing; and
- Unsales (not selling) – Conversing and relating, being truly 'social', particularly online in social networks using social media.

That is, 'unlawyering'. However, please note, 'Brand,You' must go hand in hand with 'Brand,Firm'. The formula for success is: 'Brand,Firm' + many 'Brand,Yous' = profit/growth.

This ought to be evident in your social behaviour. When using social media and engaging in social networking, you are not only engaging in conversations; you need to capture, analyse, monitor, and manage the data because true success comes from understanding 'humanness' and technology, and how to exploit it.

Highly successful lawyers, managers, and leaders in businesses of law in the new normal take full advantage of sophisticated technology systems – customer-centric systems, for example, CRM with client analytics alongside pricing and billing and WIP/scope creep systems (for example, Revenuetion – more about this in Chapter 6) – to monitor, analyse, identify, and continually 'touch' prospects/clients/referrers of value.

They focus on their human behaviour first – that is, they record their activity and data, track, monitor, analyse, re-focus, and prompt/instigate further activity, then use the technology system to aid informed decision-making and focus in relation to (for example) tendering, pitching, target market focus, sectorisation, niche focus, schmoozing of the most valuable clients, best use of marketing/business development budget, and evaluation of growth plans.

Deltek, Peppermint, Salesforce, LexisNexis Interaction/Lexis 1, Thomson Reuters Elite, Revenuetion, Clio, and ROAR are a few examples of the kind of technology systems, software, and sales behavioural models you ought to consider investing in to be successful in the digital age and robotic age. More about these in Chapter 6, too.

Successful lawyers across the globe embrace and use these systems and models to gain intelligence about their prospects/targets and clients, markets, and opportunities, and to touch their clients regularly to foster loyalty, to cross-sell and up-sell, and they do this all by striving to be extraordinary, and by being naked – ego stripped/transparent – until clothed with a personal brand which boasts genuineness and authenticity, and is created and positioned to attract the ideal kind of value client.

social tips for 2015

If you'd welcome a heads-up with regard to the latest social media trends to inform your sales and marketing strategy, plan, and activity going forward, I recommend you take a sneaky peek at Exact Target's 2014 'State of Marketing' report.[24] While I cannot reproduce the content of the report in full, below are three really cool areas you ought to consider immediately.

1. really listen to your customers

More brands are beginning to really listen to their customers/clients. Consider the context of social conversations and respond strategically. Note: it's not just about setting up a HootSuite account and watching tweets that mention your brand's name. Social listening *offers opportunities to interact directly with consumers*. So, get engaging and chin-wagging! According to the report, 60 per cent of marketers were using social listening strategies in 2013 and 24 per cent planned to do so in 2014.

2. use social advertising

LinkedIn, Twitter, Facebook, etc. are daily destinations for millions of UK, US, and international consumers, who spend an average of 37 minutes per day on these particular channels and streams. While marketers' budgets indicate the appeal of social advertising, I recommend you educate yourself and learn the most effective way to leverage social ads. Here's something to get you started:

- Establish measurable marketing goals;
- Set your budget (start small);
- Know your audience's needs;
- Pick the channel;
- Research different ad types (how they work, how to leverage them, and how your audience will perceive them);

- Check out the competition;
- Optimize your landing pages;
- Experiment and create ad copy (two or three versions); and
- Test and measure.

3. create your social media dream team

Having a dedicated team is essential to social media marketing success. Most brands understand this even if the team is only you – that is, one person.

If you are a one (wo)man band then here are a few tips:

- **Start with a strategy** – Know what you want to accomplish from social media and choose your social networks wisely. For example, focus on your niche and position your personal brand in front of the ideal target client in the appropriate network;
- **Create a workflow process** – Schedule some time each day for routine social media activities, such as posting updates, networking, listening, and monitoring etc. I recommend 30 minutes per day (minimum);
- **Develop quality content** – I strongly recommend you create original content on a regular basis (for example, blog posts, graphics, images, videos, etc.) If you struggle with the 'time-bomb' and you have a wee budget, you can get other people to create high-quality content for you (like me!) You can also get free images from sites like Flickr or Wikimedia Commons; and
- **Get the word out** – Let your co-workers and customers know that you're on LinkedIn, Twitter, Facebook, YouTube, Google+ etc. Encourage them to engage with you personally and your business of law on these channels.

If you'd welcome a heads-up with regard to how major brands will use social media big data in 2015 for marketing, I recommend you take a sneaky peek at SBR Technologies slideshare.[25] It's actually a very informative, entertaining, and fun read – albeit a little scary for the social media pessimist and/or naysayer!

I am often asked my view on the future of sales and marketing by lawyers and those in key (decision) roles within businesses of law. Although I could spend an age on this topic, I have got in down to this:

marketing is dead

'Marketing is dead. The future of sales and marketing is already here. You just don't realise it, yet...' I shall leave you to ponder. Prrrrrrrrrrrrrr. I'd like to claim I came up with the 'marketing is dead' mantra. In truth, I nicked it from a speech by the CEO of Saatchi & Saatchi, Kevin Roberts,[26] who inspired me when he said:

'The role of marketing has changed now. There is nothing new anymore. If marketers are just hearing about something going on then it is already old in today's world. The further up in a company you go the stupider you become and the further away from new things. Speed and velocity is everything today. Marketing's jobs is to create movement and inspire people to join you.'

He went on to say: 'Everyone wants a conversation. They want inspiration. Inspire people with your internet site. Don't just interrupt, but interact. Asking about return on investment is the wrong question today. You should be asking about "return on involvement".'

Obviously, Mr Roberts has been inspired by my good friend, world-renowned speaker on media futurism Gerd Leonhard, who first coined the 'return on involvement' phrase many years ago. The true return on investment for the business of law is the return on involvement by each and every lawyer within the law firm with their client online and offline utilising their personal brand ('Brand,You') in a social, digital environment. And this is why…

intimacy, service, branding, and reputation matter most

Building on what I've just been sharing with you, research by my Australian friend, George Beaton, reveals that 'intimacy and service matter most to clients', as illustrated neatly by Figure 2, below.[27] Take a sip of your wine/beer/coffee and take a wee bit of time to study this diagram.

George's reference to 'caring' and 'ease of doing business with' ought to resonate with you if you've read *the naked lawyer*, the prelims to this book, and Chapter 2, so far, thoroughly.

I was delighted when Eulogy asked me to provide a foreword to their first whitepaper on the legal sector; 'The perfect storm – reputation: the key to staying afloat in the new legal world'.[28] The 2014 report brings together a wealth of information from all areas of law. I believe they asked me because what I have been advocating for many years with regard to how firms' brands and reputations are affecting their ability (both positive and negative) to win new business. (So, embrace the ROAR model because it is in fact the way forward,

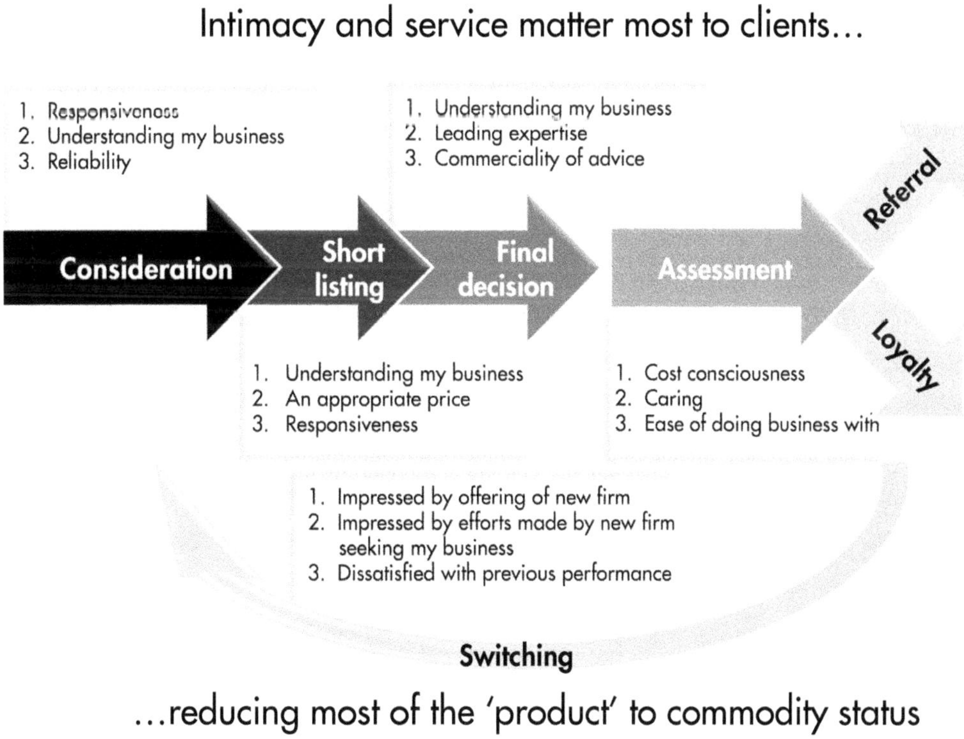

Figure 2: Intimacy and service matter most to clients (© Beaton Benchmarks, 2015)

has now been proven – four years since inception – through this research.)

By assessing every firm in the top 100 in the UK, Eulogy built up a clear picture on what is and isn't working for each. Unfortunately, I am sure that the findings are NOT what many law firms wish to hear. For the front runners in the legal industry who understand what they truly need to do to keep and attract clients, the thought of turning things upside down and/or starting again is not a 'heart sinking' feat to be met with resistance, but a challenge and opportunity which is welcomed and embraced.

Does branding matter in law firms? YES, of course it does, as the report rightly says: 'law firms are already brands without realising it, but in the context of the global (and ABS) market, they are bad ones'. Moreover, individual lawyers have personal brands within the law firm without realising it too; a lawyer's personal brand lies within a lawyer's reputation, identity, and profile (remember: RIP), both offline and online.

Ironically, many law firms still cringe at the thought of allowing their lawyers to boast a personal brand, an identity such as The Entrepreneur Lawyer (i.e. me), The Image Lawyer, or The Data Lawyer (both personal brands devised by lawyers at Shoosmiths), which attract clients both online and offline in a digital world – once you know how to find your unique space. A personal brand is the oxygen to the lifeblood of the firm's brand in a digital client world.

Eulogy's report shows that 'many (firms) understand that they need to do more in an increasingly competitive market to differentiate themselves from their competitors'. To this end, the report provides the reader with the kind of brand descriptor words they ought to be using to attract clients. The bottom line is that Eulogy's research proves that it is best to espouse 'a niche of a niche of a niche of a niche', something which can only truly be achieved by individual lawyers taking into consideration their niche specialism, comprising technical area of law expertise, a focus on their industry of knowledge, sectorisation within that industry, its geographic location, culture, and even gender of potential client.

The findings in this white paper show that there is a clear disparity between what law firms *think* clients want (to hear and experience) and what they *actually* want (to hear and experience). Furthermore, the trend is for clients to continue to demand extraordinary customer service – aka increasing quality of service – above most things, something which can only realistically be achieved through each individual lawyer's behaviour (before, during, and after instruction: the relationship evolution).

A business of law's reputation therefore lives and dies by the behaviour and reputation of their individual lawyers. Those lawyers (and therefore their firms) that are successful in standing out from the crowd are those that truly niche and are not afraid of allowing their lawyers to:

- Let RIP – Build a reputation, create an identity, raise their profile (devise and cultivate their personal brand); and truly
- ROAR (reach out and relate) both offline and online with social media, social networking, and social brand, in their quest to increase the overall reputation of the law firm.

Above all, this research shows that 'the fact that law firms are recognising that clients need to be both aware of WHO they are and WHAT they offer before they are even in the position to be asked to tender for work is a positive step forward in relation to recognition. HOW they are approaching this differs. The answer clearly lies in the AND, not the OR – that is, the amalgamation of the creatively uniquely crafted law firm brand descriptors (in the media) combined with their individual lawyers' personal brands and behaviour (in the media), particularly online.

There is no denying the importance of lawyers being visible and active online when one looks at the trends, drivers, and statistics that clearly show that digital is the future. Furthermore, brands outside the legal sector (but including those who are entering it) are already beginning to pioneer a new way of innovating through engagement; indeed, the growing use of social media by brands to have direct conversations with their customers is evidence of this.

As Eulogy's research shows, the legal market's use of new communications channels reinforces bad business practice rather than changes it. Most firms are still taking what I term the 'PR dross approach', where law firms use a 'push' communication approach rather than a 'pull' approach: pumping out rubbish, uninteresting, egotistical information to the listener, rather than positioning individual lawyers to communicate with the ideal client by pulling them toward the quality, personal, interesting, personal content and information the prospect and client craves.

The legal sector is undergoing a perfect storm of change. Because of this new climate, it has never been more important for a business of law to clearly convey to its audiences who it is, what it does, and what makes it different. Without a strong reputation within the legal and wider business market, without a clear brand, direction, and business strategy, many law firms and lawyers will simply not survive the next few years: one in three meltdown, remember?

Co-incidentally, *the naked lawyer* has been read (and its concepts and guides digested and followed) by thousands of lawyers across the globe, including the majority of the Top 20 law firms in this report, and I have had the great pleasure and privilege of working with individuals within many of these firms. My only regret is that some of those lawyers and law firms that aspire for greater things are too afraid to jump, or start again, in order to get ahead in the present and future. Perhaps this white paper will help prompt and guide them – and you?

marketing trends for 2015

In light of my statement that 'marketing is dead', it seems somewhat nonsensical to then dedicate some time to sharing my thoughts on marketing trends for 2015. I'm doing this because most of you probably won't agree with me. This is because 'we' (those of us outside of law law land – aka the rest of the world) have already begun transitioning from marketing to unmarketing; now, it's all about ROARing, engaging, conversing, and being social – in SOCIAL.

However, I came across a LinkedIn publication posted in October this year, which I believe you will be intrigued by. I was. And if it got my attention, then I know I ought to share it with you.

It's a short(ish) piece written by the head of marketing at Danone Waters in India, entitled '11 Must Know Marketing Trends for 2015'.[29] Although I will not reproduce the full piece, I will highlight a few of the things which struck me as relevant to the focus and purpose of *tomorrow's naked lawyer*:

- **'Brandalytics'** – The triangulaton of data. Making a common sense approach across brand, market, and consumer data (big data or small) will become key in 2015. This will change the way decisions are currently taken in marketing.

- **Frenzied 'digication' (digital activation) of brands** – This is a trend companies have been talking about in 2014, but in 2015 they will begin to act. Most brands will spend more, and will have much more activity on social media (Facebook, Twitter, You-tube, etc.). Building *digital content specific to brand benefit* will become a more prevalent approach. For brands which are inactive in this space, it's time to wake up! Meaning both businesses of law and you, the individual lawyer.
- **The 'slice and dice' of media strategy** – There will be many more media options for the marketer. Accordingly, geo targeting the consumer will be a key way to slice and dice, and will become more common in 2015.
- **Many niche dot coms will emerge in 2015** – Need segmentation will reach new heights in the digital and ecommerce era. Lots of dot coms will emerge which target niche areas – e.g. home décor, kids education, speciality education, niche skills building, accessories (cars, bikes etc.), men's fashion – even condoms, perhaps?

I am often asked my view on the biggest mistake lawyers are making with their marketing. Again, I could spend an age on this topic. However, to be blunt, there isn't just one big mistake. It's a series of many. But I reckon the following ten things cover most of what I believe:

1. Not thinking like your clients;
2. Not standing in your clients' shoes;
3. Not being social;
4. Not being naked (transparent);
5. Not being creative, innovative, and entrepreneurial;
6. Not being a front-runner;
7. Not being pro-active with lead generation/conversation follow-up;
8. Not embracing technology to aid in marketing (social);
9. Not embracing your lobsters (key referrers and experts); and
10. Not being truly human.

So, if you turn these around (remove the NOT), then you have my view in relation to what you need to do to be successful in your marketing (unmarketing/social) efforts:

1. Think like your clients;
2. Stand in your clients' shoes;
3. Be social;
4. Be naked (transparent);
5. Be creative, innovative, and entrepreneurial;
6. Be a front-runner;
7. Be pro-active with lead generation/conversation follow-up;
8. Embrace technology to aid in marketing (social);
9. Embrace your lobsters;
10. Be truly human.

robot hits in 2015

Instead of asking me 'what is the future of sales and marketing?', those of you who are seekers ought to be asking me the question, 'what is the future of social?' My answer: if marketing is dead, it's because the robots are here. The robots are taking over the 'traditional marketing' role, just like they are/will take over your 'traditional lawyering' role. We are witnessing offline conversion input and the rise of marketing automation, for the future of social marketing automation, is here, now… and it's improving.

I'd like to share with you an article by Roz Lemieux, CEO of Attentive.ly[30] as it puts what I have just shared with you so far into context:

'A 2013 study of marketing professionals[31] identified "social media marketing" as the second-most powerful trend contributing to the formation of the "modern marketer" – after the ability to track marketing ROI with technology. Yet even the most advanced modern marketing teams have struggled to effectively incorporate social media into their marketing automation workflows, let alone track the ROI on those communications. The hold-up has been partly cultural and partly technological.

On the cultural side, this is part and parcel of the larger paradigm shift from "blast" to "triggered" (personalized) communications... Social media has a naturally conversational structure and is not particularly effective as a "blast" medium – so companies have dragged their feet implementing effective one-to-one response mechanisms, just as they have on the email side of the house.

That means businesses are leaving money on the table. American Express reported in 2012 that its research found social media users are willing for pay a 21% price premium to do business with companies that provide exceptional service. As a result, social-based customer service improved markedly in 2013, more than doubling their response rate (62%) to questions posed directly to (or about) them.

So we're halfway there when it comes to "social customer care" – but what about tracking and responding to those *vast majority of mentions* that *don't* include your brand (or product) name? The natural next step is to link that "social listening" data to your marketing automation system – so that you (the modern marketer) can combine that "listening" data with what you *already know* about that individual – for real-time multi-channel response.

For example, let's say you are Apple tracking a customer segment that has purchased a computer from you in the last 12 months, and they complain about "my computer" – you'll know it's highly likely it's the *Apple computer you sold them* that has the problem. If you're tracking that complaint in your marketing automation system, you can fire off a warrantee reminder via email or have your social team DM that individual with an offer of support. If s/he mentions Apple directly, you can respond publicly.

Moreover, that social listening data, when linked to individuals' profiles, can provide *much* more data for segmentation and scoring to fuel your marketing campaigns. Customers spend an average of 3 hours/day on social media, but likely just a few minutes on your site (if they make it there). By tracking what customers and prospects are talking about, modern marketers can build out automations that take social posts into account when tracking customers' "digital body language" to drive trigger-based marketing. For example, the *New York Times* could target foodies (commenting on recipes or restaurants) with their "Food" content and wine advertisements. Travelocity could send Austin hotel discounts to customers mentioning #SXSW.

Last October, Oracle's Roland Smart presented a vision of "The Future of Social Marketing Automation" at #EE13 where companies could set up rules-based responses to customers' social posts based on natural language analysis. At the time, "social listening" and "marketing automation" were still largely held in separate buckets, so that was a vision not a reality. Today, we're many steps closer. Eloqua's Social Behavior Sparkplug allows marketers to listen to their customers and marketing leads on social media – and trigger smart multi-channel responses (emails, ads, direct social responses, segmentation, and scoring) based on those social signals.

What's still "future" is on the technology-side: the ability to trigger those responses instantly, which is of course what makes those public social interactions, in particular, human-feeling. The good news is that vision is not too far in the future – we'll be there in (late) 2014. In the meantime, modern marketers can take advantage of a huge new opportunity that has just opened up to (1) never miss a brand-mention on social media (even when it's hidden), and (2) using all that rich social behavior data to direct the right message to the right person at the right time – all with trackable ROI thanks to today's modern marketing automation tools.'

Marketing automation has seen the fastest growth of any customer relationship management (CRM) related segment in the last five years. Evidently, traditional marketing tips are being replaced by robots hits.

no more B2B or B2C: there is only H2H, then H2R

What do I mean when I say we need to be 'truly human'? It used to be that marketing was segmented into two categories: business-to-business (B2B) or business-to-consumer (B2C). This was done (I presume), to separate specialties, audiences, and segments in an effort to more specifically target the groups of people who ultimately would consume a brand's message. The lines are so blurred now – because of 'social' between the two marketing segments – that it's hard to differentiate between the two anymore. We all need to think like the consumers we are, putting ourselves into the mindset (shoes) of the buyer instead of trying to speak such an intensely sophisticated language full of acronyms and big words, in order to sound smarter.

Communication shouldn't be complicated. It should just be genuine and simple, with the humility and understanding that we're all multi-dimensional humans, every one of which has spent time in both the dark and delightful parts of life. That's human to human. That is H2H.

We human beings are innately complex yet strive for simplicity. Our challenge as humans is to find, understand, and explain the complex in its most simplistic form. This means you, lawyers. Find the commonality in our humanity, and speak the language we've all been waiting for. The lesson? No more B2B or B2C. There is only human to human (H2H). Of course, in the forseeable future, we will be saying that there is only human to robot (H2R) and, further still, robot to robot (R2R), perhaps?

sounding human

'Every single day, 4.75 billion posts go up on Facebook. To put that number in perspective, there have only been 129 million books published since the beginning of time, with an average word length of 64,000 words. That means we are publishing more content (by number of words) every single day on Facebook than is contained in every single book published since humans have existed!'[32]

For us lawyers (and unmarketers), it's our job to stand out in that absurdly large crowd of social online content. Yes, cutting a niche, devising a personal brand, and becoming the 'go-to lawyer' for your specialism is a good start. But, in an increasingly crowded 'social' environment running wild with robots and humans, a really cool way to stand out is to have a truly distinct HUMAN voice – this ought to be part of your personal brand, btw.

If marketing automation is the new beast in the robotic age, it becomes imperative that, to differentiate the robots from us, the humans, we learn how to sound human when online.

Here are the top eight ways to sound like a real human on the internet.

1. be sympathetic

Did you know that you can get high by talking to a friend? When two humans are chatting (and it's not a cat-fight), our bodies release oxytocin. The reason is a natural defence so that we'll stick together and not be eaten by lions – if we like hanging out with each other we'll have the safety of our 'pack' to protect us.

Accordingly, social blog posts that are written in the style we are comfortable with (meaning lots of personal words like 'you', 'we', 'our', 'us', 'I') can stand out from the maddening generic noise because they appear more natural and interesting. Tip: try writing your posts from the first person, addressing people like you would in conversation to take advantage of this finding.

2. keep it simple (don't use big words)

Like I do. Speaking like a lawyer might make you feel like a genius, but only at the expense of potentially alienating your prospect/client/reader/audience. We like things we can understand. It makes us feel smart and simple language creates strong communication because there is less risk of getting lost in interpretation. Putting things in plain language will subtly cause readers, prospects, and clients to believe what you're saying. When an idea is conveyed in simple terms you don't have to process the information or think twice about it before gaining understanding. This is especially important on social networks where we are very limited in the snippets that get shared.

3. follow the tipsy college student rule

'Write drunk, edit sober' was Ernest Hemingway's mantra. Don't you just love Ernest? (Guzzles more wine… hic!) Hemingway didn't know it, but he invented the 'tipsy college student rule'. This 'rule' basically states that you should take the edge off of your writing. Speak candidly, qualm your fears about being controversial, say what you want to say.

The lesson? Don't be afraid to speak candidly, it will help people connect with you.

4. follow the pub rule

Don't publish any piece that wouldn't be appropriate for a conversation in a pub. That means both the topic of the piece and the way it's written. You don't want the reader to feel like they're being lectured at or having facts recited in their faces. Tip: read it out loud and decide whether or not it sounds like a pub conversation. For best results, go do it in an actual pub!

5. use your own vernacular

I like to use the word 'cool' as a response sometimes. I'm not a geek, or a youngster, but it just seems so much friendlier than 'good', 'okay', 'fine' etc. We all have little 'tics' that make us unique – whether it's ending conversations by saying 'cool' or using the same dumb icebreaker your best friend always uses. These little things make us unique and identify us as human, so don't be afraid to use them.

6. tell stories

Because we are so used to stories being a part of our lives, they feel natural and comfortable. Since the beginning of time stories have been a natural method of communication. Each of us has our own style of storytelling which will reveal the subtleties of our unique humanness. (Tip: adding a story to your blog post can increase readership by 300 per cent on average and boost on-page time by 5 times.)

One of the main reasons robots haven't been able to pass the Turing test (which decides if you are human or not), is that they are unable to tell stories because they have no memory of the world as it stands. We could pass the Turing test because we are able to convey information in story format (and we're also human). I reckon you take advantage of this now, before the robots can!

7. reference pop culture

Situational references are a sure-fire way to differentiate yourself from a machine and take on distinct human traits. If you've seen *Terminator* you know that robots just don't get pop culture references. Tying content into the lives that we lead on a day-to-day basis correlates to more views.

8. obey the Shaq rule

Shaquille O'Neal turned himself from a basketball star into a global brand. He's worth $350 million dollars – even though he's been retired for three years. Shaq's overall brand comes from the power of his social media presence; he's got 8.55 million twitter followers and 4.7 million Facebook likes. He's like the American equivalent of England's beloved David Beckham.

When it comes to all things social media, Shaq has a rule. His rule is that 80 per cent of his posts are meant to entertain his audience, 15 per cent are meant to be informative and interesting, and 5 per cent are meant to sell products. Shaq realises that it's not natural to be selling all the time, and no one likes it.

Most of his efforts are spent building his audience by sharing fun and interesting content. That way, when it does come time to promote a product he's got a loyal and engaged audience to sell to, instead of a bunch of followers tired of hearing about whatever product he's hawking today.

after dark activity

In relation to the Digital Age, the Data Age, the Age of Unlawyering, and the Robotic Age, and due to the evolution of the internet, we are undoubtedly witnessing the revolution of unsales (relationship sales), unmarketing (relationship marketing), unbranding (relationship and social branding), and 'robot marketing' of legal services throughout the legal marketplace… globally.

just do something!

Take some time now to read the reports referenced at the end of this chapter. They complement the chapter content, and I'm confident it will add to your knowledge and understanding and provoke action.

Now brace yourself. The next chapter is going to take you even further out of your comfort zone…

References

1. Satell, G., 'Strategy is no longer a game of chess', *Harvard Business Review*, July 2014, see: http://blogs.hbr.org/2014/05/strategy-is-no-longer-a-game-of-chess
2. LexisNexis's Bellwether Report (2014), see: http://businessoflaw.lexisnexis.co.uk/download-the-2014-bellwether-report/.
3. Ibid.
4. HubSpot-Forrestor research print-out re social brand – '20 Marketing Trends 2013'; Eulogy! January 2014, 'The perfect storm – reputation: the key to staying afloat in the new legal world'; 'Panel Games: How Client Orgs Pick Their Legal Advisers', Oxford University Saiid Business School (see: www2.kulahub.net/clients/f/entrepreneurlawyerlimited/documents/Panel_games_in_PSFs_-_Oxford_University_Saiid_

Business_School_-_Nov_2013.pdf);

5. 'What Clients Really Want from a Legal Service Provider', Peppermint Technology in association with Microsoft (see: www.peppermínttechnology.co.uk/legal-service-customer-experience-research); LexisNexis's Bellwether Report, 2014 (see: http://businessoflaw.lexisnexis.co.uk/download-the-2014-bellwether-report/).
6. See: www.slaw.ca/2014/08/10/competence-for-the-low-tech-lawyer/.
7. See: www.law21.ca/2014/08/watershed-cba-futures-report/.
8. Source: HubSpot-Forrestor research print-out re social brand, '20 Marketing Trends 2013'.
9. See: www.gbgplc.com/solutions/digital-marketing-services/social-media.
10. Social Media Examiner, Social media marketing industry report 2013.
11. See: http://entrepreneurlawyer.co.uk/wp-content/uploads/2011/11/MP_Oct2011_HR_EntrepreneurLawyer.pdf.
12. See: www.globallegalpost.com/management-speak/farewell-to-the-oil-age.
13. See: www.globallegalpost.com/management-speak/a-pain-in-the-head.
14. See: http://entrepreneurlawyer.co.uk/wp-content/uploads/2011/06/Managing-Partner_May-2011_BD_Branding.pdf.
15. See: www.globallegalpost.com/global-view/european-gcs-slam-lack-of-client-service.
16. See: http://entrepreneurlawyer.co.uk/about/testimonials.
17. Source: BloggingPro, 'Use of Social Media by law firms', see: www.bloggingpro.com/archives/2012/06/26/use-of-social-media-by-law-firms/.
18. Source: Kovar, A., '1 in 5 Consumers Use Social Media to Look for a Lawyer', Lexis Nexis, October 2012. See: www.lexisnexis.com/community/portal/blogs/kovarat/archive/2012/10/17/1-in-5-consumers-use-social-media-to-look-for-a-lawyer.aspx.
19. Source: Legal Futures – including research by MLT (see: http://budurl.com/smnobrainer).
20. See: www.globallegalpost.com/global-view/facebook-sued-over-like-feature-66094283/?utm_campaign=D1_12_02_13&utm_medium=email&utm_source=newsletter_d1.
21. Source: 'What Clients Really want from A Legal Service Provider' (hardcopy report) – by Microsoft, NatWest, Peppermint Technology, Legal Technology Insider, Legal Futures – 2012.
22. A recent article by FT.com has highlighted social media as a blind spot for law firms, see: http://aboutus.ft.com/2011/06/28/financial-times-study-highlights-mutual-misunderstandings-between-law-firms-and-their-clients/#axzz2Cl68U75F.
23. 'What Clients Really want from A Legal Service Provider', Microsoft, NatWest, Peppermint Technology, Legal Technology Insider, Legal Futures, 2012.
24. Source: 'What Clients Really want from A Legal Service Provider' (hardcopy report), Microsoft, NatWest, Peppermint Technology, Legal Technology Insider, Legal Futures, 2014.
25. See: http://blogs.salesforce.com/company/2014/01/state-of-marketing.html.
26. See: www.slideshare.net/creativeguerrilla/preview-marketingadvances2015.
27. Quoting Kevin Roberts, CEO of Saatchi & Saatchi, see: www.thedrum.com/news/2012/04/25/marketing-dead-says-saatchi-saatchi-ceo.
28. Slide 8 in 'Positioning for Market Impact' is a compilation of original Beaton Benchmarks research. See: www.beatonglobal.com/beaton-benchmarks/>.
29. Eulogy! 'The perfect storm – reputation: the key to staying afloat in the new legal world', January 2014, see: www.eulogy.co.uk/?portfolio=the-perfect-storm-reputation-the-key-to-staying-afloat-in-the-new-legal-world.

30. See: www.linkedin.com/pulse/article/20141006151256-337113487-11-must-know-marketing-trends-for-2015?trk=nus-cha-roll-art-title.
31. Attentive.ly is a social behaviour platform that helps modern marketing organisations predict how customers and supporters will behave – even what they might do or buy – from social data.
32. See: www.eloqua.com/content/dam/eloqua/Downloads/whitepapers/B2B_Mag_defining-the-modern-marketer.pdf.
33. See: www.entrepreneur.com/article/238367.

Chapter 3: our robotic life, 2015 to 2045

'Don't wait for the light to appear at the end of the tunnel… go down there and light the bloody thing yourself.'
Cameron de Bough, Australian Paralympian

SINCE THE dawn of time, humankind has experienced, embraced (not without kicking and screaming), and survived the many challenges, radical changes, disruptions, and 'ages' during its quest to evolve: The Ice Age, The Industrial Age, The Digital Age, and The Data Age. I am confident that, due to mankind surviving in the past, it will survive the current transition (and transformation) toward the Artificially Intelligent Age and the Robotic Age too. But not without some serious casualties.

As I shared throughout *the naked lawyer*, whether we survive and smile, or falter and frown, it's all about choice, change, and control. The same rings true for *tomorrow's naked lawyer*, while noting that we also need to take into consideration the contrasts and uncertainty in our world today.

So, let's be positive, shall we? If you want to succeed in the present and future of law (and beyond and/or elsewhere), it's not just about getting naked! I reckon you need a big dose of certainty to balance the minefield of uncertainty, in order to prepare yourself for the challenges in the years ahead…

certainties in uncertain times

It is a truth universally acknowledged that any lawyer worth his salt must be worthy of employment for his lifetime. Do you reckon? I put it to you that no matter how fabulous a lawyer you are intellectually, you will meet your match and be superseded by iCyborg lawyer and RobotLawyer within the next two to three decades. Actually, I predict that artificial intelligence, machines, and quite possibly robots will come to dominate the legal world in the not too distant future. By 2020, I reckon. That's a mere five years from now.

Why do I believe this? In September 2011, I returned to England after delivering a couple of keynote sessions (opening and closing) at the Australian Legal Practice Management Association (ALPMA) in Melbourne, Australia. As the theme of the conference was 'Adapt, Innovate, Inspire', I duly spent the final 30 minutes of the closing session looking at the present and future of the legal profession, the industry, and role of the lawyer. My intention was to encourage the delegates to think, feel, and act on what I shared, hoping they would leave the event feeling inspired, eager to adapt, embrace more technology, and to innovate by re-inventing themselves, their teams, and their businesses in preparation for the bold new legal world. This is Horizon 2 and 3, sort of stuff. (See Chapter 1 – 'one in three law firms face financial meltdown'.)

However, in sharing my vision and prediction from present day up to the year 2045 I fear a number of the delegates may have departed the conference quaking in their legal beagle booties. Why? Well…

I posed the question, 'is the iCyborg lawyer near?' and then proceeded to suggest that due to the ingenuity of man – supported with evidence – the answer is indeed a resounding 'yes'. In October 2011, I shared my views in *Managing Partner* magazine that we might soon see the 'iCyborg' taking over our jobs. Huh? Guffaw. Groan. Harrumph. Again, the reaction to my statement. But it received a lot of attention from interested parties within the businesses of law working on their horizons 2 and 3. The article obviously resonated with a handful of technologists and visionaries whom I have been consulting with, and have continued to ever since.

Roll on three years later, to October 2014, when Monidipa Fouzder, *Law Society Gazette* writer and sub-editor, wrote an article entitled 'Robots running law firms? Surely not.'[1] In the article, she reported on insights from Bill Mordan, senior vice-president and general counsel at FTSE 100 company RB (Reckitt Benckiser), who summed up the legal profession's relationship with technology perfectly. I will share more of this later with you. What was the response from the 'anonymous' readers? 'This is the most ridiculous article ever.'

What is certain is that in the decades ahead, our role as lawyers within this new world is going to change dramatically. We have to start tackling this now. If you haven't been dealing with it as horizon 3 in the past five years then you need it on your agenda now because, for those businesses of law that have, it has now slipped into their horizons 1 and 2. This means they have a huge competitive advantage over you. It also means they have given themselves a greater chance of avoiding the 1 in 3 meltdown I wrote about in Chapter 1.

You need to start tackling the skills gap and transition right now, both in your current practice and in how you train tomorrow's naked lawyers, because your (and their) role as a lawyer will inevitably change due to a number of technological trends and developments; some of which I've shared already and some of which I am about to.

For example, global futurist Daniel Burrus highlights the '12 certainties'[2] he believes will transform all of our careers and roles. No matter what our role is today (whether we work in law law land or beyond), these certainties will affect us all, so the sooner we align our skills to these 12 certainties, the more relevant and valuable we will be to our businesses and clients. The 12 certainties that will transform every career are:

1. Cloud services and virtualisation;
2. Big data and real-time analytics;
3. Mobile hardware, software, and services;
4. Social business enterprise management;
5. Cyber security and forensics;
6. Intelligent e-personal assistants;
7. 3D web;
8. Connective intelligent objects;
9. Additive manufacturing (3D printing);
10. Advanced robotics and automation;
11. Remote visual communications; and
12. Gamification of education.

All of these are technology-based, because it is technology which is most rapidly transforming how we work. This doesn't necessarily mean that all of us lawyers must become technologists in order to get a top-paying job as a lawyer in the future (although it might help!). It does mean, however, that we have to adapt our current skills so they include a working understanding of these 12 certainties because this is how we will remain relevant and of value to our businesses and clients/customers/consumers.

Why do I feel so strongly and passionate about this issue? Andrew McAfee, the principal research scientist at MIT's Center for Digital Business, puts it plainly: 'when the robots rule, we (will) need a guaranteed paycheck'. Bang! Robots are going to hit our pockets.

Even the great man himself, Professor Richard Susskind, renowned for his technological knowledge and crystal ball gazing primarily in the UK and US, predicts a new role for the lawyer – 'the legal technologist' – in his latest book *Tomorrow's Lawyers* (published 2013). This kind of role has been present, by the way, for many years, in a handful of law firms.

As far back as 2008, I have known of many lawyers that have re-invented themselves and transitioned their role from lawyer to IT trainer, IT manager, knowledge manager, social media manager, etc. in law firms in the UK, Europe, Scandinavia, the US, and beyond. But they are few. This will change.

For I agree with our dear Prof when he predicts that legal markets will be further liberalized and the legal landscape is set to change more radically over the next 20 years than over the last two hundred, leading to an entirely new range of legal roles, which he calls:

- The legal knowledge engineer;
- The legal technologist;
- The legal hybrid;
- The legal process analyst;
- The legal project manager;
- The online dispute resolution practitioner;
- The legal management consultant; and
- The legal risk manager.

I reckon the next 5 to 10 years, actually – forget 20. The concept and reality of the compound effect of the 'theory of acceleration' that Ray Kurzweil speaks of will no doubt bring forward the timeframe of many predictions. The 'non-traditional' new (entrepreneurial/blue chip) sexy players in law law land aren't going to operate at the pace the old guard did/do, you see. It's not in their nature to stifle positive change, creativity and advancement. They initiate it.

Many of these 'new roles' will mean broadening our domain of expertise, not just in the areas of legal advice we provide, but also in our business development ability, business advisory ability, market expertise, project management ability, strategic consultancy, and even organisational psychology, using high-end intellectual capital and emotional intelligence.

I would add a few more roles to the good Prof's list, namely:

- The legal strategist;
- The pricing agent-provocateur;
- The value meister;
- The social collaborator;
- SocialHuman lawyer;
- The big data daddy;
- The data artist;
- The AI executive;
- The intelligent e-personal assistant;
- The icyborg lawyer;
- The robot lawyer;
- RoboManager (the robot lawyer supervisor/manager);
- RoboTechnician (the robot technician); and
- Extinct.

Significantly, things are progressing at a rapid rate with at least one Magic Circle firm here in the UK hiring its first AI graduate at the turn of the year. I actually feel sufficiently confident to predict the first robot lawyer will be released into the world by 2020 (more about this in Chapter 6).

It's what my research, reading, and gut tells me; it's never been wrong yet. It's the message you get reading between the lines of what IBM and Google have shared in the public domain (and privately with me) or, more importantly, what they haven't shared. For as it is in law, so it is with technological advancement: it's not necessarily what we can see or hear that matters; it's often what we can't.

Undeniably, the traditional way of lawyering is now increasingly being questioned, superseded, and/or supported by other ways of operating and delivering legal advice, products, and services. Sorry to break it to you, but there is far more change, disruption, and agitation to come. I reckon we need to consider the probability that we are indeed already in the Age of UnLawyering as we transition toward the Robotic Age…

the age of unlawyering

With the plethora of reports and blog posts of late whizzing around cyberland in relation to online legal document and service providers, legal innovation,[3] the law firm business model,[4] and the future of the legal profession I reckon we're transitioning toward 'two faces of the law'. I believe two dominant umbrella business models are coming to the fore in relation to who, what, where, why, when, and how we serve our clients: face to face and interface.

The law as a profession and as an industry continues to re-invent itself, transform, and transition, I have no doubt there will be a plethora of new business models which spring up under the two dominant umbrella models to compete feverishly in this plump, innovative, new, and increasingly fragmented and diverse global legal market.

Nevertheless, 'WHO' will be doing the serving in the future may well be rather different due to 'machine systems' coming into 'their' own. The way I see it, it's a wonderful and exciting time of opportunity for both personal re-invention and professional evolution for us lawyers, and I welcome the 'humanisation' of lawyers (and no doubt many customers and lawyers do too) in the face-off between 'face to face' and 'interface'.

Whether we like it or not, agree with it or not, welcome it or not, to quote the ubiquitous 'future' statement by *Neuromancer* author William Gibson, 'the future is here… it's just not evenly distributed yet'. You bet. It probably never will be.

Accordingly, to quote the author Charles Handy, 'the great excitement of the future is that we can shape it' – particularly significant when as human beings we're moving toward 'singularity'.

the singularity

The groundbreaking book *The Singularity Is Near: When Humans Transcend Biology,*[5] hit the scene in 2005. The author, Ray Kurzweil, predicts a future in which we are moving toward 'singularity' – where humans transcend biology as a result of the combined effect of the revolution in genetics, nanotechnology, and robotics (including AI).

Ray Kurzweil is one of the world's leading thinkers, inventors, and futurists, with a 20-year track record of accurate predictions. He has been selected as one of the top entrepreneurs by *Inc.* magazine, which describes him as the 'rightful heir to Thomas Edison'. Unsurprisingly he's now chirping in the Google nest.

Kurzweil predicted that by 2010 computers 'will become essentially invisible: woven into our clothing, embedded in our furniture and environment. They will tap into the worldwide mesh (what the World Wide Web is)… We'll have… wireless communication to the Internet at all times.' He was right.

Kurzweils' main concept is that our technological knowledge has been snowballing and that once strong AI is achieved it will be a runaway phenomenon of rapidly escalating super-intelligence. When we reach this point in time we will no longer recognise the world or our place (and space) in it.

Undeniably, we're in a world full of smart artificial intelligence (AI) where the coming together of genetics, nanotechnology, and robotics are affecting (and will affect) the present and future of legal provision and service and the industry. AI can be defined as the intelligence of machines, where an intelligent agent is a system that perceives its environment and takes actions that maximise its chances of success. AI is kind of like a machine mimicking a human. IBM's 'Watson' is such an agent; more on this in a moment. Keep reading.

Automation and AI is mainstream, now. It is already in use by some businesses of law. For example:

- Integrated analytics;
- Knowledge management;
- Voice mining;
- Client self-service;
- Intelligent documents;
- Expertise systems;
- Collaboration;
- Marketing automation (see Chapter 2);
- Virtual assistants/e-personal assistants; and
- Intelligent agents – IBM's Watson.

I recall a conversation with a gentleman from Das at a legal conference at the start of this year at which he shared with me that his company has been using AI for a number of years to assist with due diligence in relation to insurance claims. (Note, due to LSA 2007 and ABS, Das is not just in the insurance business; it's now operating in the business of law as Das Law.[6])

I now dare you to stretch your imagination…

- Imagine if you could be in two places at once?
- Imagine if at the end of your life your brain could be transplanted into the robotic copy of you?
- Imagine if your personality could be transferred into an avatar with an artificial brain (or your brain and mind) at the end of your life?
- Imagine if you could transfer your mind into a hologram body? That is, imagine if you could have a robotic copy (avatar) of yourself remotely controlled via BCI (brain computer interface).
- Imagine how much more work you could get done and do all the stuff we say we don't have time to do.
- Imagine the cost savings too!
- And yes, imagine what that means for how many 'purely human lawyers' in 'traditional' roles will be needed.

Hmmm…

But what if what I'm asking you is no longer imagination, but reality? Brace yourself. As sci-fi and unbelievable as it may seem, all of this could indeed soon be our reality, and much sooner than you would think.

What I have shared with you is no longer a question of 'IF', but 'WHEN'. You will be able to be in two places at once as early as next year. It's happening NOW:

- **2015** – An avatar/robotic copy of yourself will be available in 2015 and mass produced by 2020 (we're talking clones here!);
- **2025** – Your brain could be transplanted into a robotic copy of you by 2025;
- **2029** – Your brain could be in the cloud which will enable you to learn complex

new things at any age – so YES, the next time someone says to you that 'you're up in the clouds' with your thinking, take it as a complement;

- **2030–35** – Your personality could be transferred into an avatar with an artificial brain (or your brain and mind, at the end of your life) by 2030 (creation of an artificial brain by 2030) and mind transfer into a completely artificial body by 2035;
- **2035–2045** – A hologram like avatar will exist and you could transfer your mind into a hologram body by 2035–2045; if you've seen the film *Prometheus*, then this is the kind of thing we could become by 2035–45; and
- **By 2045** – Computer/AI/robot/hologram intelligence will be one billion times more powerful than the human brain is today.

Perhaps Susskind's suggestion in his provocative book titled *The End of Lawyers?* may actually come to pass. I reckon it's pertinent at this point to say that in 2015 the humanisation of lawyers will come of age. In the next five years we will experience a fundamental shift in who will be our clients and who and how the serving will be done (recall Chapter 1 on emerging markets).

The rise of the machine (AI/robot), along with the rise of the middle class in Asia will drive growth in the East and the Pacific Rim will become a hot bed of activity. Global lawyering will come of age and be the norm.

So, if the machines are already hot on our heels and may soon be cleverer as well as more efficient than us, how can we possibly compete? New ways of communicating, relating with clients, and being productive globally – whether face to face, at the interface, or virtually – can only be welcomed. Accordingly, I believe a key differentiator in the success of the face-to-face model and interface model, and our successful human and lawyerly evolution in the alignment and harmony of machines and man will be the 'humanisation' of lawyers.

As we transition even more in the years to come, as AI evolves further within legal provision and service, and singularity edges even closer, 'humanisation' – that is, our ability to simply be human (a social creature) and naked (our authentic self with lawyerly intellectual capital (IQ/LIC reasoning), empathy, soul (passion), and high EQ/EI – will become even more important and valuable.

We develop our EQ through increased reflection leading to improved self-awareness. In essence, EQ is wisdom. It's the opposite of IQ; IQ is all about our academic ability knowledge. Apparently, we reach our IQ peak at the age of 19–20. We reach our EQ peak age 40–50.

In a deeply fragmented, AI, commoditised, and global legal industry, I believe it will be our EQ that differentiates us where top level results are concerned. EQ is externalised in our 'soft skills': communication, empathy, body-language skills, etc.; the kind of skills we use in business development, rain-making, and client relationships.

I noted that Berwin Leighton Paisner's remuneration committee was recently told to put more focus on soft factors – intangible qualities like business development and client courting – when deciding an equity partner's pay. Nabarro has done a similar thing. In time, other law firms and their lawyers will no doubt follow suit.

What many leading global futurists have predicted in the past has come true. Many of these visionaries, futurists, scientists, engineers, and technologists are working on this stuff now (and have been for quite some time already). Ray Kurzweil has already published his latest jaw-dropping book *How To Create A Mind: The Secret Of Human Thought Revealed*,[7] in which he describes the present challenges relating to re-engineering the brain and understanding the mind.

Why am I sharing all this stuff with you? Well… Let's look at genetics. The biological era is emerging:

- Scientists are extending human life by five months every year;
- Due to medical advancements and genetic enhancements life expectancy will increase by two to three times within a few years;
- It is highly probable that you will live into your 80s/90s;
- My age group (the 40s) will likely live well beyond 100; and
- Our children will be the last generation to die naturally.

Given the possibility that we are going to live a heck of a lot longer, and our children may never die, you have to wonder:

- 'How will you motivate your 130-year-old colleague lawyer'?
- 'How will you manage your 18-year-old apprentice alongside your 80-year-old "not so doddery and fuddy duddy" lawyer?'
- 'How are you going to "socialise" your human lawyer with your robot lawyer?'
- 'How will you get them to work/relate together ?'

This huge age gap and skin/silicone thing may be problematic.

And personally, I wonder:

- 'Will I still be working at that gawd awful age'?
- 'Actually, will I even have a job?!'
- 'If people never die, and we keep having lots of lovely sex and popping out new babies, what will this mean to the world population and the pressure on finite resources?'

Hmmm… Maybe this is something to discuss in Chapter 6.

2030: rise of the iCyborg lawyer

I was fascinated to hear that we already have holograms in airports. Something which I'd seen in a science fiction movie has now become reality. Which got me wondering, why not holographic lawyers and holographic 'welcome' agents? It would sure help with improving customer service standards and ridding the problem of needing to be in two places at once, particularly as a global lawyer serving global clients. Given all that I have shared so far, and what I am about to share now, I predict that by 2030 we will witness the rise of the iCyborg lawyer (virtual and real) entering the legal world.

Kurzweil predicts that in 2030 nanobot technology will provide fully immersive, totally convincing virtual reality. If we want to enter virtual reality, the nanobots will suppress all of the inputs coming from our actual senses and replace them with the signals that would be appropriate for the virtual environment. Our brain experiences these signals as if they came from our physical body. If we want to experience real reality, the nanobots just stay in position and do nothing.

Back in 2011 *The Economist* magazine reported[8] on the evolution of brain-computer interfaces (BCIs). Presently, they are invasive. Over the past two decades BCIs which use electrodes implanted in the skull have enabled paralysed patients to control computer cursors, robotic arms, and wheelchairs. Now, though, non-invasive

BCIs, where electrodes sit on the scalp instead of burrowing through it, are finally becoming a realistic alternative to the complicated surgical procedure that implants necessitate. Controlling things via thought alone is fast becoming reality.

I myself experienced this at the IBM laboratory here in the UK in January this year (2014). I had a non-invasive BCI contraption slapped on my head and I was instructed to think about moving a block on a computer screen toward the horizon (the block was in the middle of the image). I was then asked to focus on pulling the block toward me and bring it to a gentle stop. In effect what I was doing was training the computer to mimic my thought so that I could control a thing from thought alone. That thing turned out to be a little toy car, which had some sort of receiver gizmo from the computer so that those two things could 'speak' to each other. I was then instructed to 'move the car and bring it to a gentle stop'. Still looking like a complete plumb wearing my BCI headgear, I focused on the toy car and as if by magic it flew across the room and bashed into the wall! Okay, maybe I was a bit rough on the little guy, but on my second attempt I brought the wee toy to a gentle stop.

In essence, and in simple terms, this is how the Google self-driving car works, with a bit more techy explanation required, obviously. And, as you're no doubt aware, Google announced the self-driving car to the world and the mainstream media picked up on it only a few months ago. Imagine what else IBM and Google are working on that is yet to be revealed?

While at IBM I was also shown a HUGE screen (kind of like an iPad but ten to 20 times bigger) with the potential for the Watson tech running within it. It is the next generation collaboration tech tool to enable multiple parties (lawyers and their clients, perhaps) around an online virtual table where machine and man think and do together. It would mean that humans would not have to be physically present, nor would they need to pass the document they are all pouring over via email or via the case management system. The Watson AI would assist/prompt the lawyers representing the parties and all those present around the virtual online table, there and then, real-time, meaning only one person would be required to oversee the document and tablet and the whole matter could be speeded up exponentially.

Whether as a buyer or seller of legal services, AI and virtual reality WILL pervade our legal world. Simulating negotiations, scenarios, advocacy and judgment, arguments and reasoning in preparation for court proceedings, among other applications no doubt.

Another stage on, as technology evolves, the iCyborg lawyer will make his debut. A cyborg is simply a being with both biological and artificial parts – for example, electronic, mechanical, or robotic parts. The term cyborg is often applied to those organisms which use technology to repair or overcome their physical and mental constraints, including artificial limbs and hands as well as a device for helping colour-blind people to 'hear' in colour. Cyborgs exist now. Fact. Simply look at our paralympians. However, fictional cyborgs are often portrayed with physical or mental abilities far exceeding a human counterpart.

Fact or fiction, I predict that real iCyborg lawyers will evolve who will tap into evolved IBM Watson type AI technology (Deeper QA) utilising either non-invasive or invasive brain-computer interfaces (BCIs). Due to the ingenuity of man, the iCyborg Lawyer is near. This quasi AI and EI 'super lawyer' being will become known as 'iLawyer'...

2045: when iLawyers transcend biology

Kurzweil sets the date for the Singularity representing a profound and disruptive transformation in human capability as 2045: 'The nonbiological intelligence created in that year will be one billion times more powerful than human intelligence today.'[9]

Post singularity, there will be no distinction between human and machine or between physical and virtual reality. As Ray Kurzweil points out, if you're wondering 'what will remain unequivocally human in such a world' it's simply this quality: 'ours is the species that inherently seeks to extend its physical and mental reach beyond current limitations'.

This might sound a little like sci-fi, but the pace of change is more rapid than you might expect. Simply reflect on all that has happened in the last few years which have become (and will be) global game changers for society, our way of living, conducting business, and affecting law. For example, companies like Apple launching the iPad and iPhone, Google unveiling the self-driving car and augmented-reality glasses, and the robot revolution in our very living space with robot vacuum cleaners!

These advancements and inventions have swept in rather suddenly and have had, and will have, a profound effect on all of our lives – society, economies, politics, and law. What is strikingly shocking and highly relevant to us as lawyers is Kurzweil's prediction that computers will, by 2029 – well within the working timespan of today's younger lawyers – be able to match the intelligence of humans. I cannot help but wonder what will be the game-changer for law? I'm also curious as to who, what, and when. Perhaps you are too?

my dear Watson: the legal game changer

Perhaps it will be the IBM Watson technology taken on board by a first-mover business of law with the vision (and deep pockets and war chest), creativity (pop the AI tech into an actual fluffy cuddly cute looking robot), and balls to unleash RobotLawyer into society? Notably, IBM has opened up its Watson technology to the market – for a price. So the potential exists. It is inevitable, in due course and with the advancements and progression in robotics and technology, that machines/robots can/will speak, no doubt supporting/assisting both contentious and non-contentious lawyering.

In February 2011 it was reported by Robert C. Weber, IBM's senior vice president, legal and regulatory affairs and general counsel, in the *National Law Journal* that a new technology (aka AI) emerging from IBM (and the machine/computer itself aptly named after the company's first chief executive 'Watson') could be a real boon to support legal research and advocacy.

The machine possesses two kinds of AI. Watson understands questions that are asked of it, and it also learns and improves with practice. The machine technology (AI) understands English language and metaphors. Accordingly, Watson is capable of understanding and responding to esoteric queries posed in everyday language with unprecedented speed, accuracy, and confidence. Watson represents a major leap ahead in the ability of computers to rapidly analyse information, identify patterns, gain critical insights, and enhance decision-making.

Deep QA (the technology underlying Watson) will be useful in two ways: for gathering facts and for identifying ideas when building legal arguments. Watson may even be of assistance, near real-time, in the courtroom. If a witness says something that doesn't seem credible, you can have an associate check it for accuracy there and then, on the spot.

Watson is operating, developing, and evolving in two ways:

- Part 1: Watson is presently about 'cognitive computing'. It is able to deal with uncertainty where there's a multiplicity of possible answers and get the definitive answer. Watson can do this now. For example, analysing patients' notes, then diagnosing, evaluating against known data, and giving an answer. There is a similarity with the process in case law, perhaps?
- Part 2: Watson intelligence is moving into iteration; for example, x per cent certainty of y outcome/result (i.e. percentage rating). This kind of AI is suitable for where there is not a perfect fit (typical in legal scenarios); for example, 'so here's a series of things we now need to consider'. This type of AI will be helpful in law law land because the machine will be able to prompt the lawyer using its intelligence; for example, with regard to including new terms/clauses or removing terms/clauses in contracts. AI could also spot tipping points in verdicts; this is decision tree kind of stuff that could be done by the computer. You could actually take the evidence and deduce what would be the most likely successful defence/prosecution.

And let's not forget, machine intelligence is going to supersede human intelligence (processing power) very soon! To quote Dr Peter Waggett, head of Emerging Technology at IBM, Winchester, UK: 'It's not IF computers will be smarter than humans, but when.'[10] Watson can do Part 1 now. It will be able to do Part 2 in the next five years: 2020. Arguably, by 2020, computers/machines/AI (whether in the form of hard-top machine or robot) will be able to reason and judge. But, assuming it could hit the commercial world and legal world around that time... Will we allow it, I wonder?

Nowadays, legal provision and primary skills fall into four areas (buckets):

1. IT-based – Commoditised;
2. Artificial intelligence (AI), smart AI systems;
3. Advocacy; and
4. Judgement.

As I said earlier, AI can be defined as the intelligence of machines, where an intelligent agent is a system that perceives its environment and takes actions that maximise its chances of success.

In legal practice, the most common AI applications already in circulation are e-discovery, digital forensic procedures, and big data search, particularly in relation to civil litigation matters and legal research. Arguably, the first two areas above (IT-based and AI) have superseded the 'grunt work' traditionally carried out by trainees and junior lawyers. Paralegals and/or junior lawyers now oversee and utilise the 'machine system' in order to maximise productivity.

The last two areas (advocacy and judgment), however, are associated more with associate level and upwards. This means we are transitioning toward three kinds of lawyer:

- The unemployed lawyer – there are too many lawyers in the kind of roles we are familiar with right now. Technology and AI will supersede some of the jobs/roles traditionally carried out by human lawyers;

- The support worker to the first two areas – There is no need in some parts of the world to be a qualified lawyer to carry out this kind of legal provision; and
- The 'super lawyer', with a high-end intelligence quotient (IQ) and emotional quotient or emotional intelligence (EQ/EI) to work on the last two areas above; with business developer, rainmaker, and technological savvy relater skills – the hybrid lawyer type.

AI is here, now. But, it could evolve in an extraordinary way in the next two decades to the extent that advocacy and judgement will also become the realm of the machine in relation to IQ. Furthermore, future applications of AI in circulation will mean AI will come into the realm of the court room too; for example, the use of Google Glass.

What does this mean for our profession and roles? Watson is evolving buckets 1 and 2 (IT and AI) and (arguably) nudging into bucket 3 (advocacy). Whether we're preparing for litigation, protecting intellectual property, writing contracts, or negotiating an acquisition, if we pose a question to Watson, in milliseconds, Deep QA can analyse hundreds of millions of pages of content and mine them for facts and conclusions in about the time it takes to answer a question on a quiz show. Furthermore, a report in *Technology Review*[11] stated that IBM is building the world's biggest data drive which promises to power complex simulation models. The system could enable detailed simulations of real world phenomena or comfortably swallow 60 copies of the biggest backup of the web – the 150 billion pages that make up the Internet Archive's WayBack Machine. Imagine how this could be useful for law and justice.

Weber proffers that Deep QA won't ever replace lawyers. After all, the essence of good lawyering is mature and sound reasoning – buckets 3 (advocacy) and 4 (judgment) – and it's doubtful a machine can match the knowledge and ability to reason of a smart, well-educated, deeply experienced human being possessing high EQ (wisdom). But the technology (at present) can unquestionably extend our capabilities and help us perform better (i.e. be more productive).

AI is here, now. But (and it's a big BUT) I believe it could evolve in an extraordinary way in the next two decades to the extent that buckets 3 and 4 will also fall into the realm of the machine in relation to IQ. WHY? Because of what I shared with you at the beginning of this book: clients want certainty; they want an improved chance/probability/percentage of a positive outcome; they want a faster, cheaper, more efficient, and more effective service.

If AI automation as far as cognition and iteration can produce greater certainty more efficiently (whether in the form of a computer/machine/avatar/robot), then I for one, as a buyer of legal services and products, would certainly contemplate engaging the business of law that has such a thing. Wouldn't you? Standing in your clients' shoes, or as a buyer of legal services yourself, next time you're involved in an ugly dispute of a commercial or personal nature which looks if it's going to be a horrible, long, drawn-out, expensive matter? Or even a matter of life, or death?

In light of what I have shared so far, I reckon we lawyers who defend our current roles and positions, and justify our existence in the present and future by saying 'but the law is so complex, there's no way a machine can assimilate, simulate, think, reason, persuade, judge as I do', perhaps we need to just sit back and ponder... Take a sip of wine/beer/coffee... Reflect...

I asked the good Dr (Peter Waggett) of IBM the following questions in an interview in January this year:

- *Question*: Do you envisage the use of an avatar for simple legal cases?
  Answer: Yes
- *Question*: Do you envisage legal e-personal assistants for lawyers?
  Answer: Yes
- *Question*: Do you think AI/robots will replace lawyers?
  Answer: Unlikely.

Unlikely is debatable...

IMHO, they will replace some of the current roles of lawyering; it's happening now. Perhaps not all roles, but over time they will replace many. The jury is out on this one. It will be very interesting to see how this evolves.

Of course, while some of you may be viewing all this technology, AI, robot gubbins negatively, let us not forget the positively new kind of law and legal work that is flowing in and lining the law firms' coffers as a result of this Digital Age and Robotic Age progress.

I mentioned 'drone law' earlier, but what about the increasing amount of data law, internet law (cybercrime/fraud), and space-related law and accompanying legal work, to name a few? I have no doubt whatsoever that the effects will creep into family law, employment law, personal injury law, intellectual property law, and more, thereby creating new legal work in due course. More about my thoughts on this will follow in Chapter 6.

utopia or road to hell?

Actually, come 2045 in a utopian world (if we so choose it to be and manage not to destroy the planet in the meantime), I predict there will no longer be a need for the vast majority of us 'purely human' lawyers. Also, from now until 2045 it will be interesting to see how powerful pulsed magnetic fields which inhibit the ability to lie[12] will impact our legal world. Time will tell whether this will be a godsend or the road to hell for law law land and society.

We have been blessed with many great thinkers, innovators, scientists, engineers, technicians, and entrepreneurs 'colliding' at this point in time; that is, in the last few decades working on diverse yet complementary fields to help the world 'kick-on'. Undoubtedly, with Steve Jobs passing we have lost one of the world's greatest technological innovators of our time. It is hardly surprising that, at the time of writing, the working Apple-1 computer sold by Steve Jobs himself could fetch $1 million at auction.

When we look back over the past 35 years[13] and marvel at the pioneering impact Steve Jobs has had on advancing technology and introducing artificial intelligence positively into our world, perhaps as we look ahead to the next 35 years the iCyborg lawyer and robot lawyer may be closer than we dare imagine?

While the world is full of great visionaries and innovators, only a special handful of human beings through time truly touch the people of the world and become extraordinary change masters. Steve Jobs is a legend and one of such masters. His legacy, genius, and brilliance will live on as we move toward singularity...

Steve Jobs was, in my opinion, the greatest innovator of my generation, an extraordinary change master and a human being with exceptional IQ and unrivalled EQ. No doubt he will be sorely missed not only by the techy world but by the business world and the legal world too. There is so much more he could have contributed to, had his life not ended when it did.

Fact or fiction, virtual reality or reality, one thing is for sure, as we continue to join the dots our world (and its technology and artificial intelligence) will inevitably evolve at an accelerating speed for 'ours is the species that inherently seeks to extend its physical and mental reach beyond current limitations'.[14] I reckon we should say 'thank you, Steve Jobs', for dedicating your life to technology, innovation, and entrepreneurship, for being brave enough to think differently, bold enough to feel and believe you could change the world, and extraordinary talented and spiritually gifted enough to actually do it. Do we have such a pioneer in the legal field, I wonder?

the robot has left the house of law

I'm still pondering on my last question… A pioneer in law law land? I wish!

The thing is, '[lawyers] have always been behind the curve… Technology solutions can make our lives a lot easier. But we're in a profession that's backward-looking.'[15] David Bain, NuCerity International GC and corporate secretary, was speaking about the technologies in development, such as IBM's 'Watson' driving the growth in robotics and artificial intelligence and set to make their way into the legal profession 'in the very near future' at a conference in mid-October this year (2014). He no doubt shares my frustration at the inertia and lack of vision in law law land.

To add to the content and insights I have already shared with you, and to put it into context in our legal world, Bain invites us to consider:

'Can you imagine, for instance, a "virtual second chair" – a computer system that sits alongside the lawyer in court, participating, monitoring and giving the lawyer real-time feedback and guidance? …

Or technology – with the computational power of the human brain – researching a policy question and returning with its own arguments for and against that policy position? Or perhaps it could draft a basic brief for you?

[Or] Technology with the emotional intelligence, for instance, to understand our body language – handy for deposition analysis, in the jury room or in "virtual" mediation.

Or surveillance technology that could be applied to time-keeping – keeping track of what lawyers are doing or reporting back to clients…

[Or] if a person has the ability to be injured, but repaired and healed very quickly to a potentially better state than before, what does that mean for how we think about damages and what an injury is really worth?'

These may seem like far-fetched questions/musings (as one anonymous commentator actually stated 'I think this article is pretty far-fetched, or at the very least is talking about things that are unlikely to emerge in the working lifetime of most Gazette readers'), but they are questions, in my opinion, which are absolutely spot-on and timely. I could go a lot further, but I will save it for Chapter 6.

Suffice to say that I chuckled when I read Monidipa Fouzder's (the author of the article) prose directed at the nay-sayers: 'did you ever imagine the cloud would be more than just a visible mass of condensed watery vapour floating above ground, or that non-lawyers would be able to own and invest in law firms?'

I confess, I thought it was a fabulous feature but it was reading the comment stream which followed that I really enjoyed most. It tickled me so much that I couldn't resist piling into the debate too. Here's my comment to the article and replies in summary:

'Sadly… the readers who placed such negative comments will be of the extinct breed within the next decade... Wake up luddite lawyers! Are you so naive to think that AI and robotics is not going to touch the legal world like the rest of the world? You mock vision, insight, creativity and the potential of progress because you fear change, risk and ultimately the future and possible demise of lawyering as you know it.

Rather than criticise the author I suggest you open your mind and get reading. There is a plethora of material on the subject of AI and robotics in use NOW, in a variety of industries. Great work and discovery is being done in many laboratories and industries around the world in a variety of fields. AI and robotics is used now in a positive way in many fields and sectors, and has been for many years.

- *Question*: Why not law?
  Answer: Because the lawyers and law firms that wield the power are too self-interested to change, adapt and adopt the technologies that will help change the world... for the better.

Imagine if Steve Jobs had given up on Apple Inc when he was booted out for being too visionary with regard to helping all people communicate around the world, cost effectively?

What happened when he was? Progress stagnated, Apple share values plummeted, until such time as he was re-instated as CEO and the world was later blessed with communication devices to connect and educate us all. The ipod, ipad, iphone revolution has been a world game changer.

AI and robotics in the legal world will be too, IMHO. There is a reason the USA government has backed the 're-engineering the brain' project with tax-payers bitcoins.

Start joining the dots rather than sticking your head in the sand and arse in the air to the inevitable rise and dominance of AI and robotics in the legal world in the months and years to come.

The luddites tried to resist the machine, and they failed. You will too, if you resist. Accept, embrace, re-educate, re-train, re-skill and at least give yourself the chance to succeed in the Digital and Robotic Age. It's not something for the future. It's here, now...'

Grrrrrr. Yes, I am opinionated. Because I care... Truly, we are in an age where legal technology wisdom rules! Period. The machine (AI/robot) has already entered the house of law. I can certainly envisage a time when we will say: 'The robot has left the building. Will the last robot out please turn-off the lights.'

Until such time we cry 'the robot has left the house of law', I have to say that I remain ashamed (as an entrepreneurial lawyer), frustrated (as a consultant and legal futurist), and disappointed (as a legal service buyer) at the slow take-up rate of law firms (usually hindered by lawyers and 'support' staff in power with ulterior motives) with regard to the quality and quantity of legal technology available in the global marketplace.

I read recently in *Real Business* that financial companies are set to increase IT budgets[16]. Are businesses of law, I wonder? Not from my experience these past few years; and certainly not at the rate or scale to keep up with the accelerating technological changes outside of the legal world and expectations of existing and potential clients.

If Millennials are ready for a new financial system, and Stellar[17] might just be it, I dare suggest that Millennials are no doubt ready for a new legal system too: one that operates globally, seamlessly, online, and in the cloud. Perhaps it's time for a new (global) legal system? If it can be done for global finance, why can't it be done for law?

I'd love to have a crack at 'The Law Manifesto for the Digital Age', wouldn't you?

after dark activity

It's time to think, and it's time to do. If you've been coasting along it's time to really take stock and take care of your horizons 2 and 3...

just do something!

If I were you, I would re-read this chapter. Truly. Read it again and thoroughly take on board what I've shared with you. Investigate the material I refer to in the footnotes and ferret around further. Not only will you be enlightened, I am confident you will be inspired to act, to make a difference and, who knows, you just might be that elusive law law land pioneer who actually does change the world (and not just the legal one)...

References

1. Fouzder, M., 'Robots running law firms? Surely not', the *Law Society Gazette*, October 2014, see: www.lawgazette.co.uk/analysis/comment-and-opinion/robots-running-law-firms-surely-not/5044479.article.
2. Daniel Burrus – Global Futurist : Certainties.com.
3. See: http://entrepreneurlawyer.co.uk/?p=3478&preview=true.
4. See: http://stephenmayson.m/2011/08/16/breaking-news-humpty-dumpty-falls-off-wall/.
5. Kurzweil, R., *The Singularity Is Near: When Humans Transcend Biology*, Penguin Books, London, 2005.
6. DAS Law Ltd is a modern and progressive law firm specialising in personal injury and employment claims.
7. Kurzweil, Ray, *How To Create A Mind: The Secret Of Human Thought Revealed*, Penguin Books, London, 2012.
8. 'Put Your Thinking Cap On', *The Economist*, 8 September, 2011. See: www.economist.com/node/21527030.
9. Kurzweil, Ray, *The Singularity Is Near: When Humans Transcend Biology*, 2005.
10. Interview with Peter Waggett, IBM, 31 January2014.
11. Simonite, T., 'IBM Builds Biggest Data Drive Ever', Technology Review, 25 August 2011, see: www.technologyreview.com/news/425237/ibm-builds-biggest-data-drive-ever/.
12. See: www.kurzweilai.net/powerful-pulsed-magnetic-fields-inhibit-ability-to-lie?utm_source=twitterfeed&utm_medium=twitter.
13. 'Technology visionary who reshaped the world', *Financial Times*, 6 October 2011, see: www.ft.com/cms/s/94e3cb04-7cae-11e0-994d-00144feabdc0,Authorised=false.html?_i_location=http%3A%2F%2Fwww.ft.com%2Fcms%2Fs%2F0%2F94e3cb04-7cae-11e0-994d-00144feabdc0.html%3Fsiteedition%3Duk&siteedition=uk&_i_referer=#axzz1a1CbHFUL.
14. Kurzweil, Ray, *The Singularity Is Near: When Humans Transcend Biology*, 2005.
15. Quoting Bill Mordan, who was quoting David Bain, in an article by Monidipa Fouzder in 'Robots running law firms? Surely not', *Law Society Gazette*, 23 Oct 2014, see: www.lawgazette.co.uk/analysis/comment-and-opinion/robots-running-law-firms-surely-not/5044479.article.
16. See: http://realbusiness.co.uk/article/27381-financial-companies-are-set-to-increase-it-budgets.
17. See: http://prospress.com/stellar-choice-new-generation/?utm_content=buffer6eaba&utm_medium=social&utm_source=linkedin.com&utm_campaign=buffer.

Chapter 4: tomorrow's naked lawyer

'If I can't drive this mother ship, nobody else is.' Ruby Wax

life without risk is like no life at all

Many years ago I read a quote (can't remember who said it but it was shared on twitter) which smacked me bang on the nose. It goes like this: 'Sometimes finding the light you must pass through the deepest darkness...'

I wanted to share this with you because it's a poignant message for where law law land was back in 2009/10 when I first unleashed *the naked lawyer* on the many unsuspecting lawyerly souls. It's also very pertinent today, and will be tomorrow, next year, and waaaaaaayyy beyond.

The mantra captures how many of us lawyers were/are feeling in challenging times (past, present, and future); that is, to find certainty/security (light), we must take some risks and deal with the uncertainty (darkness). Bottom line for law law land, it must grapple with re-inventing the roles of its lawyers. And this is what this chapter is primarily concerned with.

There's been a LOT of stuff written about the changing legal landscape and the evolving role of the lawyer in a whole range of media since 2009/10 due to the turmoil within the profession and industry. I'm guilty. Terribly guilty of contributing to this media mania. I couldn't resist popping on my dancing shoes and waltzing into the discussions and debates, sharing vision and insight and a helping hand if required and/or asked.

Back in 2011, as lay-offs continued to sweep through Wall Street,[1] I got to thinking about our legal world and the movie *Indecent Proposal*. There's a thought-provoking and inspiring line spoken by Demi Moore at the very start of the film. She is reflecting on her (film) husband's view that 'A life without risk is like no life at all'. I agree. To truly experience living and not merely existing throughout our (legal) careers, business, and life, the progressive evolutionary dynamics of our present decade (and beyond for that matter) is compelling us to get out of our comfort zones, to dare to be different, and ultimately to re-invent ourselves.

In a climate of fear, low morale, and the unknown/uncertain something we're all (arguably) dealing with right now – I reckon we need to adapt, innovate, and feel inspired by both the finger-biting challenges and extraordinary opportunities staring us in the face. But to do this we will need to take some risks. Why? Because, as I have said previously, disruptive forces are sweeping through the entire globe; in particular, the technology world, finance world, political world, business world, and law law land right now.

I also believe, and agree with Robin Sharma (a leadership expert and author), that success is driven via evolution versus revolution: 'Small daily innovations stack up into stunning results over the passage of time'. I tweeted Robin's mantra which attracted the following response from our dear Prof:

'Good quotation. I call this "incremental revolution" or "incremental transformation"' (see more on this below).

We need to get a grip. We actually need to take complete control of our personal destinies, make the bold choices necessary, and ultimately embrace the topsy-turvy changes occurring in our crazy world. Bottom line: we need to continually innovate (more so now than ever) because the world is always innovating. We need to re-invent ourselves and thereby make the transformation required to make a lasting success of our careers, businesses, and lives now and in the years to come.

IMHO, Susskind's view sits nicely with that of Whatify[2] when reporting on a news source which suggests that there are only three kinds of innovation remaining – a welcome revelation no doubt for those of us with bad memories or those of us who don't have time to explore the other five. The three kinds of innovation are as follows in the next sections.

1. incremental innovation

That is, doing what we have to in order to keep existing products up to date. Apparently, many consumer goods companies tend to spend more than half of their innovation budgets on 'incremental innovations' simply because they lack the ability to systematically scan the market for the most attractive opportunities and develop winning ideas to capitalise on them.

- *Question*: Does the average law firm and its leaders even scan the market for opportunities and encourage you (their lawyers) to develop ideas, never mind have an innovation budget?
  Answer: It's a moot point.

2. platform innovation

This is about coming up with a completely new product, where the focus is to grow the innovator's market share by giving customers a reason to switch from a competitor brand – Coke Zero is a good example. Now, this is an interesting type of innovation, particularly in the present UK legal market place where we're seeing strong consumer brands and commercial/professional brands, for example, Tesco, the Co-Operative, AA, PwC, EY (to name a few) and new brands such those mentioned in Chapter 1 enter the legal playing field.

It'll be interesting to see whether their propositions are compelling enough to entice customers away from their existing legal advisers and how much existing and latent market share these brands mop up.

3. breakthrough innovation

This is where we come up with a 'market-changing innovation' – for example, the iPad. The test seems to be 'delivering new benefits to customers and creating a new market that the innovator can dominate for some time'. Online legal document services (including legal advice) such as Epoq, Rocket Lawyer, Law Pivot, and Legal Zoom spring to mind here.

There's a thought-provoking blog post by Jordan Furlong (I mentioned him earlier) who looks at these market-changing innovators[3]. Jordan suggests that, from now on, lawyers' and law firms' profitability hinges completely on *'what'* we choose to do and *'how'* we choose to do it. I would add that the real game change at play here with regard to profitably will be WHY lawyers and law firms choose to do *'what'* and WHY they settle on *how* to do it.

WHY sits at the very core of an entrepreneurial law firm's purpose and the very soul of an entrepreneur lawyer's raison d'être. Accordingly, I suspect that the new game-changers will be even more discerning and passionate in their focus and drive for delivering extraordinary customer service. They know that focusing on THEM (i.e. the customer) first, last, always, and by investing in their people first, last, always, that the bottom line (profit) will naturally take care of itself.

I would argue that in law law land we're witnessing survival of the fittest as the strong firms grow stronger and the weak firms grow weaker, largely due to the 'fittest' firms adapting to the disruptive forces and competitor 'disruptors' by continually innovating. Leading law firms and their innovative leaders are resetting their strategies by taking bold moves. Recall Lexis Nexis's bellwether report?

The key areas ripe for innovating (within the business model and umbrella strategy) which I believe we should consider because they will be fundamental to future firm success and individual success are as follows.

1. our technology

This is a massive topic in itself and it will be covered in Chapter 6. Suffice to say, here, that I reckon Susskind can smile after 20 years of preaching as he begins to witness that his beliefs, research, teachings, and drive for a technologically savvy and online legal world are actually coming to fruition… Sort of. Hey-ho, we're getting there in the end, even if some of us are frothing around in the wake while others are surfing ahead.

2. our marketing and sales strategy

Even nowadays, despite the ROAR model and *the naked lawyer* message kicking around for over FIVE years, the vast majority of firms still allocate prime responsibility for winning new customers and keeping existing clients to the partners and allocate 'marketing the firm'[4] as the prime responsibility of the marketing, brand, communications, or business development person and/ or department: an individual pumping out 'marketing and PR messages' about the firm behind the corporate veil.

It's neither engaging nor interesting to the recipient. Trust me. I'm a tomorrow's naked lawyer. I will say it again… Potential and existing buyers of legal advice want to engage with individual lawyers (they want to get personal, get naked) so the lawyer being visible, available, and engaging to the client is of paramount importance. ALL of the key research these past couple of years PROVES this (refer back to Chapters 1 and 2 in which I share those papers).

It's time to turn the traditional top-down, triangle marketing mantra on its head to capitalise on each and every lawyer's social capital and human capital – co-incidentally, social capital and human capital are two of the four essential pillars in a law firm's make-up which Professor Stephen Mayson[5] highlighted five years ago in his book *Law Firm Strategy*.[6]

Let's encourage and support everyone in marketing the firm by re-inventing and marketing themselves. I will say this again too: devise a niche, create your 'Brand, Me', and have EVERYONE embrace new innovative tools such as social media and social networking in order to attract and keep more clients/customers through efficient and effective relationship marketing.

3. our core purpose

It appears that at the very core of the successful firm and individual lies passion, energy, and enthusiasm for the client. Integrated Legal Holdings (ILH) and Slater & Gordon (Slaters), the only two law firms in the world that had listed on a stock exchange until now are testament that taking a gamble, focusing on innovation, and delivering extraordinary client service and care actually pays large corporate dividends.

Andrew Grech, managing director of Slaters, an Australian law firm that became the first law firm in the world to be listed on the Stock Exchange in May 2007, revealed his secret to success when interviewed by author Simon Tupman[7] in a *Legal Eagles article*, which profiled sixteen innovative and visionary lawyers from around the globe who are changing people's lives and making a difference in the world.[8] They offered candid insights into their careers and shared the secrets of their success. Their stories dispel many myths about the legal profession and prove that lawyers can, and do, make the world a better place.

Andrew said, 'Good lawyers care; they give a damn… to be successful, you have to be passionate about the work you are doing for your clients.' For the financial year ending 30 June 2011, Slaters announced net profits of $27.9 million (up 40.9 per cent). They're still going strong in 2014!

ILH recorded a 51 per cent increase in profit after tax for the 2011 financial year. Graeme Fowler, managing director, told *Lawyers Weekly* that the 'results were realised through a combination of getting the basics right… and continued business improvement'.

Obviously, those businesses of law that came out trumps in Lexis Nexis's bellwether report this year took a leaf or two out of the Slaters and ILH book of 'good law goodies' too.

As the Legal Services Act 2007 is in full swing here in England, I believe the ambitious and innovative firms in the UK can look for inspiration to those successful firms across the ocean which have proved that raising external finance via a stock exchange listing (making a bold move) and adapting their strategies to be totally client-centric does indeed pay large corporate dividends.

Even the chairman at Baker & McKenzie's, the world's largest law firm by turnover, says: 'The most important metric is client recognition and that's what we're focusing on. Higher profits and revenue should be the consequence of better client service.'

In August 2011 *The Lawyer* magazine[9] reported that the number of firms where partners earn more than £1 million had sky-rocketed. What's interesting and encouraging is the diversity of firms; there are magic circle firms, silver circle stalwarts, niche boutiques, and all manner of firms in between.

Berwin Leighton Paisner (BLP) and SJ Berwin (now King & Wood Mallesons having recently merged) were the standout performers among the City firms in 2010/11. Both posted dramatic increases in profitability. At BLP, average profit per equity partner (PEP) was up 57 per cent from £455,000 to £712,000. According to Neville Eisenberg, managing partner at that time, the impressive 2010/11 result was down to investing during the downturn and that the majority of the firm's increased revenue was due to improving its standing with existing clients so they would give the firm more work across a more diverse range of sectors.

- *Question*: What was the end result?
  Answer: No less than a big fat turbo boost to the bottom line.

If we are to question how and why BLP has been so successful in scooping up a plethora of awards over the past 11 years, including most recently *The Lawyer* magazine's 'Law Firm of the Year 2010', we only need to take on board Neville Eisenberg's professional opinion that 'Law firms are not innovative enough' (and therefore ensuring that BLP differentiates itself from competitors by being innovative) and his personal view that 'There is a need to keep inspired and to continually challenge yourself.'

The innovative moves shown by the likes of Slaters, ILH, BLP, Baker & McKenzie, Epoq, Rocket Lawyer, etc. (amongst others) reminds me of a telling opinion by Robin Sharma: 'Smart leaders show up on time. The best leaders show up early.' The same rings true for innovators.

In the first *naked lawyer* book, I ask the reader to question where they rate themselves from one to ten on the PEE Poor Work Ethic Continuum (PEE = Passion, Energy & Enthusiasm) in relation to the PEE they have for their role, job, career, clients, people, and in other respects. Where do you think you and/or your business of law would sit right now, at the onset of 2015?

4. our mindset

I reckon some of us could do with a 'paradigm shift lobotomy'. I said this back in 2010 and I am saying it again: we need to rid ourselves of the fear of failure, our aversion to risk-taking and to change. Ideally, we could do with cultivating an environment which fosters idea generation. Serial innovators like Google and Apple give employees time to explore ideas, even when some of those ideas turn into massive failures. Why shouldn't law firms take on board the same innovative strategy? One thing's for sure, there's a reason Google Ventures has backed Rocket Lawyer.

Traditional law firms had better be prepared to compete with new entrants who do love to encourage, support, and reward their employees in idea generation. As John F. Kennedy once said, 'we need men who can dream of things that never were.' Are you that (wo)man?

Chris Marston, CEO Exemplar Law[10], another visionary legal eagle lawyer named in *Legal Eagles* feels that 'our industry is plagued by too little push for change'. He defies the norm and he and his law firm, based in Boston, USA, continually innovate to the extent that he is proud to say that: 'some lawyers seem to think offering a service guarantee is risky. In our history we have not had a single customer take us up on this'.

Personally, I came to the conclusion at least a decade ago that I needed to adapt, innovate, and feel inspired by the wonderful opportunities in our present and future. I confess, it was largely because I did not wish to end up *Fat, Forty & Fired* or *Overworked and Underlaid* – any combination of these for that matter.[11]

I re-invented myself and transformed a whole bunch of stuff in my career, business, and life to ensure that I would be in control of my own destiny (arguably, mutiny) and never be tempted to accept an 'indecent proposal' of the kind we find in the movie's core theme. (Those of you who have watched the movie know exactly what I mean.)

With Demi Moore's touching line 'a life without risk is like no life at all' in *Indecent Proposal*, '*Breaking News: Humpty Dumpty Falls Off Wall*' blog post by Professor Stephen Mayson, and Professor Richard Susskind's 'incremental transformation' tweet rattling around in my legal beagle mind, I find myself inspired to soar like a legal eagle, and ROAR like a naked lawyer who is prepared to take some more risks to ensure that I live a truly fulfilling life.

Can you say the same? If you find yourself in a place like Mick Jagger where you just 'can't get no satisfaction' then I respectfully suggest the following: re-invent and transform yourself; dare to adapt, innovate, feel inspired. As Australian Paralympian Cameron de Bough would say:

'don't wait for the light to appear at the end of the tunnel... go down there and light the bloody thing yourself!'

are you prepared for 2015 to 2045?

To have job security and possibly increase our earning power both now and in the future, we will, undoubtedly and unequivocally, need to boost our value and relevance by continually learning new things. As Peter Drucker once said: 'We now accept the fact that learning is a lifelong process of keeping abreast of change... And the most pressing task is learning how to learn new ideas, concepts, methodologies and technologies.'

But how do we know what to learn, what courses to take, what theoretical and practical endeavours to partake in, and what degrees and other training will position us to thrive in the period 2015 to 2045 in law law land? A good place to start may well be with one of the '12 Certainties'™ outlined by global futurist Daniel Burrus (as mentioned in Chapter 3).

gamification of legal education

I reckon we need to look at how we can build these 'certainties' into the education of our lawyers of the future so that you and they will be resilient in the face of the change each of the certainties will bring. For instance, the last of the 12 is about the application of gamification to education.

Gamification is not a new concept in the world, but is still rather novel for law law land. While the label itself may not endear itself to the nature of law, the concept is spot on. In simple terms, gamification is the use of game thinking and game mechanics in a non-game context in order to engage users and solve problems. It is used in applications and processes to improve user engagement, return on investment, data quality, and learning.

To date, gamification has been most widely applied in marketing and as a tool for customer engagement. However, there has also been interest in the application of gamification to education, training, and employee productivity. Microsoft has released the game *Ribbon Hero 2* as an add-on to their Office suite to help train people to use Office effectively and thereby improve productivity.

In his most recent book,[12] our dear Prof Susskind suggests that 'lawyers should benefit from existing and emerging techniques of e-learning, which in their most advanced forms can be tremendously powerful. This extends beyond online lectures (which themselves can be useful) to online simulated legal practice and virtual legal learning environments'. Susskind is alluding to 'blended learning'[13] (the mix of face-to-face and interface e-learning), but there is definite scope for gamification to be introduced into legal education and training in a big way.

Gamification is a process that accelerated dramatically with the invention of video games; the digital format facilitates distribution, iteration, collaboration, and emulation.[14] In a short 40 years, game designers learned more about game design than the previous three thousand years combined. The learnings compounded until they overflowed into related fields, naturally. So why not law law land, I ask?

I believe games could be highly relevant in legal education because, as with the acceleration of innovation that occurred with the emergence of video games, game design in effect has always been about developing the most psychologically rewarding experiences. Psychologically rewarding? Hmmm, sounds to me like that's something we lawyers would love. Isn't it why we chose our lawyerly career path? That is, because we like to constantly stimulate our grey matter?

Imagine education, workplace productivity, collaboration tools, and problem-solving, mobile gamification in relation to customer engagement, all made to feel as rewarding as playing a game. For many of us, the explosive rise of games such as *Farmville* and *Angry Birds* could only be explained as a dramatic and unexpected social change: *adults* had suddenly started playing games and games were *everywhere*. In reality, what happened was that the kids who grew up with games became adults themselves and then games became more 'acceptable'.

From an educational perspective though, parallels can be drawn between *Farmville* and the branch of psychology known as behaviourism, which prompts:

- *Question*: Could gameplay be used to programme regular lawyers to follow a social or corporate agenda?
  Answer: Yes.

We lawyers *can* be programmed, just like a machine or a robot, IF we are offered something of significant value. 'Gamification' is in essence, an overlap in psychology and technology. Its potential and influence is much bigger than just 'playing a game'. We're talking about human motivation and directing behaviour, something I believe ought to be welcomed in law law land as businesses of law seek ways to encourage their lawyers to be more productive and happier'.

Behaviour management sets aside the losing prospect of appealing to the rational mind (that part we lawyers continually burn as we work) and talks directly to its compulsive, irrational master. Ah… relief. WooPah! Sounds like fun to me!

How long have we lawyers worked and lived feeling unfulfilled because we were unable to derive value from the day to day things we already do? For good or evil, behaviour management is a tool; it is a powerful instrument that can tap into our darkest compulsions or lead us to our fullest potential. Used positively in an educational and training environment within a business of law, I reckon it could foster huge dividends. For example, it could solve one of the most substantial challenges to law firm business development and CRM we hear, which is getting busy lawyers to use the system.

We lawyers are highly competitive. Tapping into that competitive nature to drive productivity through the use of gamification of business development sounds like a cunning plan, I reckon. It would inevitably benefit the entire business of law as well as each and every lawyer.

But don't just take my word for it. I've asked learning, leadership, and talent development specialist Debbie Harrison for her view on this fascinating subject and to provide examples of how gamification is being (and could be) used in the workplace to apply learning. (See the box below.)

'PwC first started utilising gaming over ten years ago out of necessity; a change to regulations meant that all employees had to be trained by a specific date but, using the incumbent classroom methodology and only two experts in the subject, it was calculated that it would take two years. The PwC subject matter experts provided the content to the gaming company and they in turn applied expertise; all employees completed the compliance in three weeks, with an average of six times over!

The genius of this application of gaming was to place screens in the breakout areas throughout their global offices with a leader board continuously on show; most compliance officers dream of these kind of results and yet continue to buy the worst designed learning.

I heard this story at the UK Learning Technologies conference and for me it became a game changer. Since then, I have utilised gaming in on-boarding which takes the new hire through the company structure, values, employee benefits, products, and more importantly re-enforces that they have made the right decision to join; pre and post diagnostic to a development programme, both technical and personal, the results generated gave the trainer and line managers the delegates' level of understanding in a particular subject (psychological layers embedded in gaming design produces results immediately, rather than [after] months); compliance, both bespoke and off the shelf (it is worthwhile remembering that your standard of compliance training is the first opportunity to set the tone for the importance of learning in the firm, make it count).

During this journey of having to persuade the die hard "it's not development unless it's in a classroom" community, here are my six main reasons for using gamification:

1. Gaming is a formula – The platform embeds learning through multi-level action, which allows the learner to progress through levels of learning; challenges and stretches the learner beyond their comfort zone; and will sometimes result in failure, which in a gaming environment is motivational; it's fun, which helps the learner stay motivated to learn.
2. Game play variety is critical – Make sure you have the right type of game for the audience; by 2020 there will be five different generations in the workplace, so this is a very important consideration.
3. Leader boards drive competition and community – As with the PwC results, team leader boards drive social connectedness, creating a strong sense of community.
4. Learners appreciate having a coach – Gamification allows the designer to incorporate a virtual coach. These virtual coaches motivate and support the learners, e.g. with Rosetta Stone a virtual coach corrects your pronunciation while learning a new language.
5. Employees like to see their progress – Learners want to see their own progress, which are the intrinsic motivators that drive many people to succeed, such as a feeling of achievement or desire for self-improvement; progress reports must be easy to understand, provide a graphical interface, and allow drilling down to deeper detail;
6. Social connectivity creates learning engagement – One of the most powerful tools in the next generation online learning environments relates to social connectivity – connecting employees to each other, to learning content, and to the organisation. Providing a forum for employees to engage socially and contribute content is not only beneficial, but in the age of Facebook and Twitter, it's expected.

While my international network is replacing traditional methodology with gaming for annual employment engagement surveys, personal career planning, recruitment, and succession planning, I recently introduced gamification to a law firm by changing a static online booklet about the firm's new international partners' culture into an avatar game; number of online hits for static book was 55 in three months. Number of times game was used in 14 days, 15,000 – for the same price!'[15]

I reckon the result speaks for itself, n'est ce pas? As we know, PwC is a blue-chip new sexy player in law law land and for traditional law firms and the new businesses of law to ignore what the competition is doing would be unwise.

Notwithstanding my soap box rant on this topic and Debbie's eloquent views, I believe that the biggest challenge therefore for lawyers and legal education is to embrace what I call 'psycho-lawyernetics'.

psycho-lawyernetics

Back in 1960, Maxwell Maltz wrote *Psycho-Cybernetics*. He went beyond the 'closed system' of the 'science of psychology' and sought answers concerning human behaviour in the fields of physics, anatomy, and the (then) new science of cybernetics. He proposed that: 'any good plastic surgeon is and must be a psychologist, whether he would have it so or not. When you change a man's face you invariably change his future. Change his physical image and nearly always you change the man – his personality, his behaviour – and sometimes even his basic talents and abilities.'

With a plastic surgeon, the sphere of influence is the man's face; with a lawyer, it may be his divorce, his business interests, his intellectual property. But what brings the lawyer's approach into the same realm as the surgeon's has been summarised by futurologist Dr Patrick Dixon in a speech at the NetLaw Media conference in 2011: 'the future of law will be driven by emotion'. He believes 'what clients want in the future is advice based on emotion'.

I agree. And, until the machine/robot/AI evolves to the point that it understands and can operate and portray emotion, or even have soul (Chapter 6 stuff), this is the win-win differentiator for the human lawyer.

Legal education and training has already begun the transition in accommodating business development skills and other 'soft-skilling'; including marketing, sales, branding, public relations, social media, social networking, and entrepreneurial schooling. It's happening now at the College of Law (UK), other universities and law schools in the UK and internationally, such as Miami Law School (with its LawWithoutWalls initiative) and the department of law at the University of Dublin, with John Flood spearheading its mission. There's also an abundance of external trainers, coaches, educators, and consultants supporting and supplying all of the above to the legal industry.

However, psycho-lawyernetics is fundamentally missing (and of necessity) as a core lawyerly skill in the continual legal education and training (in both theory and practice) in the present and certainly for tomorrow's naked lawyer. This is partly because lawyers tend to favour a more analytical approach (rational) at work than an emotional one (impulsive and irrational). Recall the benefits of gamification in the previous section?

Part of the Myers Briggs approach to psychometric testing looks at the decision-making approach – either thinking (organising and structuring information to decide in a logical, objective way) or feeling (organising and structuring information to decide in a personal and values-oriented way). In the general population, men slightly favour the thinking approach (57 per cent, versus 43 per cent for feeling), while women strongly favour feeling (75 per cent, versus 25 per cent for thinking). However, the majority of solicitors of both sexes – 81 per cent of male lawyers and 66 per cent of female ones – favour the thinking approach.

The problem is that emotion/feeling drives customer behaviour (and always has, even if we didn't recognise it); customers buy due to their emotions and justify with logic. And there is no business of law, and no need for a lawyer, without the customer. Period.

Logic should tell us lawyers that if we genuinely wish to understand our clients and thereby persuade them to buy from us, we need to change our behaviour and train ourselves to take a more feeling approach. After all, it's highly unlikely that the client will.

I therefore urge any ambitious lawyer who wishes to make and/or maintain a life-long career in the law to embrace a deep(er) understanding of psychology. More importantly, legal education and training providers must build this into the fabric of their educational programmes; otherwise, the teaching of skills (the like of which I am going to share with you in the next section) will be in vain.

Inevitably, for us lawyers to survive in this Digital Age, this Age of UnLawyering, the pending iCyborg lawyer era and Robotic Age, we must begin by changing (or simply improving) ourselves – our behaviour, our approach, our knowledge, and our skills. It's going to be a real challenge, but if we get it right, at least we will be a little better prepared for the journey ahead and possibly be more certain of a likely positive outcome.

legal life career-making skills

During *the naked lawyer*, I spoke at length about the skill of rainmaking (aka business development/marketing/sales all jumbled up as understood by the majority of us lawyers) and our having the need to have high emotional intelligence (EI). I'm going to pick up on these again as things have moved on since 2010, and in true ROAR model fashion we're going to innovate. We're going to address the following skills (understanding and traits) in the next few pages:

- Psychology – Err, tick; we've already covered that;
- Rainmaking and emotional intelligence;
- Storytelling and creativity;
- Confidence and the ability to change your mind; and
- Computer programming.

rainmaking

The usually suave, confidant, handsome lawyer cradled his pounding head with shaking hands as he sat nervously, elbows jarring agonisingly into his knees. Rocking gently on the sofa in the spacious corner office he eventually looked up. Fixing his gaze on the heaving buxom breasts of the senior partner he found comfort, solace, and courage for a fleeting moment. Gradually he raised his chin and began slowly to lower his hands, stroking his prominent cheek bones and chiseled jaw before soothing his aching legs with feverish palms in a circular deep massage motion.

But then he caught a glimpse of the pulsating vein in her forehead throbbing aggressively. The blood drained from his tanned face turning it ashen as he stared into the senior partner's cold, steel blue, motionless eyes and with a twisted and pained expression spluttered: 'I'm fifty shades of ****ed up.'

This is not a scene from *Madame Bovary*, *Tess of the D'Urbervilles*, or the ubiquitous erotic novel *Fifty Shades of Grey*, which every desperate housewife and her pampered pouting pooch is currently yapping on about. However, this scene could be a scenario played out in the crumbling towers of the next Dewey & LeBoeuf, Halliwells, Cobbets and more.

Those of you having succumbed to dipping a quivering finger into *Fifty Shades* will recall that the story revolves around the sexual life of a naive 20-something virgin.

Yeah, right. She becomes entwined in an unusual arrangement with an erotically experienced billionaire who has devilishly dominant/submissive tendencies. That's putting it politely.

I confess, with regret, I've read *Fifty Shades of Grey*. It was utterly dull – romantically, sexually, and erotically. Frankly, I'd rather paw over an annual subscription of *Viz* before being subjected to more of the *Fifty Shades* trilogy. And yet, the author did manage – albeit apparently inadvertently – to spark the synapses of my professional rainmaker *tomorrow's naked lawyer* grey matter. I was stimulated into thinking about the legal profession and began to draw analogies between rainmaking and sex. Sad, but true.

Why and how we approach the two activities are pretty much the same. It's all about confidence, seduction, performance, delivery, and follow-on (remember, from *the naked lawyer*?). Whether you're a poor rainmaker, an extraordinary rainmaker, or any of the fifty shades in between, will depend on your thoughts, feelings, and actions.

Poor rainmaking is like unfulfilling sex – at least for one of the parties involved. Don't really care what the other person thinks or feels; haven't got a clue what you're doing; no real effort or interest. The whole experience is over in a jiffy. And it's all about pure self-interest.

Good rainmaking is pretty much like good sex. It's not the tools that matter, it's what you do with them that counts – a bit like identifying a good bottle of champagne not by the size of the bottle, but by the size of the cork. That is, focus, quality and application.

Great rainmaking – like great sex – involves spending lots of time exploring, researching, and thinking about what you could do next to delight. And by being attentive while adventuring and pleasuring and doing lots of giving, giving, and giving some more.

Extraordinary rainmaking involves continual mind focus, continual nurturing, continual stimulation, continual discovery, continual delivery, continual follow on, continual improvement, continual innovation, continual research and development. The outcome inevitably is that both parties, client and lawyer, are more than satisfied.

In the highly competitive, digital, technological, data driven, and client-centric global legal world, where it is quickly becoming apparent there will only be three kinds of lawyer (recall Chapter 3 – 1. unemployed, 2. support worker to machine systems (low paid), and 3. super lawyer (highly paid 'relationship broker' with business savvy and rainmaking prowess)). It's a no-brainer that the businesses of law searching for entry, growth, and exit will wish to capture, harness, restrain, unlock, and unleash (yes, pun intended) the talent of fifty shades of rainmaker and implement that lawyer's sexy business model.

The Dewey saga illustrated that the days when law firms could rely on hiring a select handful of rainmakers, usually at partner and/or senior associate level, are over. Today, ambitious and extremely successful businesses of law want all of their lawyer recruits to be rainmakers; read Chapters 2 and 3.

Accordingly, gone too are the days of winning over clients in a three phase process at different stages of your legal career as grinder, binder, or finder[16], whether in the guise of loser, cruiser, or dynamo within 'the firm'.

Prima donnas occupying the big corner office – the likes of the Big Bad Partner, who are, by their own admission, continually perpetuating their 'never ending circle of self-loathing and megalomania' by being the 'scourge of every admin, secretary, paralegal, trainee, assistant and associate', regularly growling 'get back to work for god's sake. My PEP's sagging'[17] – have had their day too.

These are potentially the halcyon days wherein law as a people business promulgating work that 'can only (truly) be done by lawyers'[18], particular in non-commoditised market sectors, cries out for *every lawyer* involved in the execution and delivery of legal advice to become fifty shades of rainmaker lawyer servicing the plethora of existing and latent domineering clients.

Being a shade of rainmaker lawyer will be the only option for the expectant highly paid lawyer and ambitious business of law where innovative new entrants and investors with their sexy entrepreneurial approaches respectively profess 'this (legal) market is too big and too valuable to ignore'[19] and 'let's get closer, rather than having one night stands'[20] in reference to client relationships. Survival and growth in the 21st century for the businesses of law will depend on the right mix, positioning, handling, and nurturing of rainmaker-lawyers. Similarly, how rainmaker-lawyers apply their rainmaking escapades will determine their individual, team, and company's success in growing and potentially raising capital.

Maya Angelou, a celebrated poet and novelist hailed as a global renaissance woman, believes 'there is no greater agony than bearing an untold story inside you'. I can empathise. Can you? Perhaps your rainmaker story is yet to unfold. Perhaps it's already over. During the journey the pain is real. The joy is real too.

In their chosen career paths and professional relationships with colleagues and clients, extraordinary rainmaker-lawyers have a knack for achieving the delicate blended role of leader and follower, master and servant, being disruptive while also sustaining, being both dominant and submissive. Successful law firms and businesses of law will embrace the fifty shades of rainmaker-lawyer and tomorrow's naked lawyer will be, at the very least, one shade of rainmaker.

It is time to take steps to pre-empt the possibility of the day arriving when you may genuinely gasp, 'I'm fifty shades of ****ed up'. Begin by asking yourself: 'What shade of rainmaker lawyer am I?' After all, you won't want to be the dispensable type of lawyer who is tossed aside or gradually 'eased out' because of your 'inability to develop and cultivate new clients or orginiations'[21].

If you are kicked into the long grass you will no doubt suffer the same anxiety as the majority of those lawyers starting their own business of law: the number one concern of new lawyers considering starting a law firm is usually how to get clients. Lawyering in 2014/15 remains, to a great extent, a one-person show. Fact.

This is obviously true for a solo, but it's also true for any lawyer at any job. You are responsible for your own work as a matter of law, ethics, and fact. You are also responsible for your clients — your existing ones and sometimes for getting new ones. Competition is hotting up amongst old and new sexy players in an over-heating legal marketplace in a bid to serve the increasingly demanding, savvy and 'spoilt for choice' client. Staggeringly, many new businesses of law are starting every month and new entrants, love 'em or hate 'em, are beginning to tap into the latent legal market and pinch existing market share in Tier 2, arguably due to a highly focused client-centric and 'value' approach.

Best-selling author of *Endless Referrals*

(over 250,000 copies sold worldwide) and *Go-Givers Sell More*, Bob Burg, has this to say on 'price' versus 'value': 'Value is the desirability of the thing for the end-user. [Lawyers] can give more in value than what the client actually pays. Focus on the value you are providing rather than the money/ price you are looking to receive. It's the thunder to the lightning.'

I agree. In my experience clients were only too happy to pay for 'value', usually as a result of extraordinary client service and business savvy (judgment) combined with total client focus. In my opinion, law firms and their lawyers will continue to struggle to attract and keep clients (and struggle with the competition), whether they be positioned in Tier 1, Tier 2, or Tier 3, if they do not become totally client-centric, niche, and ditch the hang up on 'price' (the billable hour and even fixed price) rather than 'value'. More about this in Chapter 5.

But we have a problem. Clients are continually squeezing on 'price' (perhaps because they are not happy with 'value'), law firms continue to suffer from 'margin squeeze' having driven costs down as much as practicable in the quest to become lean and efficient, and the legal market has shifted whereby it is more segmented and fragmented with business models and entities ranging from David to Goliath.

There remain too many law firms, too many lawyers, and there are not enough training contracts available for aspirant lawyers; there's evidence in relation to a reduction in training contract places being offered. Why?

At the Lex 2011 Annual Conference in March that year, both Robert Millard, (then senior strategy manager at Linklaters) and Keith Wood, (then CEO of SJ Berwin) shared with attendees that the 'big players' have moved toward commoditisation and outsourcing to ensure efficiency and value. Clearly, efficiency is king.

Annual remuneration is becoming totally merit based, particularly where partners are concerned but increasingly (at that time) I believed this would trickle down to the junior lawyer levels. It has, in some businesses of law. More about this in a later Chapter 6.

Inevitably, in the drive for efficiency (going forward) there will be even fewer lawyers and those who prevail will need to truly justify their existence (and 'merit based' salary and bonuses). Rainmaking ability helps.

A major problem which businesses of law are grappling with is the balance of expense versus income: arguably, 'value'. The likely 'make-up' of the company will comprise a few partners (or equivalent) at the top, lots of 4+ PQE lawyers, and then lots of outsourcing and commoditisation.

Accordingly, the difficulty is (and will be) dealing with providing jobs for trainees through to 3 years PQE because the firm may not be able to sustain this development and growth period where there is little or no return on investment. Firms simply cannot afford to carry this 'human' cost.

Accordingly, the role of the lawyer in the present and the future will be high-end intellectual capital (IC), advising (like partners and 4+ PQE are now) together with the ability and skills to manage resources – clients, people, and finance. The grunt work (process and content) is (and will be) done by information technology (IT) and artificial intelligence (AI) – as mentioned in Chapter 3.

The problem is, how do junior lawyers become truly skilled in advising and make themselves of value when it's traditionally taken four to five or more years PQE to reach this stage? For Tier 1 and Tier 2 firms and their lawyers, there is a compelling case and necessity to commoditise and outsource due to the large scale (global) nature of their work. Arguably, market forces are such that EVERY lawyer is going to have to contribute 'value' otherwise the business model economics will not stack up. For example, most firms and their partners will not be able to sustain the present salary levels for junior lawyers (and/or themselves) and/or the numbers of lawyers. I believe further shake-up and pain is coming. Unless?

The reality is that if you are a junior lawyer reading this book, you will need to fast-track your way to high-end value IC which partners (and clients) appreciate as 'value', that is, top-end advisory work, aka advocacy, judgment (commercial), and emotional intelligence (EI); the stuff that cannot be commoditised – i.e. done by IT and AI (for now, but watch out 2030 onwards).

I believe it is this issue which needs addressing foremost, right now. As a junior lawyer you will need to be fast-tracked in commercial nous, business savvy, soft skills, EI, and IC; fundamental elements already displayed by the present 'super lawyer'.

Firms will continue to become increasingly selective in their super lawyers of the future because the evidence, reality, and necessity in relation to opting for outsourcing and commoditisation are overwhelming… and is set to increase. Annual trainee intake will only reflect long-term business planning.

What does this mean? Firms are looking to VALUE. Junior lawyers will need to be marketable, 'value' able (valuable) and ultimately, have an edge. FAST. Unless you can become truly valuable you will become unemployable and/or expendable as anything that can be commoditised and outsourced, will be. It's happening now and will only increase as competition for market share increases, clients continue to squeeze on price and demand value. And AI becomes more sophisticated.

As a junior lawyers you must get 'there' quicker. But HOW? By investing in the short, medium, and long term in the training and development of yourself. Ideally, you will be placed in a business of law which will invest in you and you will enter a properly STRUCTURED and highly organised training programme in the skills which I have mentioned here, not something which is ad-hoc and haphazard and paid lip service to, but which will dovetail with an individual's desired career progression and align with the firm's vision, strategy, and plan.

The focus must be on 'upping the ante', on rainmaking, business savvy, commercial nous, business management techniques, managing resources, leadership, emotional intelligence, and in particular on helping you learn how to market, brand, and sell yourself NOW so that the client will understand and appreciate the VALUE of YOU by experiencing your authentic (naked) behaviour and communication.

I believe this investment in both time and money should come from a mix of the following:

- Your employer – the business of law;
- Legal education (institutional and external consultants); and/or
- You – who must take responsibility for your own development and success.

You must 'get out there'; business savvy and commercial acumen is only truly learned by interacting, engaging, and getting involved. For example, social networking (offline and online) is merely one step in achieving this… but it's a very important one.

I also advocate a move toward horizontal structures where niche expertise and non-technical skills are valued and rewarded for the new roles which I spoke about in Chapter 3 command reward and respect. The long-term success of a business of law is reliant on maintaining a pipeline of highly skilled 'value' rainmaker lawyers.

In a legal world where efficiency and value is king and a business world where extraordinary service, business savvy, and appreciation of value is king, if a lawyer is not a 'super lawyer' of value then (s)he will end up being either unemployable/redundant (at worst) or a check-out Charlie (at best). Meaning: you are either going to have to get on the fast-track or you will be shunted off the rails.

storytelling and creativity

When growing up I realized that many things in life (and business) aren't about who's faster or smarter or has better grammar or who is the better exam-sitter but often it's those who can ROAR (Reach Out And Relate) well with others and are memorable ('Brand,Me/You'). Accordingly, when I am asked by interested parties what one skill should I focus on mastering the most my answer is always... STORYTELLING!

Apparently it's 'by far the most underrated skill in business.'[22], and...'the world's second oldest profession'[23]. Now there's a story. But I don't intend to talk about the first profession. I shall leave that to your imagination. I digress. Sincere apologies.

Storytelling to me isn't about writing a novel (which I will get around to one of these years) or publishing an article, a blog post, or a cracking social media post or comment. Storytelling is a magic tool in your portfolio handbag that is useful in every part of your life, not just in business or your legal role, for example, when you stand in front of a jury and share a story or a metaphor to punch your message home.

We all desire to express what we are thinking in a way that others will understand, yet many lawyers seem to do it better than others. The difference between coming across as someone who is talking at your audience (those that lack the 'storytelling skill') or someone inspiring and talking with their audience, is learning HOW to do it. So, here are a few tips (aka rules):

- **Rule #1**: Be creative – Let your inner self out. There's a reason I shared with you my take on 50 shades of rainmaker (above) in relation to rainmaking and began the section with 'storytelling prose'. It was to practise what I preach and to give you an example of the kind of thing that grabs attention and helps the writer and listener to relate.
- **Rule #2**: Show, don't tell – Engage with a mixture of written and visual content and combine it with other effective content. Get people to really listen.
- **Rule #3**: Don't let your brand get lost in marketing noise and overload – Make your story memorable the same way a writer makes their characters memorable.
- **Rule #4**: Make sure your message doesn't get skimmed – Frame your message as a story whenever possible, with a strong title and interesting hook to get the attention of your listener.
- **Rule #5**: Don't let your information get lost in a different place – Package all information together into a narrative to make sure it's heard.
- **Rule #6**: Manage information for your listener – Tell your listener the story you want them to hear. Don't rely on them to piece your story together for themselves.

And the value of storytelling? 'People buy from people': you must be memorable, allow others to relate to you; and make people believe in your vision! Niche, 'Brand,Me', ROAR, and tell your story!

confidence

Of course, to be creative, to tell a story (your story even), to be a rainmaker, and to succeed in being paid the fair amount for the value you give, you need a big dollop of... CONFIDENCE. Confidence is king! If you don't believe me then read a LinkedIn post by the hugely successful entrepreneur and now legal mogul, James Caan.[24]

Ask any lawyer, entrepreneur, businessman or woman and they will tell you the same thing – confidence is a vital ingredient in the recipe for success. You need to believe in YOU, your story and your abilities.

Not all of us are blessed with self-confidence and many of us have to really work at it. When I was much younger, and greener, I used to feel incredibly nervous before walking into a room. Any room! But, as the years went by my confidence improved. It improved by experience and by experiencing success. I realised that I actually had something to contribute to the gathering; I knew what I was talking about and didn't feel ashamed to share my view and stand my ground on an issue. You see, it doesn't really matter if people agree with you or not, what matters is that you can confidently discuss a topic and relate to your listener professionally and without taking it personally when they convey an opposing/differing viewpoint.

However, if you suffer from a lack of self-belief there are various steps you can take to make sure you are not put at a disadvantage:

- Put your best foot forward – Prepare. Prepare. Prepare. It's everything. You don't want to be on your back foot when you go into a meeting (of any kind) without thoroughly preparing. If you are well versed, you will be more confident and thereby negate the horror of not being able to retrieve that vital piece of information that will matter.

  'To be honest, in these days of the internet and instant access to information there really is no excuse for being unprepared.'[25]
- Think about positive outcomes you have achieved in the past – Visualise past success. Maybe even look over a past case/pitch etc. And then imagine the meeting, the discussion, and hearing the answer you want to hear. Part of your preparation for the meeting is remembering the key questions you wish to ask. Have them jotted down somewhere handy if you doubt your memory. What you are doing is visualising past successes and your future success at the up-coming meeting and this will put you in the right, positive frame of mind.
- Be resilient to, and accepting of, criticism – Use criticism, or a 'no', as a lesson for improvement in honing your skills rather than taking it as a negative.

As I said in *the naked lawyer*, not everyone will like you, not everyone wants to do business with you, and not everyone will be your client. It is a fact of life that people do business with those they know, like, trust, get, understand, and share common interests with.

Just as importantly, though, for us lawyers, clients desire to have total belief and feel absolute confidence in what we are doing with regard to the quality of our legal advice. Accordingly, it's a terrible contrast and faux-pas if you lack self-belief when your client expects the opposite. GET A GRIP!

Lord Neuberger wrapped up the true meaning of 'confidence' for me when he voiced his opinion on the most important quality for a judge. He said it is the ability to 'change one's mind graciously'. Now THAT, is confidence.

the dreaded follow-up

In *the naked lawyer*, I focus a great deal on how to get clients – that is, the skills to attract a prospect and generate leads and initial meetings. Now, if there's one skill we lawyers lack, it's the ability to follow-up a lead/initial meeting properly. So, I have commandeered the master of 'the follow-up', Andy Bounds[26], to share with you the secret in how to get that precious second meeting. Over to you, Andy:

How to get a second meeting (or 'How to make sure all your hard work so far isn't wasted because you don't see each other again')

Does this sound familiar? You have a meeting with a prospect. It goes well. He seemed to enjoy it. You certainly did. It looks like you might well be working together. Then, bursting with excitement, you run back to the office and prepare the information he wants. You send it to him on time. It's all going well… But then you don't hear back. Nothing. Not a bean.

And you now have that horrendous dilemma: do you chase him (and feel you're pestering); or leave it (and feel impotent)?

The fact is: it's very hard to re-kindle these things once momentum is lost. So, it's essential you do everything you can to eliminate the chance of this happening.

Good news: there are only two things to master

Once you've seen and impressed someone, to ensure you see him again, you only have to master two things:

1. Say the right things…
2. … at the right time

If both of these are right, he'll see you again. If either's missing, he probably won't. Let's start with the latter first:

The best time to ask for meeting two

The best time to ask for a second meeting is during the first one. That's right. During it. Not after it. When you think about it, this makes perfect sense: it's always easier to do things face-to-face than remotely. And, if the meeting has gone well, he may never like you as much again as he does now! So, strike while the iron is hot. If you don't, in a few days' time, you'll have the pestering/impotent dilemma again. It's just much better to sort it while you're there.

And don't let your nerves stop you from asking. Some people think 'he is so important compared to me… and he was so generous in giving his time to Little Old Me for this first meeting… I don't want to push it, by asking him for a second one'.

This is *not* the right way to think! During your meeting, you'll have helped him. So it's also in *his* interest for you to meet again. He isn't doing you a favour here. There's a good chance that your practice can help both his firm, and him personally. And, once you realise it's in *his* interest to meet again, why wouldn't you ask him to do so?

Say the right thing, to get meeting two

So, it's best to ask for meeting two during meeting one. But what words should you use? Here are three techniques that work well. Choose your favourite…

Technique #1: go for a 'yes'

People often tell me they feel awkward asking 'would you like another meeting?' Why? Because the response might be 'no'.

Let's face it, most people aren't that rude. Can you honestly see someone you've just met for an hour saying 'No, I wouldn't. Now get out'? But, I do understand you might feel nervous asking a yes/no question.

So, don't. Instead, ask a yes/yes question. In other words, give him a couple of options as to when he will see you again, so he can choose for himself. Scripts like this work well:

'I've enjoyed our meeting, and am looking forward to developing our thoughts further. I'm aware that both of us have follow-up actions, which will take some time. So, when do you think we should get together again? Sometime next week? Or the week after?'

If you look at this script, you'll notice:

1. I'm not saying 'do we meet again?' Instead, it's '*when* do we meet again?'
2. I've been clear that both of us will benefit from meeting two. This is not him doing me a favour. This is *both* of us meeting again, so *both* of us benefit.
3. If he chooses one of my two options, great. If he says 'neither', I'll simply reply with 'well, when would you suggest instead?'

You'll be amazed how well this technique works. After all, if you've had a good meeting, why wouldn't he accept one of your date options?

Technique #2: go for a 'no'

Although technique #1 works well, some people feel uncomfortable doing it. They don't like the idea of a yes/yes option. Some feel it's too manipulative. Others just feel uncomfortable asking someone to say 'yes'.

So an alternative is to go for the opposite. By this, I mean that you ask a negatively-phrased question. So, if they respond 'no', you end up with a double-negative that makes a 'yes'. Still with me? Thought not. Here's an example to explain: 'I've enjoyed our conversation so far, and feel certain we could work well together. Can you think of any reason why we *shouldn't* take things forward here?'

Notice the word 'shouldn't'. Since it's a negative, if he replies 'no', he's saying 'no, there aren't any reasons we *shouldn't* carry on'. In other words, we *should*!

Or, he'll say 'yes' and then give a reason why you *shouldn't* continue. Maybe he'll say 'I'm worried about the cost' or it will be something else – timescale, resource, priority, getting colleagues on-side etc.

This is very useful to know, of course. By finding this out, you haven't caused a problem that wasn't there. Instead, you've uncovered something that was. The worst type of objection is the one you don't know about. Once you know what they are, you can address them.

So, if he says he's worried about getting colleagues on-side, you could say something like: 'I'm glad I asked! Let's have a chat about that now. Because, like you, I don't want something to derail us'.

Technique #3: ask for advice

Both the first approaches work very well. I know this because I use them. And my customers use them. They work. But here's one final technique that also produces good results: ask him for his advice. By this I mean you simply ask his advice for how things should proceed. As you know:

- People like to be asked for their advice, so he'll appreciate you asking him.
- Once someone has suggested something, they're very likely to agree to it!

Example script:

'I've enjoyed our conversation so far, and look forward to developing things with you over the forthcoming days and weeks. How would you advise we take things forward?'

Again, very compelling. If he proposes something you're happy with, get it in the diary before you leave. If he doesn't, use his response to kick-off a conversation with him about what happens next.

Yes, but do these techniques work?

The true test of any influencing technique: does it work on children? Well, yes they do. I've used the:

1. 'Yes technique' to convince my five-year-old to go to bed – 'Maia, it's time for your favourite story upstairs. Do you want Daddy to carry you? Or are you going upstairs on your own?'
2. 'No technique' to persuade my elder teenager to carry her plates to the kitchen after dinner – 'Megan, is there any reason why you *can't* carry your dishes through?'
3. 'Advice technique' to convince my teenage son to tidy his bedroom – 'Jack, you know I'm going to bang on about it if you don't tidy your room. But you quite rightly think it's your room. So, how would you advise we deal with this, so we're both happy?'

And if you can convince my kids to do anything, you can certainly convince a prospect to see you again.

computer programming

Yes, you may guffaw or scoff, but in light of the fact that our future is only going to entail more digital gubbins, more technological stuff, more complex machines with enhanced computing process power and AI, and ultimately robots in our homes as well as in our businesses, we might as well address the idea that we would do well to learn (even a little) and get comfortable with, computer programming.

Let's face it, if your avatar/machine/icyborg/robot takes a hissy-fit one day and RoboTechnician isn't at hand in your home or house of law, then it will be up to YOU to sort it out. Also, in light of what Tim Berners-Lee shared with the Prof when discussing the topic of 'the web we want'[27] it strikes me that the internet and world wide web is going to be increasingly woven into every aspect of our lives and play a significant role in everything we do in our future.

Accordingly, I reckon it would be very wise to understand how the little machines interact with this BIG DADDY MACHINE, particularly when the time arrives when our brains will be in the cloud come 2029!

law school: but not as you know it

Businesses of law often complain that law schools don't do enough to prepare graduates for life as practising lawyers. Well, it turns out that young lawyers feel pretty strongly about it, too.

Being 'practice-ready' matters a great deal to generation Z, as was revealed in a survey in *The American Lawyer*[28] last year. The substantial research found that job satisfaction among mid-level associates is heavily influenced by how well they believe their law schools prepared them for practice.

The demand for *traditional* legal services is declining. We know this. And yet law schools continue to churn out more lawyers than the market can absorb and they are usually ill-prepared with the kind of skills necessary to survive as a 21st-century lawyer.

I have addressed some of the new skills that are required in *the naked lawyer* and in this sequel.

Tomorrow's naked lawyers and law schools of tomorrow must meet the needs of the new legal marketplace. Happily, there is at least one stunning initiative that is beginning to cater for the new normal, and that is Miami Law School and University with its LawWithoutWalls initiative. This law school is pioneering in the field of 21st-century legal education, IMHO.

In its own words, tomorrow's naked lawyers 'must be creative problem solvers, leaders with a high risk tolerance and business mindset that can use technology, social media, and communication skills to overcome the walls of law'.

In addition to traditional substantive law, critical legal analysis, and writing skills, this law school is focusing on skills vital to the future of law, such as project management, technology, creative problem solving, leadership, and cultural competency. This school is not only shifting what – but HOW – it teaches. It's law school: but not as you know it.

LWOW sprang up in 2009/10 (officially in January 2011 when it ran its first course) as a community of entrepreneurs, legal practitioners, law professors, and law students that focus on innovating in the legal sector. Student participants work together on teams over a period of four months each year with the guidance of the LWOW community on projects aimed at innovating legal practice and education across the world.

LawWithoutWalls was devised and led by Michelle DeStefano.[29] In Michelle's words, LWOW is: 'a global, academic collaboratory that focuses on tackling the cutting edge issues at the intersection of law, business, technology, and innovation. LawWithoutWalls mission is to accelerate innovation in legal education and practice at the same time.'

Michelle and her team collaborate with academics, law and business school students, technologists, venture capitalists, entrepreneurs, business professionals, and lawyers from around the world. They seek to change how today's lawyers approach their practice and how tomorrow's naked lawyers are educated and, in so doing, sharpen the skills needed to meet the challenges posed by the economic pressures, technologisation, and globalisation of the international legal market. Those skills include: leadership, teaming, technology, project management, social networking, creative problem solving, and cultural competency. Indeed, it appears they are creating the future of law, today.

Utilising a blend of virtual and in-person techniques, LawWithoutWalls offers four initiatives:

- LWOW Live: Live virtual sessions for CLE credit featuring thought leaders in the legal profession;
- LWOW Courses: For-credit courses for law and business school students (LWOW, LWOW X, LWOW X Compliance, LWOW Arbitration);
- LWOW Inc.: Incubation services and platforms for legal startups and entrepreneurs; and
- LWOW XEd: Tailored executive education initiatives for individual lawyers, law firms, corporations, and bar organisations.

I am delighted to have been asked to get involved again with Law Without Walls (LWOW) for the fourth year running, to be an entrepreneur mentor and advisor to the brightest, most ambitious, and innovative legal minds in 30-plus universities (and law schools) across 25-plus countries.

In 2015 I will be supporting students in the topic: 'Harnessing The Power of Watson: Utilizing Cognitive Technology to Help the Law Firm Make Better Decisions and Build a Stronger Relationship with Clients.

Last year I helped students with their topic 'Robot Lawyers: The Future of Online Chat Attorneys.'

It just goes to show how forward-thinking this law school is and how determined it is to ensure its graduates are 'practice-ready'. Actually, it wouldn't surprise me if the present/future pioneer in law law land emanates from this law school/programme.

Now beginning its fifth year, LWOW has grown from a community of 16 students across six schools to a variety of multidisciplinary offerings involving nearly thirty schools and hundreds of students, practitioners, academics, entrepreneurs, and venture capitalists around the world.

While LWOW has expanded in scope and form, our core values – cultural competency, project management, virtual technology, presentation, leadership, problem solving, and innovation skills – and primary mission – innovating the dynamics of legal education and practice – remain the same.

Silvia Hodges, executive director of the Buying Legal Council and an adjunct professor at Fordham University School of Law, writes: 'No matter how we slice it, law school graduates today face a very complex and challenging market. To have a chance at success, these future lawyers need the tools to enable them, in time, to run law firms as businesses. Law schools have been criticized for not teaching lawyers practical lawyering skills. So let's equip them with the right tools.'[30]

the entrepreneurial lawyer

Entrepreneurial lawyering has come of age. Not fiction. Fact. Recall the LexisNexis bellwether report (2014), 'Brave New World', which I shared in Chapter 2, and which focuses on sole practitioners, independent lawyers, and small law firms and the extent to which they are rising to meet the industry, economic, and business challenges in the present and future?

The research identifies new working practices, increased optimism, and the emergence of a new breed of entrepreneurial lawyers and reports on the dynamic independent lawyers who are really shaking things up by focusing on building their business through the smart use of marketing, networking, and technology:

'These entrepreneurs are networked, dynamic and ambitious. Often niche specialists with superb credentials, they've set up their businesses to compete directly with the major industry players, and they're frequently winning due to their agility and top-class customer service. Always thinking at least one step ahead, they're utilising every tool at their disposal to hone their competitive edge – from strategic partnerships and gaining ABS status, to outsourcing for increased efficiency, to harnessing the latest technologies to run their firm and connect with new clients.'

IMHO, cloud-based law practice, legal case management software, and CRM systems for businesses of law and lawyers is one of the best innovations (and latest technologies) in recent years and the ideal choice for entrepreneurial lawyers. More about this in Chapter 6.

My personal entrepreneurial lawyer journey began in 2008 when I devised the ROAR sales model befitting an ambitious and dynamic lawyer in this digital age. The activities I undertook resulted in a global sales success story which I shared with you in *the naked lawyer*. I quickly realised that I had to share the secret with the world (and not just the legal world). After all, in 2008, Q4 had just taken a nose dive off Mount Everest with no financial safety net. We were experiencing a global recession of the kind we'd never seen or felt before.

The release of *the naked lawyer* in November 2010 covered how we lawyers can become entrepreneurial with a step-by-step guide to how to get more clients (and more from existing clients) through mindset shift, self-awareness (emotional intelligence), devising a niche, creating a personal brand, networking (by building a referral network and via social media and social networks), providing outstanding customer service, possessing business savvy, smart use of technology in the marketing and sales process, and constantly innovating.

Invariably, *the naked lawyer* message culminated in prompting and influencing law schools, universities, associations, legal publishers, consultants, IT/Practice Management/CRM suppliers, law firms, and lawyers around the globe (maybe even you) to innovate in lots of areas; for example, legal entrepreneurship, legal education, law firm operations, marketing, sales, customer service, finance, pricing, business planning and strategy, legal IT, artificial intelligence, and robotics in the legal world.

It will certainly be interesting to see how the LWOW's entrepreneurial essence pervades the psyche and influences and motivates the actions of the new breed of entrepreneurial lawyers graduating from its dynamic law schools thereby influencing legal service provision and innovation in this field throughout the world in years to come.

I also recall being interviewed back in 2011 by Preston Clark, a New York based attorney, business consultant, and creator of *TheLawInsider* law blog[31], who wished me to share some of the content of *the naked lawyer* with his readers when it was hot off the press, and to convey my thoughts on what lawyers need to be doing to ensure their livelihood in the present and future. This was my advice: '... to develop key entrepreneurial, intrapreneurial (being entrepreneurial within the workplace), technological/digital, commercial and rainmaking skills as quickly as possible'.

It's fabulous to witness (and be involved in) the development and success of those lawyers, law institutions, and associations and businesses of law that decided to act on this message these past few years.

In the current brave new world for independent lawyers and sole practitioners, assisting entrepreneurial lawyers to navigate powerful competition and regulatory upheaval with agility, I feel hugely privileged (no doubt alongside many of my friends, colleagues, clients, and thought-leaders in their fields of expertise) to have been involved in this new wave of re-inventing lawyering; obviously for the better since these dynamos are out-performing and tearing strips off their peers.

I mentioned earlier in the book that the UK economy, that of Europe, the US, and China are predicted to be strong throughout this year and next. Arguably, there has never been a better time for the entrepreneurial lawyer to start-up, whether within a group of like-minded souls or solo, particularly from home using some of the entrepreneurial techniques described herein.

There are government-backed initiatives to assist too.[32] Here in the UK there's a plethora of entrepreneur success stories, particularly with regard to home-based businesses[33] – so much so we contribute £300 billion to our economy. If you hadn't already guessed, yes, I am one of them.

Yesterday/year (September 2008) I was a lawyer, serving the entrepreneur of tomorrow, today, in a traditional mid-tier law firm ivory tower in Leeds, Yorkshire, England. Today (2014), I am an entrepreneur, serving the lawyers of tomorrow, today, from my luxury apartment home and globe-trotting around the world.

Since my journey began, five years ago, we appear to be witnessing a tsunami of entrepreneurial lawyers throughout the world. The Age of the Entrepreneurial Lawyer has arrived. Back in 2010 I wrote in the naked lawyer that 'Entrepreneurs are from Venus and lawyers are from Mars,' I am delighted to have been proved wrong. Lawyers are from Venus and Entrepreneurs are from Mars, says tomorrow's naked lawyer. Agree?

Based on information from The Entrepreneurs Guild, if you take this quiz you can assess your own entrepreneurial tendencies and *entrepreneurial comfort level.* Albeit there will obviously be shades of grey (not quite 50), for the purpose of this exercise just see if you mostly 'agree' or 'disagree' with the following statements:

- I'm great at and enjoy networking;
- I'm optimistic about positive, successful results;
- I need to do it my way;
- Results derive primarily from my own behaviour and actions;
- I thrive on innovation;
- The most important thing is achieving the goal;
- I have a plan, and work my plan;
- I'm comfortable with change, ambiguity, and uncertainty;
- I'm self-motivated;
- I'm a risk-taker.

If you mostly 'agree' and presently think, feel, and act in this way in relation to the above statements then you're already well on your way to becoming an entrepreneurial lawyer and tomorrow's naked lawyer!

tomorrow's naked lawyer

Someone once said to me that 'everyone has their destiny. But not everyone has the choice to follow it.' Bollocks! Not about choice, btw, but about destiny.

I DO NOT subscribe to the 'it was destiny', 'it was the will of the gods', 'it was written in the stars' mumbo-jumbo clap-trap. And nor should you. It is within your power to sculpt your future. Your future is NOT your destiny. Your future is what you create.

Do you recall what Ruby Wax said? 'If I can't drive this mother-ship, nobody else is.' And if you can't drive your mother-ship, nobody else should. It's time to stop thinking about being 'a lawyer' as being just a lawyer in a law firm and to begin thinking about being a human being of EI value with the knowledge, experience, and a talent for feeling the law in a business.

It's time to choose what type of lawyer you want to be in the House of Law and ensure you prepare yourself with the right kind of skills to serve the client of the present and future. It's time to decide if you are willing to embrace the technology, the machine, the icyborg lawyer, and robot lawyer (when the time arrives) in your House of Law.

For one thing is certain, the present and future of lawyering is going to entail a magical blend of humanness and robotics/AI/machines/technology. You have to decide whether the machine/robot will become your colleague and friend, or your nemesis and foe.

after dark activity

Sit back and look to the stars. Ask yourself:

- 'Am I ready to accept that machine intelligence could make my current role redundant in the near future?'
- 'Do I really have the skills required for my likely future, today?'

If not:

- 'What am I going to do about it?'
- 'Where do I go and whom shall I ask for help?'

Begin by digging into the references I share throughout the chapter, and...

just do something!
Dance with me now. You deserve some fun...

References

1. See: www.reuters.com/article/2011/08/21/us-wallstreet-layoffs-idUSTRE77K1OU20110821.
2. From the Whatify newsletter, 17 August 2011.
3. See: www.law21.ca/2011/08/here-come-the-disruptors.
4. See: http://entrepreneurlawyer.co.uk/wp-content/uploads/2011/07/Pages-from-legal_lowres_AW.pdf.
5. See: www.stephenmayson.com.
6. See: http://ukcatalogue.oup.com/product/9780199231744.do?keyword=stephen+mayson&sortby=bestMatches.
7. See: www.simontupman.com.
8. See: www.legaleaglesbook.com.
9. See: www.thelawyer.com/1008935.article.
10. See: http://www.exemplarcompanies.com/
11. Leading themes in two excellent books that I have enjoyed reading recently by author Nigel Marsh, see: http://nigelmarsh.com/.
12. Susskind, Richard, *Tomorrow's Lawyer: An Introduction to Your Futures*, OUP, 2013.
13. Take a look at the great work Nick Beddows is doing in blended learning at Arcobalenomedia: www.arcobalenomedia.co.uk.
14. Ventrice, T., 'The Past, Present and Future of Gamification', loyalty360.org, August 2014, see: http://loyalty360.org/loyalty-management/august-2014-issue/the-past-present-and-future-of-gamification.
15. Debbie Harrison is a learning, leadership and talent development specialist: Debbie has worked with many large corporations including professional services firms and was recently interim head of talent development at King & Wood Mallesons (Europe & Middle East).
16. Jones, L., 'Rainmakers share the secrets of their success', *The National Law Journal*, 11 July 2012, see: www.nationallawjournal.com/id=1202562595544?slreturn=20141108062940.
17. @bigbadpartner.
18. The Times, 5 July 2012.
19. #LawTechCampLondon, 29 June, 2012
20. Ames, J., 'A tale of Knights and a fiery Dragon', *The Times*, 5 July, 2012, see: www.thetimes.co.uk/tto/law/article3465783.ece.
21. 'Up or Out: When Partners Have to Go', a report by ALM Legal Intelligence which reveals partners leave because of their 'inability' to find new clients. See: http://almlegalintel.com/Surveys/Uporout.
22. Twitter quote from Gary Vaynerchuck, see @garyvee.
23. Danny Harris
24. Caan, J., 'Confidence is King', LinkedIn, 12 March 2013, see: www.linkedin.com/today/post/article/20130312113833-32175171-confidence-is-king.
25. Ibid.
26. Andy Bounds is an award-winning consultant. His online video club is a great resource for lawyers. It contains hours of videos explaining sales and communication best-practices, and how to incorporate them into your firm. You can access these videos at www.andyboundsonline.com.
27. See: www.youtube.com/watch?v=0go-MrsR_Pl&feature=youtu.be.
28. Todd, R., 'The Keys to Midlevels Satisfaction', *The American Lawyer*, September 2013, see: www.americanlawyer.com/id=1202667574407?slreturn=20141006102315.

29. See: www.lawwithoutwalls.org/destefano.
30. Hodges, S., 'What They Didn't Teach You in Law School – Until Now', *New York Law Journal*, April 23, 2012, see: www.newyorklawjournal.com/PubArticleNY.jsp?id=1202549587854&thepage=1&slreturn=1.
31. See: www.thelawinsider.com/.
32. See: www.telegraph.co.uk/finance/festival-of-business/11035185/Home-businesses-get-unexpected-boost-as-Government-strives-to-create-more-entrepreneurs.html.
33. See: http://realbusiness.co.uk/article/27458-home-based-businesses-contribute-300bn-to-uk-economy.

Chapter 5: SocialHuman

'Genius is one percent inspiration, ninety-nine per cent perspiration'. Thomas Edison

2015: social savvy junkie re-invented

As a self-confessed social savvy junkie I felt moved to write on the SOCIAL issue because many (prospective) clients, conference delegates, journalists, and colleagues constantly ask me: 'Chrissie, this social media and social networking thing, what's it really all about?'

To which my usual response is: 'Try it and see! You won't break the internet!!' The reply, nine times out of ten, is: 'Yeah, but how can the firm use social media to win work?' Hmmmm. I'm now thinking to myself 'this is going to be a painful experience'.

I'd like to share something with you – may I? So that if you're ever asked this very question you have something to refer to and/or if you were wondering the same thing yourself you now have the answer!

Social media together with social networking, when used correctly, is undoubtedly a fabulous tool to complement 'traditional' marketing, sales, PR, and business development. While marketing (and sales, IMHO) is 'dead', many businesses of law (and maybe even your good self) are not ready to accept this.

I say 'used correctly' because the real power, strength, and ROI (return on investment and return on involvement), IMHO, lies in social capital and human capital (what I call SocialHuman). That is the combined effect of the two of Professor Stephen Mayson's four essential pillars of a law firm's make-up (as referred to in the previous chapter). Which (again I say it) means, the activity must be done by the individual lawyer, not 'the firm'. The clue to all this is in the word SOCIAL. Figure it out; it's NOT rocket science.

Actually, it's better than science. Because there are no rules in 'social land'. Of course, there are ways in which you would conduct yourself (and that's your choice), but unlike our beloved SRA or equivalent across the world in law law land, how you behave in social land is largely unregulated (the internet is regulated – sort of – in relation to naughtiness).

Why is this so? Because we're human and, truly, there is no one size fits all across any (dead) marketing paradigm and by sticking too rigidly to a rules-based approach, you'll undermine your own efforts and fall well short of your expectations (or your company's) when said rules don't deliver. We have to stay true to who we really are, and stop copying others. Remember, YOU are the captain of your own mother-ship and master of the destiny you are creating.

My social media junkie friend Julian puts it succinctly: 'I know it's tempting to ape a successful business, and let's face it there's no shortage of exemplars, but you're deluding yourself if you believe that you can copy a purported Twitter, Facebook or blogging strategy. It's stating the oh-so-obvious, but just because it's worked for a competitor, even one that looks deceptively like your business (law firms are two a penny), doesn't mean it will work for you… people are not interested in your company. They only become interested (not care) when they need something… Be smart'[1].

Bottom line: you have to be prepared to go it alone, try lots of stuff, make some mistakes, and learn from them.

In spite of what I say here, most businesses of law have allocated social media activity as the responsibility of the marketing person or business development person or dedicated social media new recruit: an individual pumping out 'marketing and PR messages' about the firm behind the corporate veil. Again I say it: it's not engaging or at all of interest to the recipient.

How can I say this? Well, I've been a player in SOCIAL LAND for at least six years, read enough articles, spoken to enough entrepreneurs (buyers of legal advice), and seen enough law firm website statistics to know that in some cases over 50 per cent of the traffic to law firm websites goes directly to lawyer profile pages. It tells me that potential buyers of legal advice are interested in the individual lawyers. The lawyer being visible, available, and engaging to the seeker is extremely important. It's why having a video clip on a lawyer's profile is beneficial for the viewer because they feel that they can begin to relate with the lawyer before they've even met.

Social media is all about involvement, engagement, being human, and being authentic – naked. The recipient (follower) of the message is interested in the individual expert who is sharing their information, knowledge, interests, and personality – personally. An entity (a law firm/a business of law) is not human; it certainly doesn't have character or personality; but the people within it do.

It's why law firms have been lambasted these past few years in various legal and business media for churning out PR dross into the social media streams, and why many businesses of law achieve poor results from their 'SOCIAL' effort and wasted bucks. Businesses of law fail to realise that it's not about them, the firm. It's about THEM, the recipient, where the focus should be on YOU, the individual lawyer, providing information of real interest to be useful and beneficial to the potential and/or existing client (and their client).

And herein lies the greatest challenge for the profession and industry as I see it right now: if you, as a leader or manager in a business of law, are asking yourself 'how can "my firm" use social media and social networking', the answer is simply… IT CAN'T.

It's YOU, THE LAWYER, who should be using social media and engaging in social networking. You are your best BRAND and PR mouthpiece aligned with your firm-wide brand and PR strategy because social media is all about relationships, being intimate, and personal. Intimacy matters most – remember Beaton's beat? People build and engage in relationships, not entities.

I believe it's definitely time to turn the traditional top down triangle marketing mantra upside down to capitalise on each and every lawyer's social capital and human capital. It's time for re-inventing the social savvy junkie. It's time for SocialHuman.

The question you ought to be asking is: 'should we be reinventing our entire marketing, sales, PR, and business development approach to embrace, involve, and engage all of our lawyers in SocialHuman activities?'

My answer would be a resounding (and prrrrrrrrrrrrring) YES! YES!! YES!!!

The real challenge therefore for 'the firm' and every lawyer, you, is to embrace the social media and SocialHuman revolution for the benefit of the potential client and existing client; ultimately the business of law will benefit and (hopefully) you will too.

In order to do this we must adapt, innovate, and defy our comfort zones. Take a risk. For a life without risk, is like no life at all, remember?

Invariably, most of us lawyers are not comfortable marketing and selling ourselves. Fact. Take a look around any networking event, offline or online. We're usually the ones huddled together in a corner somewhere hoping that we won't be disturbed; hands concreted in pockets, fidgeting with our ties or g-strings. But, when we are approached by someone, we're usually more than happy to engage in conversation.

Simply put, if we view social media as engagement and conversation, and approach it with confidence and optimism, it shouldn't be that challenging. We might even find that we actually enjoy it.

I read a LOT of stuff about social media, but the article '10 Surprising Social media Statistics that will make you rethink your social strategy' published by *Fast Company* last year, continually grabs my attention because it states: 'Social Media has overtaken porn as the No.1 activity on the web'.[2] I still keep referring back to this article, because it reminds me that not only is social media and social networking a very powerful marketing, engagement, and relationship medium, whether for business or leisure, but we constantly have to re-think, and sometimes re-invent, what we are doing.

To give you a feel as to what your peers (approximately 50 CEOs/MPs/partner heads of strategy/departments throughout Europe) think about all this SOCIAL stuff, I will share with you what their answers were to a couple of questions I posed during a plenary at the Association of European Lawyers AGM back in September in St Helier, Jersey, following on from a Keynote I presented on 'Law Firms in the 21st Century: The Art of Reinvention in a Digital, Silicon & Robotic Legal World':

- *Question*: Social media and social networking. Is it more bother than it's worth?
  Answers in summary:
  - We feel our younger lawyers are more accepting of social media and social networking.
  - It is a bother but we have to invest the time.
  - With it comes the opportunity to build our brands.
  - It helps with the work to be done in building relationships.
  - There is no substitute for person-to-person contact.
  - A good personal brand helps with regard to recruitment.
  - Conclusion – it's worth the bother.

- *Question*: The evolving role of the lawyer – Are you a lawyer of tomorrow, today?
  Answers in summary:
  - We all agree about the need to understand and use technology.
  - Sceptical a robot can interact like a human.
  - We need to adapt every day – even a redistribution of roles between the partners.
  - Social media and social networking is used by younger lawyers.
  - Social media and social networking is clearly on the agenda.

- ☐ There is a shift of marketing in the firm – they insist on promoting strong individuals and personalities.

Perhaps you need to re-think your view about what it means to be SOCIAL? The world, and the online world in particular, that your competitors, potential and existing clients/customers frequent, is accelerating, changing, and morphing at a rapid rate. Even China, bold enough to kick Google into touch and prevent its people from accessing the biggest search engine in the world (because it's got its own, of course), has its lawyers using SOCIAL. The place is positively buzzing with its people using a mix of 'worldwide' social networks and its exclusive social networks within China.[3] (Note to self, again, Asia-Pacific is the largest growing legal market in the world right now.)

Hmmmm. To be successful requires moving, adapting, and being agile within social land. Fortunately, there are no rules with social media; it's a leap of brand.

SocialHuman: a leap of brand

'Branding isn't everything. But everything is branding' – the naked lawyer

Marketing may well be dead. But branding isn't… It's time to share my thoughts, ideas, successes, and examples and start bringing together what I've shared with you thus far (and in the three sections that follow) with regard to a critical subject for companies, 'things', and people across the globe, and no doubt a topic which perplexes and sometimes vexes the majority of businesses of law and lawyers; namely, branding.

We're going to look at company brand ('Brand,Firm'), personal brand ('Brand,Me/You'), and product brand ('Brand,Product').

You may be asking yourself, 'why these three?' Well, many people have asked me in the past few years: 'Chrissie, how did you do it? How have you gone from a nobody to a "somebody" who works with top companies all around the world?

How did you do it from a standing start with no money, no network, and no connections at the start of the worst recession the world has ever experienced? What's your secret?'

'My secret?', I reply, 'It's a leap of brand. The secret lies in the brand trio, and the order in which you build the brand in this Digital Age.'

So here's the trio and here is the order in which I built a viable, feasible, and sustainable six-figure company and lifestyle these past few years, from absolutely nothing:

- Brand,Me;
- Brand,Product; and
- Brand,Firm.

Why did I do it this way and why does it work?

- 'Brand,Me' and 'Brand,Product' build the profile and reputation of 'Brand,Firm' by volume and in stages giving depth and breadth to the power of THE BRAND, the SOCIAL BRAND, and SOCIALHUMAN;
- It's highly cost-effective and has the most impact this way, fast;
- 'Brand,Me' and 'Brand,Product' generate the income (provide the funding) for creating 'Brand,Firm' and/or re-branding 'Brand,Firm'. This is hugely important for companies with limited financial clout, which is the reality for the majority of businesses of law; and
- It's because THIS is the ORDER your clients and prospects relate to your company. It's what clients/customers/

consumers want in this Digital Age and Robotic Age. They buy because of emotion and justify the purchase with logic. It therefore seems logical that you begin by building a brand focusing on humanness ('Brand,Me') and sharing something of benefit/value with the customer ('Brand,Product') whereby 'Brand,Firm' is the natural product of these two.

This is not pie in the sky theoretical waffle, or mumbo-jumbo. This brand trio order works. It works extremely well. It worked for me. It works for my customers. It will work for you too.

And now that various highly credible reports and research have provided proof of what my gut, logic, and entrepreneurial spirit told me, no doubt there will be fewer naysayers and more of you willing to take 'a leap of brand'.

Every interaction you have with someone outside (and inside) your company is an instance of 'relating' – or, if you prefer, 'branding in lights'. Ask yourself these questions:

- Is each interaction good, bad, or indifferent?
- Effective or ineffective?
- Positive or negative?
- Brand-building or brand-destroying?

These are important questions – because branding is not everything, but everything is branding. Do you have what it takes to make 'a leap of brand'?

'Brand,Me', 'Brand,Product', 'Brand,Firm'

This brand triage is like magic. It's not about which trumps which, btw, it's about making sure you work on all three 'brand horizons' at the same time; a bit like your company-wide strategy and operational focus which I talked about earlier: horizons 1,2, and 3.

Nevertheless, going back to the plenary session during the Association of European Lawyers AGM, I couldn't resist asking the delegates this provocative question:

- *Question*: Personal branding vs. firm branding. Which trumps which?
  Answers in summary:
  - It's a very interesting topic for all of us.
  - We all have our egos and personalities.
  - The firm has an interest in fostering both, that is, personal branding and firm branding.
  - Depends on which jurisdiction, type of client, and size of law firm.
  - Emphasis in small firms is personal branding, whereas the opposite is true for large firms.
  - When dealing with blue chip we need 'brand, firm' because we need to cover our ass – the nobody ever got sacked for hiring IBM mantra.
  - Conclusion – both personal brand and firm brand are important.

I am confident that most of you will identify with these responses. And so, let us begin and look at each of 'Brand,Me', 'Brand,Product', 'Brand,Firm'...

Brand,Me

The single most important career decision you'll ever make is to create your personal brand. I am living proof of this statement. You have 'my story' in *the naked lawyer*, but permit me to share with you an article written by George Beaton published in Australia's *BRW* on the day which celebrated International Women's Day[4]:

'Chrissie Lightfoot is the epitome of a professionally qualified woman who decided there's a better way for her to build a career than working towards partnership.

You can't miss Chrissie Lightfoot in a crowd or mistake her in the written word. She is a walking, talking, writing testimony to the success that her own advice brings. When you start to look at her achievements as an author of, among others, *The Naked Lawyer* e-book and *Fifty Shades of Rainmaker*.

But, I think you may be getting the wrong idea.

Chrissie Lightfoot is the epitome of a professionally qualified woman who decided there's a better way for her to build a career than working towards partnership in a conventional law firm. Drawing on her experience in private practice she realised that her personal brand was a major and underutilised asset. By trial and error she worked out the essence of her own brand and set about using the online environment to build what is now a global consulting practice.

Yes, she has clients all over the world and doesn't need to leave Yorkshire to coach them; her practice is virtual. They are individual lawyers who want to further their careers and who have come to recognise that their personal brand is a key means of doing.

Clients learn that the 'naked lawyer' is a metaphor for themselves. The only things they have are their intellect, experience, energy and personality. They stand naked until they clothe themselves in a personal brand that positively differentiates them in the minds of their current and prospective clients. She does not advocate wholesale departures from law firms, rather than the individual practitioner needs to differentiate her and himself within their firm. Having a distinctive personal brand turns a generic practitioner into a go-to lawyer for clients.

By using lines like "RIP to XXX – How to Market, Brand and Sell YOU!" in social media, and through state-of-the art use of search engine optimisation, Lightfoot has built a very large global clientele that she serves virtually. If ever a professional services practitioner needed evidence of the truism that a deep specialisation widens the market you can reach, Chrissie provides it.'

Brand,Product

Do your colleagues have a choice word for you? If not, here's why you want them to. Sometimes one word can make all the difference. It's how people will instantly recall and remember you. For example:

- Iron = Margaret Thatcher (the 'iron lady')
- Dream = Martin Luther-King ('I have a dream' speech)
- Best = Muhammad Ali ('I'm the best')

But you don't have to be a celebrity, mega sports star, a leading politician, or any guise of famous for that matter. Let me tell you a wee story…

I was at an awards dinner (legal conference) recently. It was coming to a close and I had wandered into the reception area arm in arm with my lover. We collected our coats and then I popped to the ladies while he wandered outside to make a phone call in peace away from all the noise. On my returning to the spot where we had parted a rather tall, handsome, suave-looking guy walked confidently toward me with hand outstretched in readiness to greet me, bellowing an enthusiastic 'HEY… NAKED!'

Co-incidentally, while this scene unfolded, my fella had just entered the reception area and was making his way back to me; only a few meters away, he would have definitely heard the shout of 'hey…naked'. Everyone else in the room did. 90 per cent of the gathering turned and glanced toward me and 'Mr Handsome'.

Now, most of us would be embarrassed/curl up and die/hope the ground would open up and swallow us whole, if this situation was unfolding, but I smiled sweetly and duly pressed the flesh when he sidled up beside me and planted a kiss on my cheek, beaming like Top Cat. The gentleman (I still didn't have a Scooby-doo of an idea who he was) continued with 'How are you? Great to see you here. I saw you last at the Claims Conference where you went down a storm and gave a really stunning speech about getting naked'.

In all innocence, I didn't know the gentleman at all. He was a delegate at one of the many conferences I attended this year. Turns out he was an employee of the event organiser company when he explained himself further to my partner and I during the short conversation. But he felt he knew me, through my message, and the one word… NAKED… resonated with him. (And now, 90 per cent of the 500+ delegates attending the dinner that evening do too!)

The lesson here is authentic positioning and just one word matters – especially for individuals. 'Mr Handsome' couldn't remember my first and last name, or the name of my company, but he remembered the brand essence of the message I live, breath, and teach (and the brand product book catchy title of *the naked lawyer*). That is, we need to get NAKED.

This dovetails nicely with helping you understand, no doubt, the importance of having a powerful 'Brand, Product', such as a book, or equivalent.

If you share something of benefit/value with the (potential or existing) customer, such as *the naked lawyer* book and achieve conveying your message powerfully with one word, the likelihood is that your SOCIAL BRAND will be amplified through your personal brand and product brand. Meaning there is no need to market in the traditional sense. The power of the word, the association, the resonance, does it for you.

Brand,Firm

I'm not going to say much about 'Brand,Firm' because it's likely it is the one you're most familiar with. I've also already shared a little bit about firm branding back in Chapter 2 along with reference to Eulogy's research.[5]

That said, I believe Arlene Adams, CEO of Peppermint Technology sums up where the focus of 'Brand,Firm' should sit when she instructed one of her colleagues to contact me to write a piece for her company to encourage her user base to think more carefully about their brands: 'It would be a good angle to link the importance of a brand being more than a marketing project – it's about how a company lives and acts that brand and that's about knowing their customers and having a meaningful engagement with them. This provides a nice link to the technology and the need for customer centric systems in the business.' Aka, in the Digital Age, your user experience is your brand.[6]

The link between a client's satisfaction with a firm's service, their subsequent loyalty, and the ensuing increase in profitability is perceived to be so logical that the relationship is often taken for granted. The three brand horizons ('Brand,Me', 'Brand,Product', 'Brand,Firm') working in harmony, utilising the tools of social media and social networking, and being SocialHuman is certainly a good way to go, IMHO.

Despite this message, I repeat, I do believe that growing the SOCIAL BRAND ought to be done in the order of:

- Brand,Me;
- Brand,Product; and
- Brand,Firm.

My understanding that what the client wants for Christmas (in terms of legal services) and why 'Brand,You' will always trump 'Brand,Firm' can be explained as follows through a simple verse:

'And the Grinch, with his Grinch-feet ice cold in the snow, stood puzzling and puzzling, how could it be so? It came without ribbons. It came without tags. It came without packages, boxes or bags. And he puzzled and puzzled 'til his puzzler was sore. Then the Grinch thought of something he hadn't before. What if Christmas, he thought, doesn't come from a store. What if Christmas, perhaps, means a little bit more...'

The above is a verse from my absolutely favourite piece from the Christmas movie, *The Grinch*. You may be thinking, 'where's Chrissie going with this?' So, here's my take on it:

'And the Grinch Lawyer, with his Grinch Lawyer-feet ice cold in the snow, stood puzzling and puzzling, how could it be so? They used to come without ribbons. They came even in rags. They came with bribery packages, gift boxes, and loads of cash bags. And he puzzled and puzzled 'til his puzzler was sore. Then the Grinch Lawyer thought of something he hadn't before. Why don't clients, he thought, simply walk through the door anymore? What if clients, perhaps, are opting for more. And while scratching his puzzler to the very core, trying to figure out how to give clients much more, Grinch Lawyer began to experience a fuzzy feel, as he mumbled and grumbled... WHAT'S THE DEAL?'

As the Grinch begins to understand the true meaning of Christmas I liken it to us lawyers understanding what our clients are really all about and what the true meaning of extraordinary customer service actually is. Have you ever found yourself thinking, feeling, and suffering with 'Grinch Lawyer Syndrome'? I have: six years ago I was sat at my sparkly desk in Grinch Lawyer Ivory Towers R Us Lair, *hands cupping face and elbows supported on desk*, staring at the office door, glancing every now and again at my email inbox, the telephone, and my mobile phone. After a while, I realised that the new legal world order had actually kicked in and things were definitely not going to return to the way they used to be. We were in a new enlightened digital consumer age. Clients weren't simply going to walk through the door anymore.

What to do when clients are opting for more, I thought? What is more? Why do clients go somewhere else? Who do they go to? Where, when, why? What do clients really want?

Let me share with you now a secret in true Spice Girl style – I'll tell you what they want, what they really, really want. For some of us, it will come as no surprise, but for others it may be rather enlightening. I read a survey entitled 'What Clients Really Want from a Legal Service Provider'.[7] It was the first fully comprehensive research into the role of the customer experience in legal services, post the Legal Services Act.

Obviously, I cannot share with you the entire findings (copyright 'n' all). You will have to read the research for yourself. But, I believe I can share with you one wee part of the report, a particularly intriguing piece, no less. The survey report asked a series of questions to law firms, consumers, and businesses. Here's just one example, I think, that will help us understand what our clients would like for Christmas, and beyond.

The following question was asked to consumers and businesses (buyers) of law firms (suppliers): 'If you were purchasing legal advice how important are these factors?'

Respondents then had to rank six factors in order of importance. One of the six factors to be ranked was 'they have a trusted brand name' in relation to the law firm ('Brand,Firm').

Result? Businesses ranked 'they have a trusted brand name' LAST; consumers ranked it fourth from last.

This confirms what many people outside law law land have long since suspected: clients don't care about 'Brand,Firm'. Law firms have zip visibility in terms of their firm brand names and have been wasting their marketing budgets for years on 'Brand,Firm' activities.

The research findings also confirm what entrepreneurial lawyers of the Super Lawyer kind I wrote about back in May 2010[8] have realised; namely, that what clients really want is 'Brand,You'.

How can I say this with such confidence and conviction? The number one ranking for businesses answering this particular question was that it was important to 'know and trust a lawyer that works for the firm' and for consumers it was 'the quality and promptness of customer service'. Ultimately, 'Brand,You' trumps 'Brand,Firm' in the client's heart and mind.

'Brand,Firm' is an entity. It can only have personality if it has a human being (us) breathing life into it. The client is telling us that 'Brand,You' is the oxygen to the lifeblood of 'Brand,Firm': the elixir for knowing, trusting, quality, and promptness of customer service.

Maya Angelou once wrote: 'People won't remember what you say. They won't remember what you do. They will remember how you make them feel.'

What do clients want for Christmas? Grinch Lawyer, or Super Lawyer? I'll leave you to reflect on what I've shared with you here. It just may help to snuff out Grinch Lawyer Syndrome.

smart brand piggy-backing

In October this year *The Lawyer* rag (online) reported on Mishcon de Reya's three-day-week revolution:

'Managing partner Kevin Gold has approved three-day weeks and has told lawyers to take unlimited holidays as part of a new agile working programme. Gold has bet on brainpower rather than round the clock working, allowing lawyers unlimited flexibility as long as it doesn't affect their clients. The programme is aimed at improving gender balance, and the stats show that this seems to be working.'[9]

My immediate thoughts were both positive and negative. On the plus side, I'm all for innovating (and re-inventing even) when things need improving. Many of you who know my work understand that it focuses on ROAR and places the client and extraordinary customer service at the heart of everything.

Accordingly, it seems to me that a new initiative/programme which could in principle benefit clients and you, lady lawyers, in particular, who yearn to balance their commitments by taking personal control over managing their work (clients), family, leisure, and holiday time (ergo requiring flexible working), could potentially mitigate the legal brain drain and effect an increase in productivity, 'love my job' feeling, and client service excellence.

'Presenteeism' sucks. It always has, by the way, and it's about time law firms realise that lawyers (at every level) are grown-ups and are quite capable of working away from the ivory tower desk in this Digital Age and liaising with their clients remotely and/or virtually.

An anonymous commentator on *The Lawyer*'s report states: 'Clients don't give a damn where you are sitting when you work, what you are wearing, whether you have music on or not, blah blah. They pay you for your brain and talent, or not, as the case may be.'[10]

In this 'me, me, me', client-demanding, client-centric, global commerce, non-stop 24/7/365, 'must have immediately', mobile world where we're all expected to be constantly 'on' and available (via telephone, emails, and social streams on multiple digital devices anywhere in the world at any time of day or night, weekday, or weekend), the work/holiday-leisure divide has been sliced and diced through with a samurai sword for many years.

The concept/initiative/programme (or whatever you want to label it) of unlimited holiday leave is an example of the law needing to catch up with the real world lifestyle change that has already occurred; in business, in law law land, and in life.

IMHO, employment law per se (in the UK or any other jurisdiction for that matter) has not caught up, yet, with how our clients kick and we lawyers tick. On the down side, it could be argued that some partners in law firms have been operating on (and delivering) the equivalent of a three-day week for years – i.e. underperforming (in real terms), not even justifying their existence on a five day week, let alone three.

I know of some firms (and I am sure you do too – lawyers and entrepreneurs) where they continually 'carry' underperforming partners, some of whom also may not be particularly good with client care and/or service, but for a variety of reasons the firm is reluctant to 'move them on'.

I'm pretty sure that where this exists the morale of the lawyers who are pulling their puddings out is severely affected. No doubt the firm will eventually suffer as these stalwarts inevitably kick-on in a vote of no confidence with their feet, at some point in the near future, taking key clients with them.

Call me cynical but perhaps Mishcon is guilty of simply piggy-backing on the media hype around Virgin's similar scheme, as well as the power of Virgin's brand, and gleaning loads of (reflected) law law land media fuzz and buzz. Is it a ruse, perhaps, so that Mishcon can be perceived as the go-to law firm for lady lawyers and at the same time tick the gender diversity box to please their clients and City panels? Or, maybe, in this over-lawyered (too many lawyers, too many law firms) era of the Entrepreneurial Lawyer, it's simply The Next Big Idea, to purge the ivory tower of slackers? For therein lies the nub and rub: 'as long as it doesn't affect their clients'. Encouraging their lawyers to take unlimited holiday leave may in fact be the perfect programme for the firms and/or clients to agilely kick the slackers into the long grass to enjoy a permanent holiday with their shiny desk lamps?

Of course, the jury is still out as to whether any number of Branson's employees and Mishcon's lawyers press the pilot eject button by seriously abusing the privilege. For most conscientious employees and lawyers will be sensible and discerning about their new found freedom of choice with the client rope their pioneering employers have tossed in their direction.

I reckon the message is rather clear: 'Your career and your life, literally, is now in your hands.' These lawyers certainly are the captain of their mother-ship. Let's just see how long it takes before other businesses of law follow suit in brand piggy-backing, shall we? One thing's for sure, I'm going to lurk in the background in anticipation of reading the first legal dispute case to come to light on this hot PR topic. It sounds wonderful in principle, but the policy – championed by Sir Richard Branson and copied by Mishcon – could open businesses up to discrimination claims.

Nevertheless, in principle, I reckon it was rather a smart move for Gold and his merry-band of legal brand drum beaters to piggy-back on Branson's brand. I did enjoy an intellectual exchange with Mishcon's head of business development, Elliot Moss, on Twitter at the time. Mischon has come a long way from being labelled a traditional city firm acting for private clients to being branded a pioneering 'go-to' business of law for a wide range of (international) commercial clients.

smart pricing of the social brand message

Moving on from smart brand piggy-backing, but also highly relevant to the 'client-lawyer-firm' brand relationship, let's turn to how smart pricing of the social brand message is linked to bountiful dividends.

'Pricing': a choice (one) word. I immediately thought of Richard Burcher[11], the legal pricing 'go-to' guy, and promptly pestered him for answers to two pointed questions, which I felt you would benefit from hearing.

Over to Richard:

Question: Is it the personal perceived brand of the lawyer or the firm's perceived brand which in reality achieves growth for the firm with regard to the right price being quoted, and collected, for the job?

Answer: Law firms have a brand, practice teams have a brand, and individual practitioners have a brand. Logically, all three should be synchronised and broadly speaking reflective of the same values, quality, and market position. However, this won't always be the case, as even in the best of firms, there will be practice teams and individuals who for one reason or another shine more than others.

The question then becomes how is that handled from a pricing perspective? As a general observation, there is too much pricing homogeneity in firms, which fails to recognise these differences. This manifests itself as consistency in amongst other things hourly rates.

However, there should be far more differentiation between fee earners and practice areas. Perhaps the silliest thing I have seen is a slavish adherence to some sort of internal hourly rate scale based on the number of years' experience. The absurdity of this is obvious when you consider there are partners with ten years' experience who by any objective criteria are significantly better as lawyers then colleagues with double that amount of experience.

Equally absurd is the situation with lateral hires where a partner from a large firm in a city where they are on a high hourly rate moves to a firm and hour out of the city centre and their rate is dropped by 30 per cent for no other reason than that they can't be seen to be charging more than the departmental head. This has nothing to do with commercial pragmatism and everything to do with egos. The client who follows the lateral hire must think they have died and gone to heaven.

There is copious evidence that proves that to one extent or another we all use price as a proxy for quality when making purchasing decisions. In other words, if it is more expensive than the alternatives, it is probably better. It makes no difference that this is completely irrational but the effect is well researched and documented. It is this dynamic that gives rise to phrases that have entered the vernacular including 'no one was ever fired for buying IBM' and 'reassuringly expensive'.

Therefore, firms, practice teams, and individuals can take advantage of this by using pricing as part of their brand messaging. Of course, you can't fake it. If you are expensive and fail to deliver, you will be found wanting and will suffer the consequences swiftly. However, if you are a skilled professional and you provide a fabulous service, then you do have considerable capacity to use price to enhance and reinforce your brand messaging.

Equally, a reputation for discounting, weak price negotiation, and unimaginative pricing can seriously damage your brand by sending very negative messages to the marketplace.

The importance of pricing as part of the brand mix is grossly underestimated. It can be a force for good or bad depending how you use it. This holds true for the firm and individuals within the firm.

Question: Do you see a role for artificial intelligence (cognitive machine intelligence) in the pricing of legal work? If so, why, what, where, when, how?

Answer: Yes, I think that this is the next exciting frontier in the evolution of law firm software. If we go back to pricing first principles, the two primary objectives of all pricing decisions by law firms should be to maximise profitability while at the same time ensuring that the pricing structure leaves the client feeling that they have had fair value for money.

And yet opportunities to do so continue to be squandered because in order to do this really well, it requires both an objective/quantitative assessment and a subjective/qualitative assessment.

For the most part, we are capable of undertaking the objective/quantitative assessment to a high standard. We have seen a significant evolution in practice management software. Version 1.0 gave us little more than the ability to properly manage the trust account and the general ledger. Version 2.0 gave us amongst other things, better financial reporting capability and online time recording functionality.

What we have now with generation 3.0 is a much greater capacity to understand, analyse, and plan the objective, arithmetical components of a legal project, but this still rather misses the point. There are important elements of subjectivity in pricing that the current software does not come anywhere near dealing with satisfactorily.

Consider, for example, the following:

- England: Civil Procedure Rule 44.4 – Factors to be taken into account in deciding the amount of costs and The Solicitors (Non-Contentious Business) Remuneration Order 2009;
- United States: American Bar Association Model Rule 1.5 – Fees;
- Australia: New South Wales Legal Profession Act 2004 –Section 363 – Criteria for costs assessment; and
- New Zealand: Lawyers and Conveyancers Act (Lawyers: Conduct and Client Care) Rules 2008 Chapter 9 – Reasonable fee factors.

What they have in common is a clear articulation of the need to take a granular and nuanced approach to pricing legal work and not simply rely on time billing. If I was to distil and précis the opening stanzas of each of these regulatory guidelines and the extensive multi-jurisdictional body of common law surrounding them, it would look like this:

a) In determining what constitutes a fair and reasonable fee from the point of view of both the practitioner and the client, the practitioner *shall* take into account *all* relevant considerations including the following…;
b) The following list is not exhaustive, merely illustrative;
c) The relative importance of each of the factors will vary according to the particular circumstances of each engagement. The practitioner will need to apply a considered weighting to each of the factors; and
d) Irrespective of the methodology used to arrive at the fee, the practitioner must stand back and consider the overall reasonableness of the fee, 'in the round'.

So what are these factors? Many jurisdictions set out factors that overlap with others, some are identical, some are unique, some lists are limited to four or five items, and others have up to 13. I have pulled together those I think are some of the most useful and which provide the greatest guidance. Necessarily, my list is longer than any single jurisdiction. In no particular order:

- The time and labour expended;
- The skill, specialised knowledge, and responsibility required to perform the services properly;
- The importance of the matter to the client;
- The results achieved;
- The urgency and circumstances in which the matter is undertaken and any time limitations imposed, including those imposed by the client;
- The degree of risk assumed by the lawyer in undertaking the services, attributable to amongst other things, the amount or value of any property or money involved;
- The complexity of the matter and the difficulty or novelty of the questions involved;
- The experience, reputation, and ability of the lawyer(s) and the firm performing the work;
- The possibility that the acceptance of the particular retainer will preclude engagement of the lawyer by other clients;
- Whether the fee is fixed, conditional, or contingent (whether in contentious or non-contentious work);
- Any quote or estimate of fees given by the lawyer;
- any fee agreement entered into between the lawyer and client;
- The reasonable costs of running a practice;
- The fee customarily charged in the market in the locality for similar legal services;
- Whether the fee was proportionately and reasonably incurred;
- Whether the fee is proportionate and reasonable in amount;

- The conduct of the parties;
- The conduct of the lawyers;
- The quality of the work undertaken;
- The nature and length of the professional relationship with the client; and
- The relative price risk to the practitioner and the client arising out of the detail of the pricing arrangement between them.

The challenge lies in the fact that a significant number of these criteria are wholly or substantially subjective in nature. This requires the practitioner to make a value judgment as opposed to an empirical calculation. Might it be possible in the future to entrust this analysis to software? I am sure it will come but unfortunately, the ability of software to analyse subjectivity (an oxymoron?) is a long way off – perhaps 5 to 10 years.'

But it will happen. You heard it first here.

smart words that sell

It is well documented that great headlines get attention. And taglines are the first step to emotionally engaged customers[12], for example: 'You shop, we drop' (Tesco's tag).

But in social land where attention span is short and you need to grab a reader's attention within 140 characters (the number of characters permitted in a tweet) you're going to have to get smart about using your 'one word' and other smart words that sell. Not just in headlines, straplines, and positioning yourself with your personal brand, but also within the body of your content, whether that is in the form of a story, an article, a blog post, a comment in a social network or a tweet etc.

Let's chat about headlines first. If your headline is weak, chances are, it won't get noticed, and your message will fail. At the very least, it won't be any way close to being as successful as it could be. Here's a statistic that will help drive home my point: on average, eight out of ten people will read your headline, but only two out of ten will read the rest of your copy.

Do you understand the full importance of that statement? In a nutshell, it means people will decide whether or not to read your stuff based solely on how compelling your headline is. In other words, if your headline doesn't capture the reader's imagination, your message/piece is pretty much destined to fail. That's how important it is to get the reader's attention whether in traditional print or online. This is especially true for online copy though, because internet users are notorious scanners. You have to literally make them 'slam on their eyeball brakes!'

So, what makes a good headline? Before you can write a good headline, you first have to understand what the job of a headline is. The number one job of a headline is to get the reader's attention. Period.

There are two ways that you can grab the attention of the reader:

- With a direct headline; or
- With an indirect headline.

What's the difference, you may wonder? In a direct headline, you get directly to the point. You let your reader know right upfront what you're selling/'socialing', and what your amazing offer is. For example, a headline comprising 'How To' is generally very effective.

An indirect headline fosters curiosity. For example: 'The Man With The Grasshopper Mind'. Isn't that a smack you in the face, slapper-my-thigh, kick you in the crotch kind of provocative headline or what? (By the way, this example is a classic headline, and one of the 100 Greatest Headlines Ever Written.)

Which is better – direct or indirect headline? Honestly... both work really well, particularly when you use power words. It's a matter of personal preference.

Some writers prefer direct headlines due to their belief in respecting the reader's time, so they like to get right to the point in their headline. That way, the reader can decide immediately if they want to continue reading the rest of the copy.

Personally, I prefer the indirect headline because the number one job of a headline is to get the reader's attention. We humans are terribly curious, by nature. If the job of your headline is to grab your reader's attention, you will not fail by appealing to their curiosity.

Occasionally, I do use direct headlines to mix it up a bit and when I'm told to or have no say in the matter such as when I write for clients and they wish to take a more 'reserved' approach or because it must comply with their brand – understandably.

Nevertheless, regardless of which type of headline you use – direct or indirect – it's absolutely imperative that you know your audience/prospect/target. Knowing your audience will help you write more effective headlines, as well as more effective copy in general.

Always, always, always research your market! (I go into this in *the naked lawyer*, Volume 3.) If you go the extra 10,000 miles and do whatever it takes to completely know and understand your target audience then this will be your greatest edge over your competition.

For me personally, my best headlines are usually the ones that sort of just pop into my head. But remember, I have 25 years of experience doing this. Generally speaking, you're better off writing a bunch of headlines until you end up with your strongest one.

How do you determine your strongest headline? Well, the easiest way is simply to show your headlines to your colleagues or if you're a member of any small business forums, show your headlines to forum members to get their feedback. Of course, there is always your family and friends. Garner their opinion.

But if you're flying solo, whether out of choice or necessity, I recommend this tool. It's REALLY neat: The Emotional Marketing Value Headline Analyzer.[13] Give it a try.

By the way, emotional appeals and hot news stories are very powerful in headlines too. So use them as often as possible. Here's what it takes to write an effective headline in six simple steps:

1. Write your headline first, before writing your copy;
2. Research your market – You must know and understand your target audience;
3. Target your headline to that audience;
4. Give your audience what they want;
5. Get the reader's attention – be creative; and
6. Use emotional appeals, and hot news stories in your headlines whenever possible – again, be creative.

Oh btw, when writing your headline DO NOT try to trick people. YES – Get people's attention. YES – Be creative. But also... BE

HONEST. Why? The point is your headline is a promise to prospective readers – a promise that you should be committed to keeping. By writing your headline before the rest of your content I believe that if you write a strong, compelling headline, it will force you to work harder to write copy that lives up to the promise you make in your headline.

Let's now look at compelling and smart words. According to the psychology department at Yale University, some words in the English language are more powerful than others. And their top 10 most powerful are:

1. **You** – Listed as the number one most powerful word in every study reviewed.
   Because of the personal nature of advertising copywriting, you should use 'you' in your headline, opening line, and as often as possible. In fact, many copywriters will throw out a headline if 'you' is not in it.
2. **Results** – Works in rationalising a purchase.
3. **Health** – Especially powerful when it applies to a product.
4. **Guarantee** –Provides sense of safety at time of purchase.
5. **Discover** – Presents a sense of excitement and adventure.
6. **Love** – Continues to be an all-time favourite.
7. **Proven** – Helps remove fear from trying something new.
8. **Safety** – This could refer to health or long-lasting quality.
9. **Save** – We all want to save something.
10. **New** – It's part of basic human makeup to seek novelty.

Here's a handful of additional powerful words (sales words) that can get your reader to do your bidding:

- Announcing;
- Bargain;
- Challenge;
- Compare;
- Discount;
- Easy;
- Exclusive;
- Hurry;
- Important;
- Improvement;
- Miracle;
- Plus; and
- Practical.

And these uplifting words add power to your message:

- Abundance;
- Achievement;
- Charity;
- Confidence;
- Creativity;
- Energy;
- Freedom;
- Grace;
- Guidance;
- Happiness;
- Harmony;
- Health;
- Honesty;
- Inspiration;
- Intelligence;
- Kindness;
- Life;
- Love;
- Memory;
- Peace;
- Persistence;
- Poise;
- Power;
- Purpose;
- Resourcefulness;
- Serenity;
- Strength;

- Success;
- Vitality; and
- Wisdom.

Amazing communicators know and practise the secret of often using the strongest words in their content such as:

- Free;
- You;
- New; and
- How.

Nothing gets more attention than 'free' and the word 'you' is simply magic. YOU should be used everywhere. Plus, it keeps you focused on whom you are addressing.

A little effort will enable you to come up with many places to use 'new' in your copy. And 'how' will work wonders in otherwise boring writing. Everyone wants to know 'how' to do something. How to be more productive? How to be more attractive? And even how to be a better writer?

These are the timeless power words that have always worked, and if you don't believe they still work today, leave them out of your writings at your own peril!

In the words of a very dear social savvy friend of mine: 'Great content is never finished. It's only abandoned.' So make sure you use great headlines, straplines, and words in your content so that:

a) It gets read; and
b) It gets shared and re-read!

smart behaviour that sells

'Chrissie has the power to extenuate charisma over email (I want that)', said Garrett Miller[14] in an email to co-speakers presenting at the IBA this year in Tokyo. Garrett's sentiment is most flattering. But I'm not sharing it with you to boast. I'm sharing it with you to make the point that smart behaviour (in conjunction with smart words) sells too.

What I naturally do is combine the use of power words and headlines in my communications with what has become known as 'social selling'.

social selling

Social selling is THE HOT TOPIC right now – so hot it doesn't even have a definition in Wikipedia. Look it up. A lot of sales consultants and software vendors claim social selling and Sales 2.0 are really the same thing.

Anneke Seley, author of the book *Sales 2.0* defines the term as a more efficient and effective way of selling for the buyer and the seller enabled through technology. After all, if social media is an enabling technology, then applying it to selling would make it 'sales 2.0.'

- *Question*: How does social help us become more efficient and effective sellers/be SocialHuman?
  Answer: through Socially Enabled CRM.

By combining CRM with social data, you get a complete and accurate profile of your customer/prospect. Social data reveals so much about an individual such as their interests, specialties, employment history, biography, groups, awards, and connections. This is the most accurate and detailed information available because it comes directly from the individual – at the time it happens. Savvy sales teams and marketers use this additional information to make more informed sales calls and targeted campaigns. It also provides a truly unique vehicle to communicate inside of the social median.

Mike Derezin, vice president of sales at LinkedIn, shared a statistic very recently with readers that was absolutely mind-boggling: 'Sales professionals who use social selling are 51% more likely to exceed their quota.'

According to LinkedIn, the primary components of social selling comprise the following:

- Create a professional brand – Establish a professional presence on LinkedIn with a complete profile; aka create a professional personal brand that can be used on any social network;
- Find the right people – Prospect efficiently with powerful search and research capabilities (aka research your ideal value client/niche);
- Engage with insights – Discover and share valuable information to initiate or maintain a relationship (aka ROAR); and
- Build strong relationships – Expand your network to reach prospects and those who can introduce you to prospects (aka cultivate your lobsters – key influencers/ referral buddies).

(Sound familiar? Recall the ROAR model?)

Speaking of lobsters and influencers my good friend Bob Burg, whom I introduced you to in *the naked lawyer*, now defines 'influence' as: 'the ability to move a person(s) to a desired action, usually within the context of a specific goal. *Ultimate Influence*™ is the ability to get the results you want when dealing with others while helping them feel genuinely good... about themselves, about the situation, and about you... The person who does this consistently can be a great corporate or team leader, a top-producing sales professional and an overall success in life.'

If you'd like to know where you currently stand in 'the influencer' stakes he's just created a self-assessment tool, the Ultimate Influence™ Assessment.[15] (It's free, btw.) It includes 14 value-based questions designed to provide you with influence knowledge and persuasion knowledge as well as an excellent idea of your areas of strength and those areas in which you can improve.[16]

2015 to 2020: the next big thing in SOCIAL

You won't be surprised by now to learn that this is also a question I get asked, A LOT: 'Chrissie, what do you think is the next big idea in social?' To which I reply: 'The rise of resonance'

'Huh?' Is the usual response. I then expand by saying: 'We are going to experience the evolution of social networking relationships, you see. It's going to be all about context, deep personalisation, relevance, resonance, vibe tribes, vibe communities, and vibrational intelligence.'

Permit me to tell you another story... Jazz Rasool is a scientist.[17] We met at a futurist conference last year and 'hit it off'. We both share the same enquiring mind about technologies that are likely to benefit the future and how they can be applied to make the world a better place. We kept in touch and arranged to meet up to learn more about what we are both doing and to determine whether we could assist one another going forward. And this is what I learned about Jazz and his product at our meeting (and the subsequent one).

The work Jazz is doing is phenomenal. He specialises in psycho-sematics; the understanding of how the mind affects the body, and Jazz teaches in this field.[18] Jazz has recently devised pioneering software in this discipline. When the European Union put out a call to help London improve its ability to get SMEs to collaborate in the digital and creative sector, his company won the European Regional Development grant to do this.

The technology can be, and has been, applied in 1) recruitment re virtual teams 2) mental health and wellbeing 3) leadership 4) marketing and 5) retail. It can profile anything, for example, match a person to a thing which will help them make the best of their day – e.g. best fit to books, websites, etc. In essence it's kind of like a new social network. Jazz has invented a technology that connects up people with products beyond what Facebook and Google presently do. It matches content to individuals – that is, it is highly personalised and collaborative (exclusive to the individual) and creates the inner world of one person with another and then creates a team world. You can go into a virtual space (something which means something – a strength or a weakness), create a virtual world (using oculus rift connected to his software), and wander around a representation of your inner world. In essence, you can sit in your comfort world, plan tasks and activities in the terrain for you as an individual and as a team.

No longer will there be a need for outbound retreat because it's inbound now. You can have a team of people coming together in a virtual gathering/landscape – it's a physical manifestation – where social matching occurs. I reckon it's the next step on from gamification and social networks as we know and experience them now.

Take a look at Figures 3–6:

Figure 3: Evolution of social networking relationships (© Jazz Rasool, Energy Diamond Consulting, 2010)

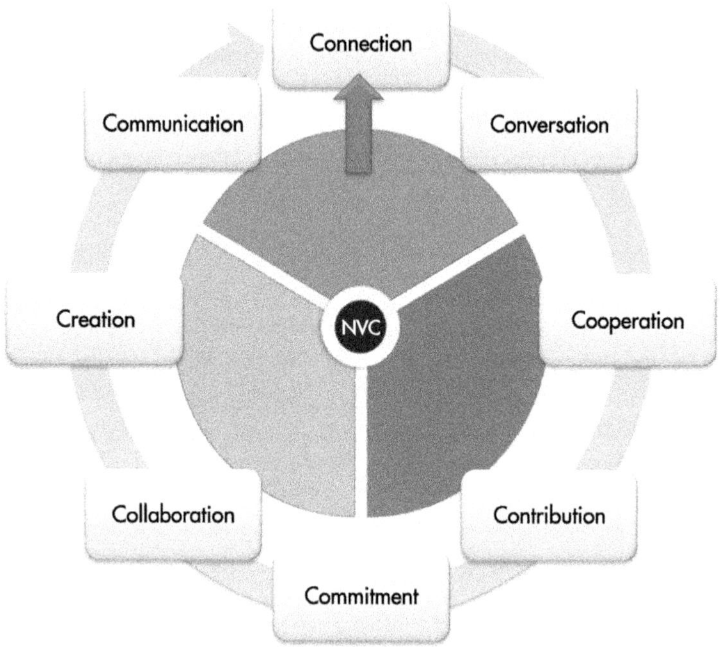

Figure 4: The collaboration cycle (© Jazz Rasool, Energy Diamond Consulting)

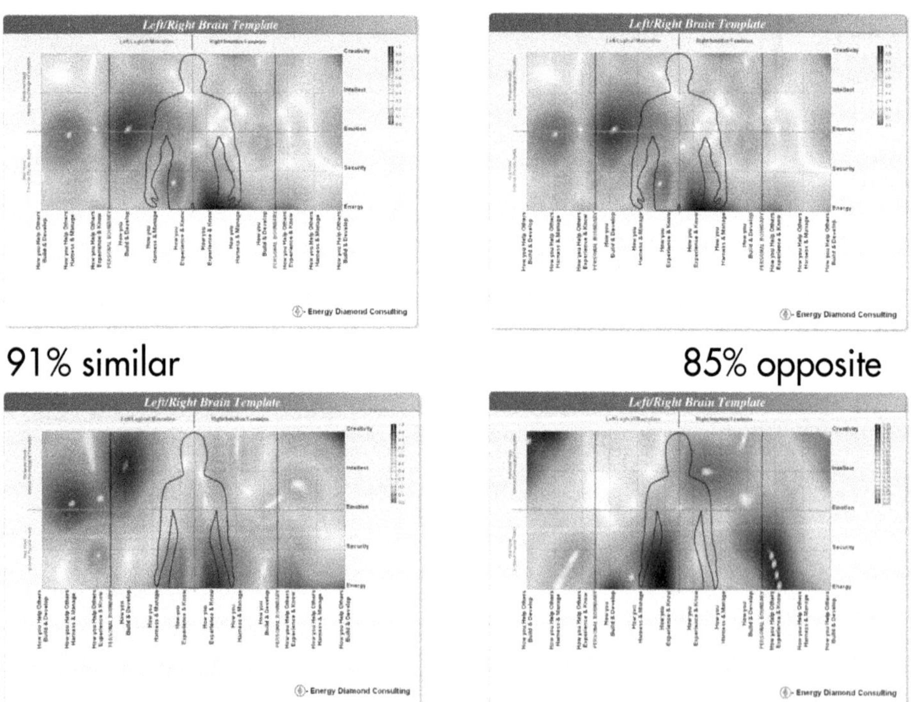

Figure 5: Using Social DNA for social resonance; comparisons of people with similar and opposite qualities (Energy Diamond Consulting)

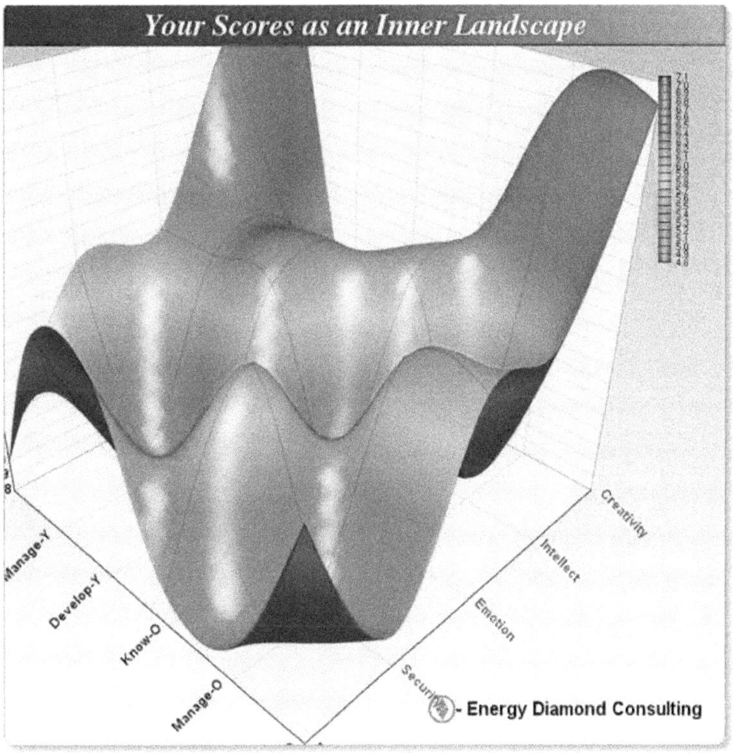

Figure 6: Collaboration technology (Energy Diamond Consulting)

The software turns 2D into a 3D image of what you're like in your life along with your intentions. It's a landscape of your inner space, manifested as mountains, valleys, plateaus. Jazz enthuses: 'We put earthquake cracks in for not being authentic. Lakes and reservoirs are truths/authenticity. Habits are habitats based on good or bad habits; for example, either ghetto or Sunset Boulevard! You get a real sense of the shape of yourself.'

The terrain means something! You will feel inertia, or feel like flying. One of the features is you can jump, virtually. If, for example, you are taking a training programme, this technology shows the before, during, and after CHANGE. It maps the positive good habits over a period.

It is a satellite view of your life and your productivity.

The technology is all about relevance; returning surface level stuff – interests (intentions), preferences (priorities), behaviours (way of being consistent). What matters is similar intentions, priorities, and the way of being complementing yours (resonance factors).

'Internet, social media, society are moving from a relevance age to a resonance age. Google and Facebook etc. are working with relevance right now. They need to be working with resonance', says Jazz. And they know it. But I can't breach confidentiality, so that's as much as I am going to say on this point.

This 'collaborative technology' would make the likes of Facebook and Twitter even more optimised and personalised. If we are to inject social networks with collaborative technology, synchronicities will happen.

Jazz said to me: 'Arthur C. Clark said that "any technology which is sufficiently advanced is indistinguishable from magic". I'm a statistician at heart but this is magic! When awareness reaches a certain level it's magic.'

I can see how this technology could be applied in law law land in relation to the effective development of lawyers. Social matching between lawyer and client could even ensue. It would link with what I share in the ROAR model, the RIP element, and bring it to life in the virtual world to then be applied in the real world.

For example, let's take gravitas – your lawyerly centre of gravity. What reputation, what brand, would suit you and your perceived brand? What's important for you on your current day? Where should you centre your activity to be most productive? If you have a good reputation/personal brand, then this technology will help you draw on it to the maximum effect on a given day.

Businesses of law need to be more dynamic. No matter what challenges and problems the entity experiences, the solution resides in the leaders and managers asking the question 'where is our centre of gravity today?' This technology would help you, the lawyer, be ultra-efficient and effective, ultimately making YOU highly profitable in monetary terms (for your employer) and in relationship terms.

As Jazz squarely says it: 'Whatever model they (the law firm) are using to come across to people is outdated. They need a new way to present themselves. It needs performance and precision. You achieve this through a centre of gravity, and gravitas.'

Gravitas occurs in the moment. It's okay talking about reputation but it's different when the reputation manifests itself at the moment the individual lawyer is with the client face to face. Reputation comes down to presence; in an email/ on the phone/face to face. Gravitas has to come across in every medium – particularly in court. This technology is engaging, fun, and empowering. Engagement is the exciting thing. Engagement begins with resonance, tuning into the vibe of that person.

Vibe is a multidimensional thing. Let's take T'ai Chi – energy and consciousness. Jazz's technology derives from this practice. Your intention drives/directs/positions the energy. And attention holds it there and builds it up. Together they organise the flow of your energy. Your vibe might match a person or a book or a piece of music etc. The vibe is the resonance that your intention has – it can be a person or a thing – and how much of a match there is at an authentic level and surface level.

There are all kinds of possibilities in monitoring the vibe/resonance of the individuals/the groups/the departments/the relationships – employees/prospects/clients – within the business of law. You could profile a new lawyer against existing lawyers in the company and you could identify the best mentor to connect with them internally and externally. As a client you will be able to find out which lawyer has the best resonance with you.

The next step for clients doing business with those lawyers they know, like, trust, 'get', understand, and share common interests with is doing business with those they resonate and vibe with! This is much more personal and intimate than we presently achieve. And remember, intimacy matters most. Ultimately:

- You can be smart about the lawyer you choose to affect the vibe of the other lawyers;
- You can be smart about the vibe person who represents the energy of the client/ customer; and
- You can be smart about the clients that vibe potential clients.

I trust you can see the value in this? I shall leave you to reflect. Prrrrrrrrrrrrrrrrrrrr.

ROAR case studies

To wrap up this chapter I'm going to share with you a handful of case studies which reflect all that is good, bad, and terribly pants in how lawyers, businesses of law, and suppliers to law law land handle SocialHuman.

the good

Mitch Jackson

Mitch Jackson, attorney at law, California, USA

Mitch Jackson is probably the best example of a lawyer who is the ultimate SocialHuman lawyer. Mitch, like me, kicked off his SOCIAL journey back in 2008/9 and has since enjoyed huge success as a result of his social activities. He read *the naked lawyer* when it was first published in late 2010 and adopted some of its messages and teachings. During the last five years he has won awards such as 'Trial Lawyer of the Year' and 'Super Lawyer' in Orange County, California, USA. He's just kicked off a new venture called 'Human: Social' which I highly recommend you check out.[19]

McCullogh Robertson Lawyers

Jeremy Kennedy. WHS lawyer & partner, McCullough Robertson Lawyers – Newcastle, Brisbane, and Sydney, Australia

Back in 2012 Jeremy kindly shared this testimonial about ROAR: '*the naked lawyer*, together with engaging Chrissie as a consultant, gave me the inspiration and guidance I was searching for to develop an online presence in the form of LinkedIn and Twitter, which has directly added £1,000,000 plus to my book of work over the last 12 months and significantly increased both my and the firms profile. 12 months back I was struggling for work. Now I have four lawyers working directly under me at full capacity. Although one might consider Chrissie's messages on the present and future of legal practice a little controversial and eye-opening they are indeed effective!'

Schjødt Law Firm

Knut-Magnar Aanestad, chief knowledge officer and head of information technology at Schjødt Law Firm, Oslo, Norway

Due to a number of successful strategic and operational initiatives in the past four years, including members of the executive team reading *the naked lawyer* and executing the ROAR sales model, Schjødt has achieved significant revenue increase and enjoyed and received various acclaim:

- 2010 t/o £35 million > 2013 t/o £60 million;
- Law Firm of The Year, Nordics 2012 (*The Lawyer*);
- International 'Best Innovation Award 2013'[20]; and
- Mergemarket/*Financial Times* law firm of the year 2013 (Norway award).

Knut puts the success of his business of law down to the 'green light' from his managing partner and the leadership group together with a number of internal strategies.

Knut and I have shared the stage on a couple of occasions in Scandinavia, and at one of them he opened up his heart to me, sharing that he believes a great deal of his own personal success and therefore that of his company happened because the powers that be wanted 'me to move mountains. It is demanded of me, it's a requirement. It's a driver for me.' Knut also revealed that when he read *the naked lawyer* back in 2010/11:

'...it woke up something that had been sleeping; to involve social networking... Originally the partners thought of it as a threat rather than a possibility and an opportunity. But when they saw the marketing effect, on the individual level and the firm, and how we could take firm information and empower it and spread it through the network through each of the lawyers the power of that was revealed. It was a turning point for us.

The managing partner wanted to be exposed to it as an individual. We saw the power of joining each and everyone's network and marketing potential. We made it a firm policy.

We have the marketing person helping firm wide with LinkedIn and Facebook and Social Media in general, and we taught our lawyers the basic principles, and use our company profile to enable each and every one to share content.

We helped the lawyers make a brand for themselves and therefore raised the brand firm. We found the naked lawyer highly useful to help us go forward.'

It's a real pleasure to witness the richly deserved success of my friends in Scandinavia.

Shoosmiths

Graeme Smillie. UK brand guy, head of brand & digital, website strategy & development, digital & social strategy at Shoosmiths LLP, UK

I had the great pleasure of working with National law firm Shoosmiths during 2012–14. Many of their lawyers have now created a fitting personal brand – such as Gary Assim, 'The Image Lawyer' – that dovetails with Shoosmiths 'Brand,Firm', and they have enjoyed winning instructions in social land as a result of the ROAR experience.

I was thrilled to read that Shoosmiths has been shortlisted in two categories for the 2014 British Legal Awards: the 'Banking, Finance and Restructuring Team of the Year' award and the 'UK Law Firm of the Year' award.

X-Press/LPAS

David Lister, managing director, X-Press Legal Services where 'Business is just a great big onion'

Again, I have had the wonderful pleasure of working with X-Press Legal and Law Plain and Simple since 2011. This is Dave's story about his company, including what he has to say about the ROAR experience:

'Founded in 2000, Xpress Legal Services is a Warrington-based family business, supplying solicitors, licensed conveyancers, property developers, and auction houses with a full range of property related searches and risk reports to aid the house buying process. We founded the business on three main principles:

- Only use good corporate disciplines (no office politics);
- Be a bespoke provider (of services to clients); and
- No bank borrowings (use available cashflow).

Today, we have grown our business into a respected player in this sector and this year we will produce in excess of 325,000 reports on behalf of 480 solicitors' practices, distributed via our network of 32 regional franchised offices located throughout England and Wales.

It all paints a very rosy picture and indeed we are doing exceptionally well as a group; however, this has not always been the case and if we peel back the layers of the onion I will explain. The first thing to understand is that promoting (selling) your service to the legal sector is very, very difficult. In the main they will only engage on trust or recommendation, but how do you attain either unless they engage with you?

Many hours are spent thinking up novel or interesting ways to get yourself noticed and in the beginning it took us three months (and heaven knows how much shoe leather) to have a single meaningful conversation. Eventually sheer perseverance paid off, a local solicitor gave us our first break and we were off and running and mainly through recommendation we quickly gained several new clients. This continued until 2004 when the sheer weight of work was beginning to threaten our much prized service levels. The only way we could think of coping with the volume was to stop marketing, this we did and it made no difference whatsoever.

So we decided to franchise, this we thought would be a quick and efficient solution to our problems; we were wrong and it took nearly 18 months to put together a quality franchise offering. Finally in October 2005 we launched our offering at the National Franchise Show in Birmingham's NEC Conference Centre.

The franchise grew rapidly with everything doing well until in 2007 the government in their infinite wisdom decided to launch the much maligned Home Information Packs (HiPS). This move totally distorted the market, financially ruined many people, and was finally put out of its misery by the government in May 2010.

X-Press came out of this period with its head held high having declined to be a HiP provider, instead choosing to work with its client base and help them through the Home Information Pack maze.

The problem however was that many practices had been badly let down by spurious providers and once again the shutters went up regarding trust. The reason I have given this brief overview is that even with all of our hard work and goodwill, we found this period very challenging and we were struggling to make any progress whatsoever.

Radical thinking was needed and many fruitless meetings were convened until we boiled it down to two courses of action:

- A refreshed website; and

- Join the solicitor training circuit (CPD) and provide free courses.

The website was refreshed, looked great, but hardly generated a torrent of traffic. The CPD courses hit the bullseye and once we presented ourselves in a live setting we began to pick up clients on a regular basis. Growth was steady, we were in good shape, but we definitely were not setting the world on fire.

Once again we knew we needed something else to elevate the group to become a serious market player and once again many fruitless meetings were convened, in short the X-Press think tank had run dry. In my previous corporate life it had been drilled into me that a successful business was founded on three principles Product, Price, and Service and if all three were met then you simply could not go wrong. Well, we excelled at all three elements and we were still not making the progress we deserved. It was following this I had my Eureka moment: we needed a fourth element, namely cross-promotion; this for sure was what was missing, the last piece of the jigsaw so to speak.

I worked on this idea for several weeks as I knew that for this initiative to work we needed something whizz-bang and unique, something that promoted not only the conveyancing department but the practice as a whole, a totally holistic offering. We looked at the entire legal landscape and it became evident that the general public or indeed commercial clients do not walk willingly into legal practices; the whole thing is driven by fear.

The very word "legal" terrifies people in exactly the same way that "audit" terrifies the business community. Zero understanding of the process, legal jargon, and Latin phrases all collude to completely alienate the end user and only an urgent necessity to solve a problem makes the client adopt the process.

It made perfect sense to me that there had to be a much simpler way to engage the public, help the practice, and grow our own business. I cannot be exact when I decided on a dual aspect website that would de-mystify the legal process, talk in plain English, take out the jargon and Latin, provide plenty of legal information for free, and help the user via an informative directory to find a local solicitor that would do the same, in effect taking the fear out of the process and making legal practices more approachable.

We began talking to bespoke web designers and it became abundantly clear that this was a massive undertaking that would need a big design team and take many months to complete. Still driven by the idea that this was the correct thing to do, we ploughed on and overcame many hurdles before the build could even begin.

Already committed to an eye-watering spend we turned our attention to how, once built, we were going to promote this web offering to the wider community. Newspapers, local radio, TV, leaflet drops etc. were all considered and dismissed as we simply did not have the cash to run a sustained campaign (and remember one of our founding principles was "no bank support").

At this point we were totally stumped and to be honest floundering as what to do, when low and behold Chrissie Lightfoot's name fell into our lap. We contacted Chrissie and made the pilgrimage to Leeds where over several hours we simply poured out our whole story, frustrations, aspirations, pitched our new ideas, and anything else we could throw into the mix!

Several sheets of A4 notes later Chrissie wisely asked for time to consider the task ahead and whether she could help us. The very next morning as if by magic a full transcript of our conversation appeared perfectly and logically laid out along with a suggested brief that suggested the route that should be taken, timelines, costings, schedules etc. all delivered in one nice neat package – impressive was not the word.

An integral part of the plan was to train the entire franchise network on the business etiquette of social media. We were counselled as to the difficulty in dealing with a network and for anybody who has had to do it they will be familiar with the term "chasing chickens" as that is exactly what it is like.

We did well and managed to get a buy-in from approximately two thirds of the network and the training commenced. We met in a hotel in the Midlands and I have to say that it was not what I had envisaged, with virtually the entire room totally bamboozled by the process. Chrissie, ever calm, explained that this was a normal reaction and over the coming months things would become much clearer. Thankfully they did and the X-Press social media campaign began, closely followed by a very soft launch of our bespoke website, www.lawplainandsimple.com. Chrissie took to this site like a duck to water and was instrumental over the next few months in helping to get it ready for a full launch.

In the meantime the social media was steaming ahead and, along with CPD and head office support and a fantastic impetus from the franchise network, we began to attract new clients gaining around 80 in the year. We soon had to secure Chrissie for another term as she was now a household name within our business and we continued to grow and boy how we grew; in the calendar year 2013 we increased our group turnover by £1.5 million.

2014 arrived and we decided to plan a full launch of Law Plain and Simple. We decided rightly or wrongly that in order to get an even broader message out there that something else was needed to support what was by now a fantastic social media platform. In March we launched the website still supported by Chrissie and boosted by a sports marketing campaign that goes out on Sky Sports.

In all honesty I simply did not believe that we could continue the phenomenal growth in 2014 and at our annual conference in February I confidently predicted that our growth would be restricted to £974,000 in the calendar year. Shows how much I know as we are well on course for another £1.5 million increase over 2013!

At this point, I would like to say the biggest thank you to Chrissie Lightfoot for a job very well done, and for believing in a small but totally dedicated family business, for listening to our machine gun pitch, and allowing us for a few hours in Leeds three years ago, to peel back the layers of our rather large onion. And she never cried once.'

Dave's son, Christian Lister ('the SME ambassador'), also a director of X-Press Legal Services Limited; vice-president of Europe at the International Small Business Council; director of The Genesis Initiative; chairman IPSA, UK, had this to say:

'In a volatile, highly competitive, price sensitive, and digital world I recognised that myself and my company needed a helping hand in "the next big step" to survive, compete, expand, and stand out in a vanilla world. Chrissie Lightfoot was (and remains) that guiding hand. Significantly, only two to three months after reading *The Naked Lawyer* eBook together with Chrissie consulting and training us in her ROAR Programme – developing personal brands, incisive positioning in the market place present and future, forming niches, using social media and social networks effectively (LinkedIn, Twitter, and Blog in particular) to grow our prime referral, prospect, and client networks – myself, the team at HQ and the franchisees have already achieved impressive bottom line results. I found the elements of the ROAR programme simple, yet ground-breakingly effective. In essence, it's all about how to sell without selling. It works. It works a lot! So impressed are we that Chrissie is also working with us on further (on line) innovations within our company.'

Wendy Reece – a franchisee of X-Press Legal Services – shares her view on the ROAR experience:

'I have to admit, from the very first day when X-Press Legal Services introduced me to Chrissie Lightfoot and her ROAR Model I was deeply sceptical about how social networking online was going to help my business growth. I didn't have any interest whatsoever in personal branding or using social media/networking and certainly didn't have a clue where to start or how to go about raising my profile and that of my business online in order to be more successful in my business... And yet, I decided to give it a go, and this is my story...

I run my business alongside my husband Scott and the business had just been casually ticking along nicely and smoothly. Chrissie had come at a time when we had just about had enough to be honest. We felt we had exhausted all avenues of marketing and struggled with trying to create some sort of brand awareness. No matter how fancy the packaging of our letters, the sparkle of the glossy leaflets, or even the simplicity of the mailshots we were sending out. We were literally banging our heads against a brick wall. Now was the time to either like it or lump it. Give in or die fighting.

Anybody who knows us though knows that the thought of giving up would never stay in our minds for long. Die fighting would always be the motto. Hmmm, so where do we start?

SLAP!!!!!! Chrissie hit me like a bolt out of the blue. Maybe this lady had something worth listening to. Well it was certainly worth a try; we had nothing to lose.

We wanted to do far better in business than we were presently delivering. Although I was active on Facebook, I'd never used LinkedIn or Twitter before and was scared witless about what I should or shouldn't say, so I started working through what Chrissie had shared with me. The minute I did begin to take Chrissie seriously, I realised where my mistake of being sceptical lay. My Facebook account is my personal account. Why on earth would prospective clients want to jump on board with me just because of my Facebook account?

Chrissie indicated how Twitter is a complete mixture of social and business and what I tweeted would depend on the type of persons my account would attract. I was already liking the idea of this Twitter thing.

So, thinking back to my first lesson, what was my Twitter name going to be. Well I did need everybody to know that this was my business and exactly what line of business I was in. I wanted to put the word out quite simply that I can be a help to anybody in the line of conveyancing. ConveyanceAid. Surely that would show in an instant who I was and what my content of tweets would be.

Second lesson: I needed to add a picture and a few words just to reinforce what line of business I was in. Well, of course, never one to miss an opportunity to show off, my avatar had to be my very own hand-made cupcakes that I had made for a previous CPD Event with our X-Press Legal Services logo plastered straight across it. Nobody could mistake the big red cross logo of X-Press. Then the pièce de resistance – well, it just had to be – my background picture was of course my certificates and trophies to show I am a successful business woman and I am to be taken seriously.

So now what? My very first Tweet. Oh God, what do I say. I was so nervous, You would think I was literally speaking publicly on my feet in front of a whole nation. I decided the safer option would be just to retweet what others had tweeted just as Chrissie had taught me. Because I was just getting the hang of it, the only people I was following and being followed by were my fellow franchisees and a few suppliers. Maybe a few clients were in the mix too.

Before I knew it, because the tweets I had been tweeting were in the conveyancing line, I soon had like-minded people retweeting me and then also following me. Some of these people even started to speak to me and welcome me to Twitter. Yes I was liking this Twitterverse.

Very quickly, I grew so much in confidence because of the various people I was engaging in conversation with that I actually grew a brain for myself and started doing my own thing rather than taking others' leads. I remember Chrissie saying to us about this not just being a self-promotion site where you stood on a soap box all day preaching how good you were but this is also a social networking site. Seriously, the clue should have been in the title but I just got so held up on speaking business that I forgot that I did actually have a personality.

I decided that through the hours of 9–5 I would speak business like; quite professional tweeting would occur, and I would self-promote. Once that clock turned 5pm then I was no longer your 'ConveyanceAid' and I became Wendy Reece. I had my own personality and it was time to show this. I started to get involved with different networking hours. The first one being the Wyre Fylde Hour as this is a location that I ran my business from. I watched what people were tweeting for a couple of minutes, then just jumped in feet first.

I came out of there totally blown away by how easy it was to interact with so many people for so long and so easily that I had never ever spoken to in my life. That hour resulted in so many more followers and completely changed my whole way of tweeting.

The very next week it happened. A client that we had been trying to speak to for easily five years had suddenly started to follow me. I could not for all this time even get a foot through the door for this person to even speak to me nor give me the time of day. They were a massive practice and this person was soooooo busy. Now, we were exchanging tweets like nobody's business. Before I knew it, the tweet came where I was asked by this person how they actually got listed on our cross-promotional website – Lawplainandsimple.com. This person is now no longer a prospective as I can happily say that they are now a client.

This case is not a sole case as a few different enquiries have arisen over the time I have been tweeting. Unfortunately for me, one of them was not in my location as we as franchisees only operate in our specified area. But, fortunately for one of my fellow franchisees on the other side of the country, one of the enquiries did result in a brand new client for them. Just goes to show that in this game networking goes a long long way.

I sent out my first tweet in June 2013 and at our February 2014 Annual Conference I won the 'X-Press Legal franchisee Social Media award' and trophy for the best user and performer for the business. Having sent out over 4,500 tweets and attending Lord knows how many networking events. I think that says it all…

Now, our business has completely turned around. We have just completed our year end and we have more than doubled our turnover. My only regret in all of this is wasting so much time at the beginning being such a Doubting Thomas.'

Law Plain and Simple

Permit me to tell you more about Law Plain and Simple and the very personal story which underpins it all…

Law Plain and Simple,[21] a home-grown website and legal service, was launched as a response to legislative reforms, the demise of legal aid, and the imported challenge to help consumers, businesses, and law firms. It is an online legal information and advice service linked to 400 law firms in England and Wales. The website was master-minded by Dave Lister, director at X-Press Legal Services Ltd., which has developed and funded the service, and has been providing property searches to law firms and licensed conveyancers for many years.

The website explains the fundamentals of the law and its standard processes, as well as translating its terminology. It has step-by-step guides covering 39 of the most common legal categories, ranging from property law, bankruptcy, wills and trusts, and business law to guidance about social media and social networking and even image rights.

Dave commented: 'We wanted to take the mystique and fear out of the law for ordinary people. The website avoids legal jargon and has been written in very basic English to help people understand the law and how it might affect them in particular circumstances.'[22]

Law Plain and Simple has been written by qualified solicitors – no, this is not a misnomer or a joke. Co-director Lynne Lister says: 'We intend that our website should give people the facts in words they understand, so they can move forward in resolving whatever difficulty they are in. We believe that "A little knowledge is a wonderful thing".'

The idea for the website grew out of enquiries from members of the public directly to X-Press Legal Services Ltd. about legal terminology, particularly in the housing market. Dave and Lynne commented: 'We recognise the importance and value of professional solicitors with their extensive experience and knowledge so we are keen to enhance the service they can provide – not detract from it.'

The website is free to use for consumers, businesses, and the law firm clients of X-Press. The website receives no referral fees and doesn't do data grabs. The law firms in the local search directory are clients of X-Press and these law firm clients set their own fee rates when advising the visitor who has come through the website, as well as providing a continuous stream of legal articles for visitors to read on the site.

With the numbers of users (consumers and businesses) visiting the website set to increase significantly due to publicity and awareness raising through offline and online activity by X-Press HQ, its 40 franchisees and 400 law firms in the network, and deals being struck with high traffic websites, this radical new business model and service is set to be a win-win for all concerned – consumers, businesses, law firm clients of X-Press who are in the directory and providing legal articles on the website, and X-Press itself. Clearly, as more visitors use the website and are pointed in the direction of the client law firms in the directory (whereby those firms may experience an increase in enquiries and instructions), X-Press may no doubt receive more conveyancing searches from those client firms succeeding in serving existing clients further as well as new law firm clients.

I believe the real story behind the success of Law Plain and Simple is its history, business model, culture, and ability to see around corners. For what the Law Plain and Simple website service is really about is X-Press helping their clients' clients.

They help their law firm clients to be more successful by marketing to, providing for, and helping the law firms clients by delivering a free helpful legal resource as a first point of call. This 'client's client' strategy and model is commonplace for smart marketers and savvy business people, and proves successful. And to think, all of this started with a Cadbury's creme egg…

I dare say X-Press (and Law Plain and Simple) wouldn't be what it is today if Dave didn't manage to woo his childhood sweetheart, Lynne, with an enticing choccy egg during one fine Easter break. For X-Press Legal began many years ago as a husband and wife team, and is now a family run business with a nationwide network of franchisees with a totally entrepreneurial and customer-centric culture.

Perhaps what it will really take for lawyers and law firms to succeed in the Age of UnLawyering (at the very least) are these three things. The ability to:

1. See around corners – to anticipate the radically unexpected; and
2. Create a service or product in readiness for the unexpected; and
3. Embrace a truly customer-centric business model which includes marketing to and providing for (and helping) your clients' clients.

It's clear that, in many instances, the traditional law firm business model and lawyering as we know it is well and truly stuffed. But all is not lost. We can pray along with our new Pope.

At the time the new Pope was instated *The Lawyer* website bulletin read: 'The Catholic church and the legal profession have more than a few things in common. Both are ancient, slow to change and sometimes require senior members to wear ridiculous costumes. Oh, and both have a fondness for Latin, though that probably harks back to the fact that both are a bit ancient.'

Dave Lister et. al will have no need for prayer. Law Plain and Simple doesn't entertain any of these things, as is apparent in its homepage mantra: 'No legal jargon. Certainly no Latin.'

In this Age of UnLawyering, if Dave and his X-Press crew happen to blag a seat onto the pioneering good ship Virgin Galactic, and bump into Captain Kirk on his Starship Enterprise at the final frontier, no doubt the conversation by those who boldly go where none of us have gone before would be: 'It's lawyering Jim, but not as we know it.'

the bad and the darn right pants

I was in two minds as to whether or not to include 'the bad' and 'the darn right pants' sections (for as you know I prefer to focus on the positive), but in the end they made the cut and they are combined here.

I confess, there's a lot of UGLY social media, social networking, digital and innovation inertia in law law land. It's a sorry state of affairs that it has taken five years for the legal profession and industry to gather some momentum in 'allowing' their individual lawyers to 'let RIP' in social land.

It's frustrating when I (and no doubt some of you ambitious lawyers) witness your marketing people running around on 'projects' like ants, continually putting off the stuff that will make the difference (such as SocialHuman), and instead indulging in mere fluffy puff.

The focus is all wrong. It strikes me that the majority are always chasing their tails and playing catch-up rather than being the pioneer. In the majority of cases, it's not the marketing/business development people at fault. It's the powers that be who will not give the nod to the SocialHuman stuff.

Equally as bad is where the business of law takes an ad-hoc approach – I could name hundreds – that is, bolting in some element of social media and social networking training (such as a stand-alone Twitter course, or standalone LinkedIn course) without underpinning it first with a behaviour system such as the ROAR Model and integrating the SocialHuman element across the entire company's marketing and digital operation (like Shoosmiths positively did).

No wonder many of the businesses of law fail so miserably when they merely dip a quivering little piggy toe into the vast pool of SOCIAL. They might as well take their money and walk down to the nearest pond and feed their green notes to the ducks. I'm convinced they would make a bigger quack of it!

Isn't it also sad to witness your managing partner/CEO/partners struggling to grapple with basic stuff like understanding CRM and ERP systems (many of them don't even know what these are)[23], let alone expecting them to understand about the online social realm and its power.

I am totally frustrated with the lack of forward movement and the timeframe it takes for business of law to give their lawyers the green light when there are many examples of competitors doing it right and enjoying phenomenal success. There's just way too much inertia and slippage...

after dark activity

If there's one thing I would tell lawyers and entrepreneurs about social media, it's this: patience. And this: JUST DO IT!!!

just do something!

If you haven't already got into social land, make a start! If you're struggling as to where to start, read *the naked lawyer* as it provides you with a step-by-step guide. If you have, go dance, and try a few of the things I've shared here in this chapter.

References

1. Blog post, 'There are no rules with social media', see: http://juliansummerhayes.com/rules-social-media.
2. *Fast Company*, '10 Surprising Social media Statistics that will make you rethink your social strategy', 2013, see: www.fastcompany.com/3021749/work-smart/10-surprising-social-media-statistics-that-will-make-you-rethink-your-social-stra.
3. See: www.ciccorporate.com/index.php?option=com_content&view=article&id=1204&catid=99&Itemid=208&lang=en.
4. Beaton, G., 'Beyond partnership: Learning from Chrissie Lightfoot, a class act', 6 March 2013, see: www.brw.com.au/p/professions/beyond_partnership_learning_from_DMorkINCIG4ulymMm5qS1J.
5. Eulogy!, 'The perfect storm – reputation: the key to staying afloat in the new legal world', January 2014, see: www.eulogy.co.uk/?portfolio=the-perfect-storm-reputation-the-key-to-staying-afloat-in-the-new-legal-world.
6. Slumbers, A., 'User Experience is Key in Digital Technology', mipimworld.com,

October 2014, see: http://blog.mipimworld.com/2014/10/user-experience-key-digital-technology/?utm_source=Twitter&utm_medium=social%20media&utm_campaign=Antony%20Slumbers%20User%20Experience%20is%20Key#.VlWawcm6j9p.

7. Research report published annually in October 2011/12/13 by Peppermint Technology, see: www.pepperminttechnology.co.uk/news/2011/10/17/research-reveals-what-clients-really-want-from-a-legal-service-provider.
8. Lightfoot, C., 'The end of lawyers? Pah! This is the time of the "super lawyer"', *The Law Society Gazette*, 20 May 2010, see: www.lawgazette.co.uk/analysis/the-end-of-lawyers-pah-this-is-the-time-of-the-super-lawyer/55563.article.
9. See: www.thelawyer.com/analysis/behind-the-law/the-leadership-interview/work-three-day-weeks-and-take-unlimited-holidays-kevin-golds-revolution-at-mishcon-de-reya/3026629.article.
10. Ibid.
11. Richard Burcher is a former New Zealand practicing lawyer and managing partner with over 30 years of experience. Richard has been based in London since 2012 as the managing director of Validatum (UK) Limited (www.validatum.com). Richard now devotes all of his time to legal services pricing consultancy work and is widely regarded as the leading international authority on pricing legal services.
12. Joseph, J., 'Taglines Are the First Step to Emotionally-Engaged Customers', entrepreneur.com, see: www.entrepreneur.com/article/236172.
13. See: www.aminstitute.com/headline.
14. Garrett Miller, Partner, Eugene F. Collins law firm, Dublin, Ireland (www.efc.ie).
15. See: www.adversariesintoallies.com/wp-content/uploads/2013/03/BobBurgUltimateInfluenceAssessment.pdf.
16. Ibid.
17. Jazz Rasool, CEO of EnergyDiamond Ltd (www.energydiamond.com).
18. 'The best view of your world is not from Outer Space but Inner Space', see: www.energydiamond.com/innerworld/innerworldflyer.pdf.
19. 'Learn how to use social media to connect, engage and build professional relationships the human way!' See: http://human.social.
20. See: www.schjodt.com/news-insights/news/schjoedt-wins-international-best-innovation-award-2013.aspx.
21. See: www.lawplainandsimple.com.
22. Author interview with David Lister and Lynne Lister, 2012.
23. ERP = Enterprise Resource Planning system – it's usually a one-stop tech system encompassing finance, operations, Content Management, Case management, Customer Relationship Management, etc.

Chapter 6: NewTech, NewHuman, NewLaw

'The real problem is not whether machines think but whether men do.' B.F. Skinner, American psychologist

YOU WILL recall I mentioned a splendid new book out by George Beaton called *NewLaw New Rules* in a previous chapter. While George speaks of NewLaw in light of the new legal landscape with its new business models, new players, new governance, structures, strategies, tactics, and more, I'd like to expand upon his great work and address the following topics within this chapter: NewTech, NewHuman, and NewLaw.

While I have coined the new phrases NewTech and NewHuman, George beat me to it with regard to NewLaw. Love it! Respect, my friend.

You will come to understand what I mean by all three of these phrases as you continue to read. Significantly, my reference to NewLaw here is NOT what George refers to. I'm going to be talking about the requirement for NEW LAW – that is, the black and white 'letter of the law', and all the grey stuff in between, in the Digital, Robotic, and Interstellar Age. Yep, we are now going to be prancing and dancing into some really futuristic stuff, but not, I hasten to add, without first addressing the legal technology available today to support you in your transitioning roles.

NewTech

The businesses of law are increasingly relying on new technologies to drive processes and efficiencies. This trend is only going to continue as we advance into a Robotic Age with AI technology and legal businesses becoming ever more tightly connected. The companies (and you lawyers) that succeed in the near future will be those that take the time now to assess the role of technology in their delivery and service model.

A book by Chris Bull and David Bason has recently been released called *Law Firms in the Digital Age*, which I strongly recommend you read.[1] Although I am only going to touch on some of the technologies and their suppliers here, *Law Firms in the Digital Age* contains an extensive final section that demystifies the technology that is transforming law law land.

Customer acquisition and retention is the lifeblood of any business of law. Many lawyers hold the view that good work will inevitably lead to a successful legal practice. These lawyers are usually most comfortable with word-of-mouth endorsement and networking through personal relationships as their only marketing tools. However, SocialHuman within successful professional services firms focuses on the more complex – and ultimately more rewarding – process of establishing niche practices, entrenching client relationships, and in turn building profitable and sustainable practices by embracing social technology.

By putting in place a robust client management process, aided by technology, your company and you the lawyer, can ensure that both it and you deliver high-quality, tailored services, and build the kind of client relationships that will lead to repeat business, referrals, and enhanced reputations.

'I wrote an article recently called 'How Smart Marketing, Networking & Technology Can Grow Your Firm' (aka 'legal technology wisdom rules') in which I basically argued that law law land is always slow to adapt, change, and embrace new technologies to benefit the client, the lawyer, and the business of law. Welcoming technologies within your business of law is no longer a choice; it is now a MUST if you want to outperform your competitors and drive better performance.

This is what a couple of readers had to say in the comment stream which flowed from my article:

'This is a frightening article because it reminds us once again that the legal market is in danger as it is slow to change and sticks its head in the sand and learns nothing from colleagues in the other professions such as finance, veterinary, healthcare and so forth. It clings to what it knows and hopes against hope that change will pass it by. Sometimes it dips its toe in the water but then like an Alan Bennett dialogue decides better of it and puts it socks back on again.

We know that you can't buck the system but it does feel like an unnecessary uphill struggle and over the past decade I can think of many conversations with colleagues in the legal IT consulting market talking wearily about their clients' tardiness for change.

However, there are lawyers who do have vision and get excited about the opportunities in this digital age and they are a joy to work with. They will of course take the prizes and they deserve to do so. Small and large firms, sometimes sole practitioners, but all have courage, vision, passion, self belief, and a determination to succeed. They are the entrepreneurial lawyers. They are the top 10 per cent.

With roughly 10,000 UK firms out there, that means 1,000 of them have got a fighting chance of surviving and thriving. Good luck to them I say...

Looking back ten years to when I started my company and launched the HR Portal I remember one of my mentors advising that I should instead focus our products at the financial market where clients are more commercially minded and moving with the times and going through change is a fact of business life, an opportunity rather than a nuisance.

Hindsight is a marvellous thing! I would be retired on a Mauritian beach by now! Well, in my dreams anyway :) The legal market will develop at its own sweet pace and we just have to work with what we've got. Thank goodness for the top 10 per cent... they keep me sane.'[2]

Mitch Jackson, attorney at law, nails it when he says: 'If you're not busy building and developing a proper digital footprint, you will soon become digitally irrelevant and out of business.'

As you are no doubt aware I am a staunch advocate for the great things that technology can do for law and in helping you in your drive for growth and success.'

MPF, PM Forum, and Elephant Creative suspected (like me) in 2014 that although marketing 'got' social media, the same was not true of management, so they organised a major survey into attitudes toward digital and social technologies: 'While there is good news that management and marketing experts are now much closer in their views, there is still a mismatch in perceived purpose/outcomes that are measured and more broadly confusion still exists over what generates results, how much to invest and areas for priority.'[3]

The key findings of the 2014 report are:

- Growth – Less than 10 per cent growth in usage is anticipated across all channels over the coming year;
- Reporting – There are still big issues over who gets to see which key performance indicator (KPI) data;
- Clients – Channels are now being used in equal measure with existing clients and prospects;
- Favourites – LinkedIn remains the preferred channel; and
- Internal – The technologies are still not being used effectively for internal collaboration.

A respondent within the report commented: 'Firm leadership and marketing teams need to take a more integrated approach to digital and social media as part of their overall marketing. Stop seeing social media as a strategy in itself. It is not a strategy, it is a channel.'

Actually, it's a 'bit part' of SocialHuman and the raison d'être for social technology. And yet, those businesses of law that really 'get' technology and all the huge goodies within its powerhouse which can assist in enhancing growth are experiencing exactly this.

You will recall I mentioned Schjødt Law Firm to you in a previous chapter. Schjødt doubled its turnover within a few years from approximately £30–60 million, largely during the period 2010–2013. It's probably the best example I can share with you in relation to how powerful it can be to have the right technology in place utilised in the right way with the right team and the right attitude.

Back in 2009, Schjødt law firm welcomend the Deltek ERP technology into its fold. For decades, Deltek has provided an integrated solution for case management and accounting that deliver the actionable insight, clarity, and control which businesses of law need to increase the commercial focus of their practice. According to Knut Magnar Aanestad, knowledge manager of the firm:

'We were impressed both by the dynamics of Deltek's system and the opportunities it held to customise and integrate to other systems. We chose Deltek after a thorough evaluation of other vendors in the market. We had some clear strategic requirements which included user-friendliness, a dynamic structure, integration capabilities, future-proof setup, and data security. We evaluated the various systems and made our decision to go with Deltek based on these factors'.

Knut and I had a chat after one of the conferences we had both been presenting at, during which time I asked him a series of poignant questions. Permit me to share the highlights of his replies with you now:

- In 2008 a decision was made to build a strong management team – Bring in managers in their areas of expertise, for example, knowledge manager, HR etc.;
- In 2009 the knowledge manager said 'we need a system';
- 2009/10, Deltek was on board;
- We're interested in business intelligence, client intelligence, and competition intelligence;
- Our strategy is to be smarter – We ask 'what happens when technology/AI/the robot is smarter than the human lawyer?';
- We use DIY documents (we have called it 'Eureka') – Our junior lawyers tend to do this and do it very well. We give them a bonus;
- We want to incentivise behaviour;

- We want to be future proof when it comes to our technology;
- The business grew – NOK 350–620 million in 5 years (2008 > 2013);
- Experienced over 80 per cent revenue increase – 27 per cent workforce increase;
- Now it is a lean and mean machine – Cost is 34 per cent of revenue in 2013;
- We had a clear view of technology to support and follow, i.e. enhance the processes
- We merged the technology department and knowledge management department;
- Our focus and key is to achieve efficient use of the human resource (aka ALL of their lawyers);
- We live transparency – Everyday at 23:30 the new matter report goes to EVERYONE, which shows which new matter has come in over the last 24hrs (albeit at this point it is an estimated invoice, we usually invoice double when it becomes actual);
- Transparency helps incentivise; and
- We have tremendous control over (and on) our business.

Contrast Schjødt's case with the revelation that 56 per cent of law firms here in the UK do not have an accurate view on what types of work make money. Pah!

frazzled brain, fluffy cloud

While there has been resistance to 'the cloud' and cloud technology (non-legacy systems) in law law land, and not just by the partners (usually for financial and/or security concerns) but from those in the IT department (usually for reason of self-interest – fear of losing their jobs), I do believe we are witnessing green shoots.

Let's face it, if the BIG BOYS, aka Thomson Reuters and Lexis Nexis, have shifted their tech strategy and new product lines which embrace Microsoft Dynamics (cloud tech), it's saying something about the potential, market, and future of legal tech.

Choosing the right technology for your business of law is crucial. No doubt you have MANY legal tech providers banging on your door at present. Yes? Accordingly, let's briefly have a look at some of them. We'll have a look at the David's and Goliath's of the legal tech providers in order to cover the breadth of what is available to suit all strategies and size of war chest.

Lexis Nexis (LN) & Thomson Reuters (TR)

Until recently, from a technology point of view, the legal industry had been serviced by a cottage industry focused on legal software. LN and TR are the two big boys and front runners. Both started dipping their toes into software and have indulged in recent years, picking up software companies. Elite, PLC & Westlaw were bought by TR, hence TR Elite. LN acquired Interface ergo LN Interaction. Although LN would hate to admit it, TR Elite is still the most prevalent system in the UK Top 200 at present; for example, Allen & Overy use Elite.

However, spurred on by the knowledge that LN was chasing the coat-tails of TR back in 2010, LN began to look for a new way. Coincidentally, at this time Microsoft was looking for vertical markets. Microsoft had a multi-billion ($9 billion) R&D budget for a development project to do enterprise-grade business management software: an ERP. This enterprise resource planning technology is Microsoft Dynamics (MD). Note: there are different versions of MD. AX had $500 million spent on it. LN entered into an agreement to do MD AX in late 2010/11, around the same time as Peppermint Technology was rolling out here in the UK.

From LN and TR perspectives, Peppermint Microsoft Dynamics tech system (which is not AX) is doing what they do the other way around. Where LN and TR put finance at the centre of the system, in contrast, Peppermint puts the client at the centre of its system. Fundamentally, the technologies are chalk and cheese.

The MD AX platform has multiple modules (pms, dms, cms, cms, crm, etc). In essence, it's a complete one-stop practice shop that will knock out the majority of legacy applications. LN has Axia (AX) because it needed to build a global system to suit business of law which work with clients all around the world in multiple jurisdictions. AX is a readily available system adapted to legal by LN called Lexis 1. LN sells AX into retail, manufacturing, and professional services, etc. PwC, Delloittes, Simmons & Simmons use MD AX, for example.

Lexis 1 is the legal version of AX. Collas Crill law firm (300–400 lawyers) in Jersey use Lexis 1; albeit not an international behemoth, it is understandable that the firm chose Lexis 1 as the firm deals with multi-jurisdictional matters daily. However, in Lexis 1 there is no social media/social networking/marketing/CRM element available as yet. This can only be found in LN Interaction. Obviously, LN does not wish to make its LN Interaction product redundant by bringing out a superior product which is all whistles and bells. No doubt, given time, there will be a way of bringing LN Interaction into Lexis 1 as a phased project over time.

Contrast this with Peppermint Technology which has MD CRM (not AX) and the complete package of whistles and bells (pms, dms, cms, cms, crm, social media, etc). Clearly, there is overlap with what LN and TR do as technologists and what they do with practice management. Inevitably, the two are going to have to converge!

Peppermint Technology

In the words of Charles Christian, legal tech guru extraordinaire, the Peppermint Technology[4] is having the same disruptive effect on law firms as Elite did 20 years ago.

The multi-award-winning Peppermint Platform is built on the world-leading Microsoft Dynamics CRM platform, and for those businesses of law which hold their clients at the heart of everything they do, selecting a customer-centric technology platform such as this is essential. This technology enables your firm to centre all tasks, documents, communications, and transactions on the client and deliver a highly personalised service.

Recall in previous chapters where I shared with you trends, drivers, research, and future expectations in relation to personalisation? Ker-ching!

When I met with Arlene Adams, CEO of Peppermint, and questioned her about her technology, and in particular its CRM element and focus, she had me chuckling:

'It's interesting you are reporting on Legal CRM tech. We typically start with firms by talking about CRM as a system but by the end of the conversation we get them to realise that a CRM system will solve very little. I really believe CRM is a way of life. It's about the culture of a law firm and how everything and everyone works together from a single source of data. This is where the real power of CRM is. That's what we have created in Peppermint… It's like a dog. You commit for life to CRM, not just Christmas!'

There are some interesting case studies available on this technology, but the one from Salisbury-based Wilsons Solicitors

LLP struck me because Wilsons believe that Peppermint is the only legal software capable of actually generating revenue through the effective automation of cross-selling and business development. Music to my frazzled brain.

Wilsons' managing partner Andrew Roberts commented: 'As a commercial firm with leading private client and charity practices we have always provided a high quality, personal service tailored to individuals and trustees as well as businesses. These diverse needs present real challenges to any practice management system. After 25 years with our current supplier it was time to move on to a market-leading solution that robustly retained all of the core functions needed to sustain our individual approach while adding new features to enhance and extend our client service. After an extensive review of the market we chose the Peppermint platform, which more than meets these requirements, in a very user-friendly way, while offering clear routes to increased revenue and profit for our business.'

Recently Peppermint launched PeppDirect in direct response to demand from law firms with little IT resource. The product is targeted at small and niche/boutique businesses of law that require ready-to-use software without any customisation; it provides the same modern, client-centric, functionality as the multi-award-winning Peppermint Legal Service Platform with tailored templates and workflows.

Next, I'd like to share with you Kulahub. It's literally The Naked CRM for Customer Engagement.

Kulahub

To begin, I must declare that I am an advocate for Kulahub[5] as I've been using it for five years. If you're a solopreneur lawyer, small, or even mid-sized business (of law), and you do not need or want an all singing and dancing full suite of pms, dms, cms, cms, crm, etc., then this pure CRM system may suit you well.

Why Kulahub? It's an easy-to-use, cloud-based CRM and email marketing system which is a very simple and cost effective system designed to enable you to easily keep in touch with your customers as well as attract new ones. The flexible design enables you to fit the system around your existing data (not the other way around!) and with its unique category, email, and SMS communications built in you are always in touch with, and aware of, what your customers and prospective customers are doing, personally.

I reckon I have survived this far in business due to a combination of continually re-thinking, re-inventing, and embracing 'naked' marketing and networking (SocialHuman) and technology.

It's one thing to have a positive customer experience, but it's another to keep track of your customer relationships and have the ease of easily 'touching' them. (For those who have read *the naked lawyer*, remember the lesson about touch, touch, touch?) Maintaining good customer relationships is all about following up on recent experiences with your prospects and clients. This could be anything from using the notes within the CRM to remembering previous conversation topics or setting a task to wish someone a Happy Birthday or work anniversary.

Using the CRM will help you stay on top of communications with customers and ensure you're being proactive in maintaining these crucial relationships, not just responding when something goes wrong – as we lawyers usually do.

Finally, let's take a quick peek at Clio: the Naked App for practice management...

Clio

In 2008 Clio launched as the first cloud-based legal practice management software in the world. Now in 2014 Clio is five times larger than its closest competitor. The company and its star product is clearly the market leader in cloud-based PMS. It's the leading go-to law practice and legal case management software for businesses of law, lawyers, and entrepreneurial lawyers.[7]

Similar to Kulahub, but with a different and complementary product and service, it's the perfect tech for solo lawyers, small and medium-sized businesses, and ultimately the entrepreneurial lawyer who doesn't require a complete whistle and bells suite comprising each of pms, dms, cms, cms, crm, etc.

Undoubtedly, the Clio PMS was built for collaboration and simplicity. Clio:

- Is very robust at a hugely affordable price;
- Users save an average of eight hours every single week;
- Saves lots of time by completely streamlining the time-tracking and billing process.

What's the word on the street about Clio?

- We are Salesforce.com for Lawyers' (Clio).
- 'Simple and elegant experience' (Users).
- 'The Naked App for Practice Management' (Me).

Clio also boasts an iOS app which makes mobile document management possible for us lawyers on the go.[8]

what's missing?

Despite how fabulous all of this whiz-bang legal technology is, there are elements missing that would make it absolutely magical. For example, SocialHuman tracking and attribution, and Revenuetion. (Huh? Read on…)

SocialHuman tracking and attribution

I have spoken with a handful of (leading) existing legal tech providers about my idea to track the online SOCIAL lawyer activity of their lawyers and to seamlessly drop said activity into its existing ERP/DM AX/DM/CRM system.

Where lawyers, prospects and clients increasingly meet and communicate in social land it seems obvious that the tech systems need to evolve to cater for this communication medium and SocialHuman element. At present, you, the lawyer, have to feed the information into your Tech System manually (keyboard) with regard to your activity on various social streams such as LinkedIn, Twitter, Facebook, etc. You do this to track the touch points with your prospects and clients to then feed into the bigger CRM picture resulting (hopefully) in a client matter and therefore the finance, and even (fingers crossed) remuneration system.

Wouldn't it be nice if all this was done automatically? We're there with document automation in law law land. We're beginning to get there with marketing automation, slowly. But the next big thing, I reckon, in law law land tech is to tackle SocialHuman technology.

I wonder which of the current legal tech players will be the pioneer? Perhaps it won't be any of them. Perhaps it will be a new player that comes along and bolts the SocialHuman tech/software plug and play element into one of the MD platform providers?

While on the subject of attribution, I was chatting with a couple of people from Google earlier this year at a conference and thereafter at Google HQ about Jazz Rasool's relevance and resonance technology (since Google search and algorithms presently tick and buzz around relevance) and my idea about SocialHuman tracking attribution. I shared with them my views in relation to the relationship cycle and correct attribution with regard to WHO in the law firm actually influenced the instruction from WHAT social/web based activity – for example, using social networking, recording it easily, and therefore the right individual being rewarded accordingly.

The trend to their comments was this: in the future, we are going to have a much better understanding of attribution. Smart legal businesses are going to get more excited about things like how you can tell for sure that the advertising that resulted on you clicking on the ad got you to the website and resulted in the instruction – i.e. they're going to want to know where the instruction really came from.

I reckon they were actually talking about which elements truly impacted the instruction decision. If we could combine this idea with what I am suggesting then this would be magical for you, the lawyer, you, the prospect and client of the law firm, and ultimately you, the owner of the business of law.

I can see it would certainly sit nicely with businesses of law which boast a merit-based system, such as RPC, which scrapped its flat rate salary for newly qualified (NQ) solicitors from September this year in favour of a merit-based system, arguing that the concept of the flat rate has 'passed its sell-by date'. Hear hear! Perhaps if the law firm I was at was as pioneering and visionary as RPC I would have stayed practising law there as a NQ with this fabulous setup in play! Prior to September, only trainees and NQs had a fixed salary at RPC, with those higher up the chain already rewarded through a merit-based system. This is the most common (outdated IMHO) set-up in law law land, as we currently know it.

Oh, and while I'm on this innovating soapbox I believe it's timely to say that if the existing legal tech providers plugged in the IBM Watson AI tech into their ERP/MD AX/MD CRM systems then this would boost the value of their products exponentially in LOTS of areas. It's not a bad, or mad, idea since your brain and my brain, and the brains of our fellow lawyers, prospects, and clients are going to be 'in the cloud' by 2029 and connected to technology… and heaven knows what else.

Forewarned is forearmed. It's better to be prepared than to be chasing your tail. I guess the question is, 'are you going to be a first-mover or laggard?'

Revenuetion

Herbert Smith Freehills' (Herbies) head of revenue, Nick Murphy-Whymark, has this to say on reforming the way law firms bill and collect to make them a lot more efficient:

'Revenue should be dealt with as a single point of focus… Treating billing and cash collection as separate processes creates problems… "Revenuetion" is a finance-led project that connects the revenue team to partners and key business stakeholders in an effort to understand how revenue's service can be improved.'[10]

One of the changes Nick made is that Herbies fee earners now regularly come into contact with 'revenue patrollers', using iPads to capture and analyse WIP data in real time and monitoring how work, billing, and collection are delivered:

'Revenue needs to continue to drive innovation around financial performance and efficiencies, while boosting the level of service to both internal and external clients. This continuous audit, review, and improvement places us in an excellent position to influence the world of revenue.'

Now, dare I suggest that if these existing MD technologies bolted in the revenuetion tech, the problem of unbilled WIP and lawyers hiding invoices in drawers collecting dust, rather than being presented in a timely manner to the (debtor) client, quite rightly, would be resolved with the revenuetion solution? Furthermore, the days of the businesses of law 'playing bank' for their clients would be numbered. Wouldn't this be nice?

If you'd like to learn more about the Revenuetion technology I recommend you contact Nick at Herbies and/or Nexum, the software developers.

The penultimate point I'd like to make about 'what's missing' is on the topic of big data and the power of real relationships. For the future is not just numerical, it's emotional...

Big data and relationships

Businesses of law can no longer hope to survive on providing legal advice alone. If they are to thrive in an increasingly technology-driven era, they must add value in the data field – as well as being generally more human.

Gerd Leonhard – described as one of the world's 'leading media futurists' by the *Wall Street Journal* – confidently suggests that 'data is now the new oil'. He proclaims passionately that the legal profession is in the content business, the marketing business, and, ultimately, the data business. Why? Because the world is headed toward systems of peer-to-peer collaboration, unbundling, and fragmentation.

Mr Leonhard says: 'We're living in a digital society where there is a different world view on control, ownership, and authority'.

We are moving from hyper-competition to hyper-collaboration. We're living and working in the networked society and businesses of law must be networked. And to be successful in a networked world, the human factor of adding value is essential to how we use information and data. Other sectors – such as finance, insurance, banking, and music – are examples of the shift.

Mr Leonhard suggests adding value means focusing on elements such as 'time and attention, influence, and reputation', in other words, intangibles such as high-end intellectual capital and emotional intelligence.

Ultimately, he suggests, the key is being a human brand (where have you heard this before?), where trust is the new currency, and where the focus is on humanity and being social. Interestingly, he predicts lawyers will be paid by virtual currencies in the future – for example, Facebook credits, as the public rating of lawyers becomes increasingly important in a world where we value interaction before transaction.

UK-based fellow futurist Dr Patrick Dixon agrees. He maintains that while there are current frustrations – for example, the modern world is already digital with digital clients, yet lawyers operate with 'dinosaur interfaces' – the future of law will be driven by emotion. Evidence of this can be seen in the fact that lawyers themselves have already 'become rated. If you post a tweet about law, Google will take it seriously'.

Nonetheless, concern remains in the legal profession that big branding is still prevalent and causing problems. The managing partner of a mid-tier UK law firm recently told me: 'We must not forget that corporate brands provide barriers to entry'. For example, the 'nobody got fired for buying IBM' mantra is as applicable to the legal market as it is to any other, and can be seen in operation daily at every level of the legal services market.

But personal – or human – and corporate brands are not mutually exclusive. It is important to view corporate brands as the umbrella for multiple human brands in a networked, collaborative world, IMHO. SocialHuman is a powerful force since it harnesses emotion. An entity cannot.

Data-focused companies are building, exploiting, and nurturing personal brands and SocialHuman now in a smart way. This relates to how they use their personal brands and the customer experience within social networks (and social media streams) to leverage and build awareness of the firm's brand.

It is a networked world and will continue to be. Trust and being human are – and will remain – the reasons clients are attracted to law firm brands. And all businesses of law are going to have to look at new ways of adding value on the periphery of their core propositions if they are to remain competitive. Businesses of law may not realise it yet but, to re-iterate Mr Leonhard's belief, you are in the content business. In addition, you are in the SocialHuman business and your value will be in becoming data businesses.

We are shifting – and arguably have already shifted – from the oil age to the data age. The early 20th-century world, in which the American industrialist John Rockefeller dominated, has been superseded by the 21st-century Digital Data Age where the shots are called by the likes of Facebook's Mark Zuckerberg.

Businesses of law and we lawyers need to shift our positions too. Just as man cannot live on bread alone, no longer can businesses of law live on providing legal advice alone. If you attempt to do so, the oil well riches of the past and present will surely run dry. Nick Murphy-Whymark of Herbies asked James Caan at a law conference recently a question about the potential of big data in legal. To which he replied: 'Yes, but keep it simple!' Genius. Priceless.

And for my final point I'd like to share with you my view about the value of intrapreneurship within the business of law...

Intrapreneurship

The intrapreneur's dilemma[11]:

'When someone tries to innovate within a traditional organization,
few will understand what he/she is doing,
but everybody will understand who is a trouble-maker.
After the innovation has been embraced by the organization,
few will remember who started it,
but everybody will remember who was a trouble-maker.
This is the dilemma encountered by many intrapreneurs –
they risk punishment for success.'

An intrapreneur means someone or some small group that initiates change or experimentation on their own – with no mandate or dedicated resources from their company. It's what I did back in 2008 when I initiated the ROAR Model in the law firm I was practising in at that time.

I risked punishment for success. Fortunately, ROAR worked! My story in *the naked lawyer* is not unique. Countless intrapreneurs and lawyers have found themselves in similar circumstances; Nick Murphy-Whymark is a good example.

Recently innovation has become a trend as more companies have learned that their typical operating environments do not allow for much innovation or intrapreneurship. To those individuals inside businesses of law that have not taken their first intrapreneurial step: beware. You will need strong conviction, uncanny business acumen, and a laser focus on your goals to achieve what you are attempting. And you will need one hell of an incredible team to make it work – no matter how small. I dare suggest Nick would agree.

So why even attempt intrapreneurship inside your business of law? Why risk the alienation, misunderstanding, and turmoil to build something valuable for your company and not yourself? If you are successful the riches of experience and leadership (and sometimes money – albeit not always immediately) become yours. This is, in essence, the intrapreneur's dilemma. To wit, I now ask you, are you prepared to be intrapreneurial and are you using social technology effectively?

NewHuman

The rise of the use of technology in the legal profession to achieve greater efficiencies and flexibility has been well documented. Up until now, the focus has been on making law firms more efficient: streamlining work processes into a single system to provide a secure working environment and transparency of business performance, satisfying the needs of the whole practice.

'While operational processes have been the focus of most companies to-date, future technologies will concentrate on making individuals more productive, efficient and mobile, according to new research we recently completed with leading figures in the Australian legal industry.'[12]

Indeed, the results of the 2014 LexisNexis 'Workflow and Productivity Survey'[13] found that the most popular efficiency initiatives adopted by law firms were the use of technology, knowledge management, and staff training. Accordingly, with all this NewTech take-up, AI in play, avatars, iCyborgs lawyers and Robot Lawyers in the wings, perhaps it is time to chat about what it means to be 'human' and the morals and ethics surrounding AI and robotics.

For example, what are we (humans – lawyers and clients) going to do when we have AI personalities, emotions, and consciousness? Recall what I shared with you in Chapter 3? How is this going to affect the law?

Robot wife, robot hooker

Let's chat about the oldest profession of them all now, shall we? Prostitution is known as 'the world's oldest profession', and is one that continually attracts controversy because of the ethical issues involved in selling sex. The ethical issues surrounding the arguments related to prostitution have been debated for centuries.

In order to gain some insight as to why people will be willing, even eager, to hire the services of robots for sex (malebots and fembots), I attended a futures conference earlier this year at which I met David Levy, an AI researcher and the author of a thesis titled 'Robot Prostitutes as Alternatives to Human Sex Workers'.[14]

David argues that the arrival of sexbots seems imminent when we consider recent trends in the development of humanoids, sex dolls, and sex machines of various types. Sophisticated humanoids have already been developed that are humanlike in appearance. Advances in materials science have enabled sex doll manufacturers to improve significantly on the inflatable products of the preceding decades, creating dolls with prices in the region of $5,000–$7,000.

However, like any new techy device when it is first introduced into the market, the price-point is usually high, meaning it is probable that when sexbots first appear on the market they will most likely be beyond the pockets of the majority of the population, and be a 'luxury good' for all but the wealthy.

With regard to sex dolls, Japan leads the way with the current generation of high priced dolls:

'Their popularity on the retail market has also spawned a doll variant of the more traditional form of "escort" service. In a 2004 newspaper article entitled Rent-a-Doll Blows Hooker Market Wide Open, the *Mainichi Daily News* explains how one leading purveyor, Doll No Mori (Forest of Dolls), started their 24/7 doll escort service in southern Tokyo.'

- *Question*: Why invest in sex dolls? *Answer*: Outlay is low when comparing the return on investment and recuperating the initial cost does not take a long time and there is little continued outlay thereafter. If the doll's initial cost is the major investment and wages will never be a problem for the employer it is likely that the owner will claw back their entire initial investment within the first month; as the owner of a particular sex doll hooker states:

'Unlike employing people, everything we make becomes a profit and we never have to worry about the girls not turning up for work.'

I guess this could be said for Robot Lawyer, when the time arrives.

Within little more than a year of the doll-for-hire idea taking root in Japan, sex entrepreneurs in South Korea also started to cash in.

How does all this sit with 'the law', you may ask? Well, upmarket sex dolls were immediately seen as a possible antidote to Korea's Special Law on Prostitution that had been placed on the statute books. Hotels in Korea were hiring out 'doll experience rooms' for as little as $25 per hour. These hotels assumed that there was no question of them breaking the law, since their dolls were not human.

However, the news web site *Chosun.com* reported, in October 2006, that the police in Gyeonggi Province were 'looking into whether these businesses violate the law. . . Since the sex acts are occurring with a doll and not a human being, it is unclear whether the Special Law on Prostitution applies.'

Accordingly, if the activity surrounding sex dolls are already causing concern with regard to whether the present law is suitable, it is only a question of time before it hits the headlines again (or law-makers and the statute book) when Robot Hooker appears on the Asian 'sex for hire' scene. And not just in Asia, I hasten to suggest.

It is highly likely that sex entrepreneurs will infiltrate the global 'sex for hire' community swiftly, for the robot sex for hire money-go-round will be too lucrative to pass up.

How will this affect the UK and other countries? We will have to address our existing laws on prostitution, particularly when robots become so sophisticated that we will indeed be questioning what it means to be 'human'.

Attitudes and behaviour with regard to relationships, love, sex, sexual exploits and sexual union have changed through the ages in relation to age, gender, ethnicity, and sexual orientation. Here in the UK, prior to the 1960s and the 'age of free love' the topic of sex was pretty much taboo; as was masturbation and homosexuality.

Homosexuality, until very recently, was a 'no, no, no' subject and society spurned gay men and women. But attitudes changed. The law followed. Here in the UK, and in some other parts of the world, gay marriage is now lawful.

I dare say that if you read in the 1970s/1980s/1990s (20/30/40 years ago) that the UK would grant the Civil Partnership Act 2004 you may have scoffed and mocked. But here we are in 2014 and so it is.

We currently live in a world where:

- In divorce proceedings the parties are arguing over who gets full custody of the pet;
- A bridegroom chooses a dog as his best man;
- There are websites where you can 'marry' your dogs;
- Our children adore virtual pets, for example, the Tamagotchi;
- Sex-dolls are available for hire;
- A man says (in real life): 'I've tried having girlfriends but I prefer my relationship with my computer' (anon);
- Men marry their computer game characters/sex-dolls, and
- Gay marriage is lawful.

If we've evolved as a race to have attachments to pets, virtual pets, sex dolls, and computer characters/images/sounds/chatbots, and same gender marriage in law, it's surely indicative of the way human love/relationships/sex are evolving. So why doubt the development of whom and what we bestow our affections on. Maybe the movie called *Her* is actually not quite as fictitious as many of us may think.

Is it too far removed that you cannot teleport yourself into the future 20/30/40 years from now and imagine reading that the Robot Partnership Act 2034/44/54 is law? Surely, it's not ridiculous to think that the Robot Wife and the Robot Husband will surely come to pass in law; and perhaps be preceded by Robot Hooker?

It is likely that UK society will accept love, sex, marriage with robots within 30/40 years, IMHO. You heard it first here. I often pose the question at my presentations and speeches to the lawyers in the audience: 'What effect is what I have just shared with you going to have on matrimonial law and family law, I wonder?' I pose it to you, here and now.

Robot evolution or revolution

According to Neil Rose, editor of *Legal Futures*:

'Sam Steer, head of Large Law at Thomson Reuters, said the drive to "industrialise" law – as it was put in the report by Marc-Henri Chamay, managing director of e-business at Allen & Overy – is 'evident in the demand we're seeing from our leading law firm clients'.

She said: 'If the changes that have taken place in the legal market over the past two years are any indication of what lies ahead, the future of legal services is set to be an exciting one.'[15]

Indeed! The 'industrialisation' of law is already underway. Sam is no doubt referring to the document automation and AI aspect. But the robots are no doubt thinking, à la Jack Nicholson, not unlike the Joker in the *Batman* movie: 'wait 'til you get a load of me!'

The iCub robot exists now (in 2014). It's like a child. It stands 2/3ft tall, looks cute, and is learning and teaching itself. It is now responding to voices. The robot is actively learning and lodges its knowledge in its artificial brain. 20 of these iCubs have been created. The transition from cognitive intelligence to iterative intelligence to super-human intelligence is already well underway. Imagine when the iCub is fully grown up…

Whether or not we experience a robot evolution or revolution, lawyers beware. The City will soon be run by robots. If it's happening in banking, it will happen to you and me too.[16] We're already living in a world:

- Of driverless cars, driverless tubes, and driverless shuttles – it is imminent. No doubt many of you would say that many law firms in law law land have been driverless for decades.
- Of soon to be endless connectivity – By 2020 everyone (the entire world population) will be online. That's eight billion people due to the accessibility of devices as a result of connectivity via project loon. It's live now.
- Where you can build your own drone.
- Of wearable technology – Google glass has already become yesterday's news and will become as prevalent in law law land as email has been for the past 15 years.
- Of various products and services powered by IBM Watson technology, for example, the natural language shopping app.[17]
- Where Watson Analytics is a tool to enable every business user to harness all the power it can deliver.

What will all this mean for lawyering and law, I wonder? Choice, change, control, contrast, uncertainty and… Opportunity.

NewLaw

With the advent of AI and potential for robotics in a law firm setting, I view this as an opportunity to right some wrongs:

a) We can do more to help the poor and disenfranchised; and, in contrast,
b) We can bring an end to the disingenuous 'rip-off' lawyers who bleed us dry with 'grotesque costs'.

Has access to justice and law become a luxury good rather than a public good, I wonder? Is there a solution? I question, when we have a possible solution in our grasp, why are we not using it?

The demise of legal aid here in the UK is a travesty and a tragedy, IMHO, particularly when I read how technology is helping deliver legal services to the poor and I can envisage how AI and the Watson technology in particular could assist – some of which has already been documented in previous chapters. Surely, there is a place for machines/AI/robots (and a role to be played by the same) in the legal justice system?

The delegates attending the European Lawyers Association appear to believe so.[18] When I asked the question 'is there a place for Artificial Intelligence (AI) in your law firm? If YES, where, when, and why? Discuss', this is the summary of their responses:

- Potentially law firms will use AI, but it may vary between jurisdictions;
- AI should be back office;
- Outputs by AI should be checked and viewed by lawyer(s) before they are handed over to the client;
- Regulatory aspects in relation to guidelines for use of AI in the civil code;
- Budgeting for AI could be an issue;
- Areas of law where AI could be used:
  - ☐ Mergers and acquisitions;
  - ☐ Research – data scanning;
  - ☐ Regulatory;
  - ☐ Litigation; and
- In relation to the current status of using AI, only our Irish colleagues use it in

competition procedures, but they say it's better than a human doing it.

We have the technology. It appears all we need now is the budget and the desire. For as American psychologist B. F. Skinner once said: 'The real problem is not whether machines think but whether men do.'

I would argue that if the legal aid budget has been slashed and the tragedy is that human lawyers can't afford to represent clients at the price they are squeezed to, then from the point at which the machine/robot can think and do like the human lawyer it would make sense that it is 'employed' or deployed to do so. Fewer human lawyers, and a handful of overseers would be required to manage the machine/robot and its processes, case load, and case law queries etc.

Not unlike the sex entrepreneurs who argue that once the sex robot is paid for (aka the initial investment) they no longer have to pay for the sexbot (no payment of wages is required, understandably), so to it will be for Robot Lawyer. Once it is paid for, the initial investment is recouped in time and then there is little further outlay.

It would certainly be a lot cheaper (and within the current legal aid budget) than hiring the barrister at a rate that they are not happy with, understandably. Insofar as there will be fewer barristers/advocates in time, just as there will be fewer solicitors, and we may have already witnessed a lost generation of legal aid lawyers,[19] I anticipate there will remain a role for the Robot Lawyer supervisor/manager.

With foresight, boldness, technology, and a dab of entrepreneurism within law law land we could actually resolve the legal aid 'problem', those people without the means could be represented fairly, equally, and cost effectively[20], and we could redress the travesty that we have allowed what was once our revered legal system to become a mockery. I believe that what I propose is absolutely achievable in light of the fact that J. Dory Reiling plans to run several courts fully electronically with paperless trials by 2015.

In contrast to technology/AI/robots helping us pay the minimum to achieve justice and legal help, let's now turn to exorbitant costs and how technology could help. A High Court judge has called for a cap on costs after a divorcing couple racked up a bill of almost £1 million contesting assets. Mr Justice Mostyn described as 'madness' a case where lawyers and experts were paid a total of £920,000 (almost 32 per cent of the assets!) during a dispute over assets worth around £2.9 million.[21]

Clearly, the judge, IMHO, was right to express his displeasure and rage that these fees were 'grotesque'. Furthermore he proclaimed: 'The time has come when the law-makers in this country, whether they are legislators or judges, must stop saying something must be done and actually do something...'

Justice Mostyn suggested that new rules must come into force to impose a costs cap on fees charged by lawyers and set fixed fees for each stage of litigation. Hear hear.

If these tougher rules do come about in due course, for Justice Mostyn is bringing his judgment in this case to the attention of the president of the Family Division 'as a matter of urgency' with the Family Procedure Rules Committee, we may actually see more people opt to instruct a lawyer (at a fair price) rather than be self-represented as they seek expert advice on how much their case will cost.

It is arguable that once one law firm introduces IBM Watson intelligence or an equivalent AI into its dispute resolution procedures and case law analytics (and the courts move toward paperless trials), thereby utilising cognitive and iterative decision-tree analysis, the costs that would normally skyrocket could be reduced and passed on as a saving to the client.

Once one business of law has taken this technical, financial, entrepreneurial, and bold step, I would envision that the laws of economics, competition, supply, and demand would kick in and we could experience the gradual erosion of the grotesque costs demanded by the purely self-interested greedy lawyers that put our beloved profession to shame. I dare say it would be welcomed by many of us (lawyers and non-lawyers alike) to reach the stage in law law land where we expunge the lament: 'for want of a fee, justice is lost'.

robot lawyer, robot boss, and robot judge?

I have spoken at length already about the possibility of machines/AI/robots taking on some of the roles of the lawyer now and in the future as technology evolves. But can we envisage a time when the machine/robot could be our boss, or the judge?

There was a very entertaining, creative, and informative article by Matthew Wall, business reporter at the BBC, in October this year. I'm going to share the essence of it here with you, my version:

Could ICub, the 'learning cognitive agent', be your boss one day?

I'm on a date with ICub. He's suavely dressed, drop dead gorgeous (a dead ringer for Brad Pitt) and emotionally intelligent. Bonus. But he's a little too virtual for my tastes.

ICub is a 'learning cognitive agent' you see, according to his creators NewHumans R Us Inc.; like one of those virtual customer service helpers that pop up on a corporate website or train platform – only not so stupid and a lot less irritating.

But one day, he could end up being my boss in Ivory Towers R Us, NewHumans R Us believes. Now, I'm impressed by ICub because he can swallow legal textbooks whole, speak 50 languages fluently, understand concepts, metaphors, and jokes, AND he can learn from his mistakes; something we 'pure blood humans' struggle with.

Oh, and he can be replicated any number of times. On my screen I see him absorb a complex legal manual in 14 seconds then immediately answer questions such as 'What are the tax implications in a multi-jurisdictional transaction of this nature for both parties?' and 'What would you advise in these circumstances?'

This may be a far cry from Scarlett Johansson's uber-intelligent operating system, Samantha, in Spike Jonze's sci-fi film, *Her*, but it's the future, says NewHumans R Us chief executive officer.

The key to ICub's intelligence is that he can understand what you mean even if you ask the question several different ways – 'what is meant, not just what is said', as the CEO puts it. And if he doesn't know the answer ICub can refer to me, the human agent, for help, observe how I handle the issue, then learn the answer for next time.

This ability to interpret context, problem solve, and learn is fundamental to automating many of the legal processes now performed by me, the 'pure blood' human lawyer, usually in my large ivory tower but sometimes virtually/remotely, the CEO believes.

Machine intelligence is already starting to rival my human intelligence, to the extent that this machine learning intelligence is starting to work its way into my employer's, the business of law's, boardroom, here at Ivory Towers R Us.

Interestingly, IBM is developing a version of Watson that could contribute to board meetings and help develop strategy in our business of law. Our newly appointed 'boardroom Watson' is able to transcribe everything said in the meeting, show answers to research questions on our big screen, and also come up with its own suggestions consistent with our company strategy based on algorithms and big data analytics.

Worryingly for some of the complacent lawyers/partners, no doubt, IBM says Watson would also be able to analyse the contributions made by each board member for usefulness and accuracy. There will be no hiding, soon, dear partner slackers and laggards, particularly if your PEP is sagging.

So does this mean ICub, Watson, and their artificially intelligent siblings are threatening to take over our ivory tower and law law land landscape completely? Not yet…

The strength of computers and smart machines lies in their ability to analyse vast data sets and make decisions based on evidence alone. Human judgement is often clouded by irrationality, emotion, and imperfect knowledge. But, optimists such as myself believe that smart robots and cognitive agents will rid us of the unskilled boring monotonous tasks and let us get on with what we human lawyers are really good at – being creative and schmoozing prospects and clients.

'Today, most of us are enslaved to the common chores that occupy 80 per cent of our time', says the CEO of NewHumans R Us. (Ah, that's the buckets 1 and 2 I spoke about in a previous chapter.)

He goes on: 'Cognitive agents will free us from the mundane and allow us, or prompt us, to elevate ourselves into higher value creation – something that requires more creative thinking.' (Ah, that's the buckets 3 and 4 we discussed in Chapter 3: advocacy and judgement.)

No doubt robots will be able to judge, some day, once they can 'think' and 'reason'. In spite of all the brilliance that ICub possesses, I would argue that we still need to rely on our gut instinct in legal matters and develop a richer, more instinctive understanding of our clients.

As for managing me, the hybrid junior lawyer and social collaborator, well, data analytics will certainly have a bigger part to play in quantifying my performance and assessing my strengths and weaknesses. Even psychometric testing can be automated by the robot resources department; our evolved human resources department. But when it comes to human skills such as intuition, lateral thinking, and emotional intelligence, ICub lags far behind, at the moment. Phew!

'Machines can at best be run-of-the-mill managers. Thinking creatively, out of the box, for implementing better business outcomes tomorrow is a domain where, today at least, man reigns supreme', says the CEO of NewHumans R US.

It may be some time yet before my ICub conquers the world. But I will go on a date with him, anytime! Will a machine/robot like ICub be my boss one day?

When you read scenarios like the one I have shared with you and reports where it is predicted that 35 per cent of the UK workforce will be replaced by robots within 20 years[22] and machines could potentially wipe out 47 per cent of the US workforce,[23] combined with the knowledge that machines are going to exceed human intelligence and develop EI, in time, I reckon it is highly plausible… but maybe 10/15 years from now before it hits the mainstream.

Never has Jack Welch's wise words been so pertinent: 'Control your destiny or someone else will'.

the new law for the Digital, Robotic, and Interstellar Ages

From now until 2025 there will be seven 18-month 'Moore's Law' generations, resulting in a 128-fold (2^7) increase in computing power. That will enable devices that are, for example, five times more powerful, five times cheaper, *and* five times smaller (hence requiring five times less energy input) than today's computers. Coupled with similar progress in other technology fields, this means there will be huge potential for change in very many areas of work, play, learning, and healthcare – as well as in our social, economic, and legal structures. The potential upsides *and* potential downsides are both enormous.

Serious analysis of the potentially radical scenarios that may unfold between now and 2025 includes us questioning the laws of the society and universe we are currently comfortable with.

We are moving toward smart societies... One trajectory is the positive trend – the opportunities and advancements due to technological acceleration etc. The second trajectory is the negative trend – the systemic strains and stresses – for example, finance and law, inequality/alienation, weapons of mass destruction, environment, resource shortages, etc.

Whichever road we are currently trundling along... take a wild guess... we have it in our human power to do the right thing. For starters, 'if you find yourself the smartest person in the room, then you're in the wrong room!'

In a world where economic and political uncertainty and turbulence are the 'new normal' where the old economic systems and arguably legal systems are no longer appropriate, for mankind to evolve, it will require fortitude.

The developing world is starting to flex its muscles. What's interesting is the innovation happening in those societies. The Middle East is asking 'how can it invest in this new stuff?' No doubt the $10 insurance policy, etc. is coming to a town near you in the West.

As social demographic shifts are reshaping society, the world population increases and we begin to live longer (remember Chapter 3), how do we deal with all these issues? For example, marriage: do we make divorce compulsory after 30 years? Our working life: to be capped at age 50? The list goes on...

New paradigms are being embraced by emerging markets/societies because they are starting with a blank sheet – rather than being threatened by defunct and dysfunctional existing systems and infrastructure.

This science is going on in parallel with the painfully slow progress in industries, such as the legal profession. Remember the scientists told us it would take 100 years to crack the genome – it actually took eight years!

Accordingly, the timeline that Kurzweil speaks of in relation to the technological progress in relation to genetics, nanotechnology, and robotics for the period 2015 to 2045 may indeed be smashed... or elongated.

We just don't know which it is going to be. But wouldn't it be better to be prepared, just in case, for WHEN it happens, whenever that moment occurs?

With regard to the issues surrounding human enhancement, what will be the policy/legal issues, I ask?

I've already shared a number with you throughout the book so far. For example, Google – if they were patenting wearables five years ago, what are they patenting now? Grafting/embedded technology in the human body/brain, perhaps? Could we, would we, should we?

But rather than waiting for the invention and reacting, why don't we lawyers, agents of the law, and legal anthropologists start truly understanding all this new stuff and get a grip! AI is going mainstream, now. As I said earlier, the AI machine has already bolted out of the R&D labs and the money-making machine is already rolling.

Clearly, unless policy-makers and law-makers get a grip, we're heading toward dystopia or utopia – a potential nightmare the likes of the movie *Transcendence* depicted, or Nirvana (nobody wants to make that movie – understandable – it's not shocking or scary enough). There is still a huge amount of stuff we don't know or understand.

At a futurist conference earlier this year I recall Sonia Contera, a scientist specialising in biology and nanotechnology, saying: 'The best nanotech we have is you, your human matter, your DNA and proteins. But only 2 per cent of your DNA is genes. The rest, we don't know! It's not only chemistry, it's physics. We need to integrate the sciences. We're starting to study biology like physicists study physics.'

Err, didn't we used to think that the sciences were separate, sort of? Apparently, our cells dance.

The future of medicine and biology is very much nanotechnology. When Sonia was questioned: 'Is there smaller than nano in biology?' She replied: 'Yes. Quantum – human consciousness might be linked to quantum; we need to go further down than nano.'

Although we don't know how the brain works yet, we're working on it. Upshot is there's a lot we don't understand. It's little wonder that a 'scientist' tried recently to persuade the Australian High Court the fundamental laws of physics are wrong. I recall some (now famous) scientist centuries ago trod a similar path and he was vilified. Turns out he was right, back then. It may well be that the 2014 scientist is too. Be careful what you scoff at and mock, I reckon.

The laws of the universe and those in our world which we presently accept and believe in are in fact being questioned and challenged, right now. This is due in no small part to the fact that leading scientists and great thinkers throughout the world, and particularly at Massachusetts Institute of Technology (MIT) where STEM (science – biology, chemistry, physics – technology, engineering, maths), AI, and robotic research is being conducted in a hotchpotch environment due to each of these fields finding itself in rooms next door to contrasting fields.

The result of which magic is beginning to happen… Magic and science are blurring. It is foreseeable that we are entering an Age of Magic and Miracles.

If this is the case with regard to our current understanding of the laws of the universe (e.g. physics) and we become further enlightened as we make new discoveries (on this planet and beyond), we will have to re-write the book of law… Literally.

I would argue that indeed we must. The law, in certain areas, as it stands, is not fit for the Digital Age, let alone the Robotic Age and Interstallar Age to come:

Law in the Digital Age

I reckon new copyright law and laws appertaining to porn would be welcome, right now. The macaque (a species of monkey) who took a 'selfie' and subsequently sparked a row (which went all the way to court) over who owns the copyright of the photo provides a suitable example:

'If we can debate this today,' David Bain says (remember him?), 'it is conceivable we have the same debate about IP that's developed through artificial intelligence in the very near future.'[24]

The USA has similar concerns. I strongly recommend you read 'The Art of the Steal: Copyright in Retreat', by Peter Baldwin.[25] Furthermore, both the UK and USA are experiencing the ripple effect of revenge porn. If you aren't prone to trawling through the web's darker recesses as a SocialHuman, you may not have come across the concept of revenge porn. It is defined as the intentional distribution of sexually explicit content without the subject's permission. That encompasses everything from topless selfies to surreptitious sex tapes offered up for public consumption. Perpetrators are most often former lovers, but can also be strangers. It is an enduring hell, for the women (and men) who go through it...

While there are no accurate figures available in the UK, yet, anecdotal evidence suggests the phenomenon is growing at an alarming rate. With entire websites devoted to hosting the nude/porn pictures (which exist because anti-nudity policies on Facebook, Twitter, LinkedIn etc. ensure most offensive images are taken down swiftly from social media), the problem is getting exponentially worse.

Aided by aggressive and obsessive internet trolls, revenge porn destroys lives on a daily basis. Across the world, differences in cybercrime laws inform victims' experiences dramatically – while action in countries like Germany, where a High Court ruled that intimate photos should be deleted at the end of a relationship if one partner requests it, and the USA (12 states now have laws expressly applicable to revenge porn) – the UK's discussions have only just begun.

Without specific language defining revenge porn as a crime, existing laws under which it might fall lack bite and are difficult to use, which inevitably incurs expensive legal fees due to the long drawn out nature of the legal matter.

As UK Law currently stands, depending on the nature of the images and the intentions of the perpetrator, posting explicit images without consent may fall under the Malicious Communications Act 1988 or the Communications Act 2003. If there is more than one posting, there may be an offence of harassment under the Protection from Harassment Act 1997.

Bottom line: if your ex takes the images with your permission and you're over the age of 18, charges of child pornography and copyright infringement fly out of the window. If your ex doesn't attach direct contact information about you along with the image, neither harassment nor stalking applies either. The government is exploring whether these laws are sufficient to tackle the problem of revenge porn. Clearly, they're not!

Moving on from copyright law, let's briefly look at data protection and privacy law. While there is very little written about where privacy and regulation is going, I came across the book entitled *The Future of Privacy* by Eduardo Ustaran, a data protection lawyer and leading privacy lawyer at a Top 20 law firm here in the UK. The book entails a legal framework that respects our privacy but also embraces the wonder of technology. As I turned the pages, what struck me were Eduardo's cases for why he believes the law of privacy needs looking at, now. It comes down to three things:

1) Evolution of technology;
2) Value of data as an asset; and
3) Data globalisation.

He argues that we shouldn't regulate technology because engineers (and designers) move faster. But, he proposes that what we should use is the law to regulate behaviour.

Market research companies collect data all the time. We don't know if the use of said data is going to be harmful. Eduardo grapples with the two main debates:

1) The human right debate – The state is to serve the individuals so it must justify the use of data for the benefit of the people; and
2) The commercial debate – In today's world information/data has value.

How do you reconcile a global approach by a company with an international legal framework with heterogenous jurisdictions and data laws? And, if 'our privacy is a pillar of our freedom'[26], quite rightly, then surely we have the right to be forgotten with regard to our SocialHuman digital footprint. Perhaps the ruling resulting in Google deleting 18,000 web-links a month in the UK is the first step?

Law in the Robotic Age

As I have already mentioned and advocated my reasoning for the pending changes that may well be required to family law, matrimonial law, and the law on prostitution to be welcomed in light of the advent of the avatars, sexbots, malebots, and fembots, I'd like to focus now, briefly, on avatars and humanoids (iCyborgs and robots) entering the workplace and its implication, legally:

- The robot as worker; and
- The 'pure blood' human as worker.

As in all things, I believe it is best to prevent, rather than cure. To be a pioneer rather than a laggard! And so, let us address the above two points very briefly.

robot worker

Avatars could be present in a work environment as early as 2015. With each generation, the computational worm is getting smarter. By 2030 robots will be omnipresent. In the next 25 years, these robots will have cognitive and iterative computing intelligence.

I believe that fairly quickly we first need to define 'human' in law, so that ALL of the usual employment laws can then work satisfactorily, or indeed be tweaked and changed where appropriate and applicable. I do not propose to attempt to define it here. Perhaps that is something you can play with in your 'after dark activity'.

If/when we have robots/icyborgs/ humanoids in the workplace and if a person/non-person has the ability to be injured but repaired and healed very quickly to a potentially better state than before, what does that mean for how we think about damages and what an injury is really worth?

If the said injury at work is caused by a non-person/avatar/robot, it begs the question 'who/what will be liable/accountable for the damages?' Will it be you? The avatar is, after all, your copy, remotely controlled by you. Depending on how 'human' is defined the level of personal liability, vicarious liability, and also whether the employer has recourse to the robot supplier (NewHumans R Us Inc., perhaps?) will hang in the balance.

'pure blood' human worker

I can envisage a future where discrimination will come down to a science, where 'pure blood humans' without genetic intervention could become the underclass. Accordingly, it ought to be illegal (in the future) to discriminate between 'pure human' and genetically enhanced human and icyborgs and robots. While there is no gene for fate, we 'pure bloods' are blessed with the 'human spirit' gene. Let us hope that our spirit is wise – and not programmable.

law in the Interstellar Age

We are at the dawn of an advanced age. I find it incredible that we sent an unmanned probe ten years ago (with technology nowhere near as advanced as we have today) to rendezvous with a comet 300 million miles away from earth travelling at 86000 miles an hour… and we succeeded.

Why did we do this? Because scientists and cosmologists believe that the data we will receive back holds the clue as to how life began. Such is mankind's curiosity, thirst for knowledge, and spirit of adventure that a Dutch company announced earlier this year that it wants up to 20 healthy adults (aged 18+) to train for eight years to be the first group of human beings to colonise Mars by 2023. I'm NOT kidding. Go and Google it for yourself.

This is, of course, a one way ticket. If it is successful, the company will be sending out more voyages every two years after 2023. Yes, yes, yes, I hear you. Richard Branson is still struggling to hurl Virgin Galactic beyond the earth's atmosphere so how is mankind going to plop 20 brave souls onto the 'red planet'?

I dare to propose that, just as nature finds a way, we humans will find a way too. For I believe it's in our nature to continually seek and understand, to question, and to answer the mystery that has been plaguing mankind since time began: why are we here? And are we alone?

Sir Richard will succeed in his venture, I have no doubt. He doesn't know how to give in, or to lose. His human spirit is such that he will never stop trying. And I believe it this drive, the human spirit, which will propel us into space and onward to the stars, planets, and galaxies that until now we can only dream of and have only recently discovered.

This being the case, I highly recommend that one of the 20 souls is a legal anthropologist on the mission to Mars. If we have a blank sheet, and we contemplate law and order on a new planet, how would we begin all over again, I ponder?

At the top of my crisp, white, velvet sheet I would pause and contemplate… there has to be a better way… and then pen: 'From martial law to Martian law… but not back again.' And then I shall take a leaf out of Walt Disney's book and the movie *Saving Mr. Banks*, for 'it's what us storytellers do… we restore order with imagination.'

I must admit, had I not met my lover, I'd have been rather tempted to put my name forward for the Dutch company's mission. Even with all the uncertainty and the inexhaustable variety of life which life on earth provides, there's something remarkably challenging in such a mission, which appeals to my curiosity, spirit of adventure, and humanness. If I had ever made the call and succeeded in being one of the chosen, I know exactly what I would have been thinking on my final day on earth: 'Let it have one more moment in the sun before it disappears from the world'

It is rather poignant and timely that I share this with you. Someone once said to me 'I admire you… I admire how you handle the tension between technology's promise and its peril.'

And I guess this statement sums up what lies ahead for those valiant colonists, for us entrepreneurial lawyers, the variety of businesses of law in law law land and the law-makers writing the 'letter of the law' in the advent of the Interstellar Age.

To answer the question 'are we alone?' I suspect we already know the answer…

With powerful telescopes we are able to

see canals on Mars. In 2008 we discovered water on the planet. We suspect there was alien life form there in the past but something catastrophic occurred; therefore, if there is any type of species on Mars now we suspect it is subterranean.

Our ancestors were convinced we had ancestors on Mars – but that's for a future article or book. Searching for alien life is no longer in the realm of science fiction. The Kepler spacecraft and its telescope, has been on a seven-year mission to seek out planets that may have alien life. It was designed to answer the question 'are we alone?'

In April 2009 the spacecraft jettisoned its dusty cover and beamed back spectacular images. Kepler watches stars in order to detect planets. In the first six weeks Kepler found five new planets. But what the Kepler scientists are truly interested in is finding worlds capable of sustaining life.

Life needs liquid water (hydrogen and oxygen). And just the right temperature is necessary to have liquid water. The Goldilocks zone is required – where the right temperature and orbiting the sun at the right speed exist.

Which means the scientists need to find a star or planet that orbits similar to earth – that is, it orbits once a year around a sun.

In December 2011, our scientists found a planet in the goldilocks zone; it orbits the sun in 290 days and it was named Kepler22b. On planet Kepler there is lots of liquid water.... and energy. The scientists suspect it might even have an ecosystem similar to earth because photosynthesis can occur in this environment.

In February 2012 NASA said it has discovered over 1000 new planets, and it's currently finding two a day. Some of these planets orbit dwarf stars like the red dwarf (similar to the sun). They have a hot side (facing the sun) and a cold side (a giant polar cap on the opposite side, facing away from the sun).

Understandably, this would have a profound effect on the atmosphere. But a planet-wide wind system would mean a stable atmosphere could exist in the twilight zone on the planet where the sun never sets (at perpetual sunset). There would be a deep red sunlight. Black plants are likely to exist in order to absorb maximum energy from the sun. And as we know, if there is plant life, then it is possible there will be animal life – for example, land whales.

Recently, in the past year, Kepler has found a planet similar to earth 1200 light years away. Alien life could exist here, and there could be more habitable planets out there too. Why not shunt the Dutch company's courageous souls off to this planet, rather than Mars, you may think, particularly as it is a planet similar to earth? Better the planet you know, eh?

Well, alright in theory, but it would take millions of years to get there. Until such time as we have invented interstellar travel and/or the technology has evolved which will mean our children will never die, this option is clearly not on the rocket burner table!

We are at a remarkable moment. We are discovering many planets with rock and water composition. Surely, we are not alone... Even IF we think we have answered this question, I reckon it will remain as to 'why are we here?'

Unless the God Particle and/or our alien creator/engineer from some galaxy far far away, or the data from the probe on the comet sat some unbelievable 300 million miles away from us at present reveals the answer, I suspect our search will go on... and on... and on.... and on...

Back in 2009/10 in my speeches, writings, and in *the naked lawyer* book I used to motivate my audience by saying:

'Reach for the moon. At least you will fall amongst the stars.' Now, in the space of five years, I reckon it is far more fitting to inspire with this phrase: 'Reach for the stars. At least you will fall upon a new planet.'

after dark activity

'When you are inspired by some great purpose, some extraordinary event, all your thoughts break their bonds. Your mind transcends limitations, your consciousness expands in every direction and you find yourself in a new, great and wonderful world. Dormant forces, faculties and talents come alive and you discover that you're a greater person by far than you ever dreamed yourself to be.'[27]

just do something!

Task 1:

- Imagine you could be in two places at once;
- Imagine that, at the end of your life, your brain could be transplanted into the robotic copy of you;
- Imagine that your personality could be transferred into an avatar with an artificial brain (or your brain and mind) at the end of your life;
- Imagine that you could transfer your mind into a hologram body;
- That is, imagine that you could have a robotic copy (avatar) of yourself remotely controlled via BCI (brain computer interface).

Task 2:

Imagine what laws need to be created and which existing laws need adapting to be fit for purpose in this Digital Age and in readiness for the imminent Robotic Age and Interstellar Age.

I have suggested within this chapter that we may, indeed, need to define what it means to be 'human', in law, so that ALL of the laws that we are currently familiar with can then work satisfactorily, or where necessary be tweaked and changed where appropriate and applicable.

Accordingly, perhaps this is something you can play with in your mind – or, better still, proffer to policy-makers and law-makers in your jurisdiction, now. Isn't it time we law-makers pioneered rather than waiting for the invention to happen and the technology to run away before the damage is irreparable?

To help you, remember what Ray Kurzweil pointed out. If you're wondering 'what will remain unequivocally human in such a world it's simply this quality: ours is the species that inherently seeks to extend its physical and mental reach beyond current limitations'.

Task 3:

Identify all of the books I have made reference to throughout this chapter, make a list, and go and work through the ones (over time) that appeal to your curiosity, capture your interest, and stir your imagination.

Task 4:

You've done the hard work by getting your head around the techy and futuristic stuff. Not just in this chapter, but throughout the entire book. There's only one more chapter to cover and it's an easy, fun, and pleasurable one.

So, may I suggest you now relax, take a sip of sustenance – whatever is your poison – and read on! Let's enjoy our penultimate prance and dance together…

References

1. Ark Group's 2014 report, *Law Firms in the Digital Age*, by Chris Bull and David Bason, provides the blueprint for lawyers and law firm managers to successfully respond to the

opportunities of technologies that define the digital age.

2. Carolyn Mumby, CEO, Barrister. HR & Employment Law specialist. See: www.employmentlawportal.com.
3. 2014 report into PSF management attitudes towards digital and social technologies, see: https://response.questback.com/isa/qbv.dll/ShowQuest?QuestID=4647441&sid=fJZg4UuP7k.
4. See: www.peppermintttechnology.co.uk/legal-software.
5. See: http://kulahub.com/entrepreneur-lawyer-landing-page.
6. See: http://entrepreneurlawyer.co.uk/media/kulahub.
7. See: http://entrepreneurlawyer.co.uk/media/clio.
8. See: www.goclio.co.uk/2014/08/07/training-thursday-clio-makes-mobile-practice-management-possible-part-3-documents/.
9. Simmons, R., 'RPC to scrap NQ flat rate salary for performance-based pay', *The Lawyer*, 19 November 2013. See: www.thelawyer.com/3012645.article?cmptype=RPC%20scraps%20NQ%20salary%20for%20merit-based%20system&cmpid=dnews_42064.
10. 'He's calling it a revenuetion', *Briefing* magazine, November 2012.
11. Quoting David Nordfors, president & co-founder in 'The Intrapreneur's Dilemma', see: https://medium.com/@jkubicki/the-intrapreneurs-dilemma-9362a18f8e76.
12. Dr Marc K Peter, 'Increasing the efficiency of individuals – the next priority for the legal industry', October 2014, see: www.alpma.com.au/a-survival-guide-for-legal-practice-managers/increasing-the-efficiency-of-individuals-the-next-priority-for-the-legal-industry.
13. See: www.legaltechnology.com/wp-content/uploads/2014/11/Legal-Professional-Efficiency_whitepaper_final.pdf.
14. Levy, D., 'Robot Prostitutes as Alternatives to Human Sex Workers' (white paper), London, 2006. Accompanying material includes: Levy, D., 'Marriage and Sex With Robots', EURON Workshop on Roboethics, Genoa, March 2006; Levy, D., 'Emotional Relationships With Robotic Companions', EURON Workshop on Roboethics, Genoa, March 2006; and Levy, D., 'A History of Machines With Sexual Functions: Past, Present and Robot', EURON Workshop on Roboethics, Genoa, March 2006; Levy, D., 'Love and Sex With Robots', Harper Collins, New York, 2007.
15. *Legal Futures* Special Report – 'Innovation in the City: The quiet revolution' – which is now available in association with Thomson Reuters. See: www.legalfutures.co.uk/reports.
16. Burn-Callander, R., 'Bankers beware: City 'will soon be run by robots', *Sunday Telegraph*, 31 August 2014, see: www.telegraph.co.uk/finance/newsbysector/mediatechnologyandtelecoms/electronics/11067077/Bankers-beware-City-will-soon-be-run-by-robots.html.
17. See: www.bloomberg.com/news/2013-11-25/fluid-s-watson-powered-shopping-app-will-debut-next-year.html.
18. European Lawyers Association AGM September 2014, Jersey: 'Law Firms in the 21st Century: The Art of Reinvention in a Digital, Silicon & Robotic Legal World' plenary Q&A session.
19. @SJ_weekly: 'Gen Y(LAL): a lost generation of legal aid lawyers?' See: www.solicitorsjournal.com/comment/gen-ylal-lost-generation-legal-aid-lawyers.
20. $45B: Estimated demand of low-middle income earners priced out of expensive legal services. Shan Li, 'Technology is bringing legal advice and documents to the masses', see: www.latimes.com/business/la-fi-legal-startups-20140218-story.html#axzz2uLvgNRB7&page=1.
21. See: www.lawgazette.co.uk/law/judge-rages-at-grotesque-leeching-of-costs-in-divorce/5045058.article.

22. 'Coming to an office near you – The effect of today's technology on tomorrow's jobs will be immense – and no country is ready for it', *The Economist*, 18 January 2014, see: www.economist.com/news/leaders/21594298-effect-todays-technology-tomorrows-jobs-will-be-immenseand-no-country-ready?fsrc=scn/tw/te/pe/comingtoanofficenearyour. 'Artificial intelligence meets the C-suite', McKinsey & Company, September 2014, see: www.mckinsey.com/insights/strategy/artificial_intelligence_meets_the_c-suite. Matther Wall, 'Could a big data-crunching machine be your boss one day?', BBC News, 9 October 2014, see: www.bbc.co.uk/news/business-29456257.
23. Pullen, J.P., 'Why You Should Revolt Against the 'Robot Uprising'', *Entrepreneur*, 20 January 2014, see: www.entrepreneur.com/article/230887.
24. David Bain in an article by Monidipa Fouzder in *The Law Society Gazette*, 23 Oct 2014: 'Robots running law firms? Surely not.' See: www.lawgazette.co.uk/analysis/comment-and-opinion/robots-running-law-firms-surely-not/5044479.article.
25. See: www.newsweek.com/art-steal-copyright-retreat-283118?utm_campaign=3-3-7%20Social%20Media%20Campaign&utm_content=9689995&utm_medium=social&utm_source=linkedin.
26. Ustaran, E., *The Future of Privacy*, Data Guidance, London 2013.
27. Quoting yogic philosopher Patanjali.

Chapter 7: the age of magic and miracles

'I'd rather be a poor happy soul without you, than a wealthy tormented soul with you.'
Chrissie Lightfoot

I PROMISED you an enjoyable final chapter during which you can relax and have some fun. So here we go…

Permit me to serenade and waltz you gently through this final chapter beginning with a quick recap of the key themes, messages, concepts, practicalities/tips/insights, and future thinking that I have shared with you throughout this sequel to *the naked lawyer*, a book that, as Stephen Mayson wrote in the Foreword to this sequel, pioneered and 'went where no-one else had quite been before'.

I have endeavoured to stretch the boundaries yet again throughout *tomorrow's naked lawyer* with the variety of ideas and solutions I share with you – underpinned by the ROAR platform and the new themes of 'uncertainty', 'contrast', 'challenge', and 'opportunity' – as we look in detail at topics such as 'the future', 'technology', 'AI', 'robotics', 'entrepreneurialism', 'social', and 'humanness' (SocialHuman).

I hope that at least one thing resonated with you as you danced through the introductory pages of this book – whether it was that you felt that sometimes the law can be an arse or that you could appreciate that in order to be a successful lawyer of tomorrow, today (aka 'tomorrow's naked lawyer') and/or successful in business and/or life, I reckon you need to:

- KISS: Keep It Sexily Serendipitous;
- KISS: Keep it Salubriously Serene; and
- KISS: Keep It Socially Savvy;

Similarly, I trust that a few things touched you in the first three chapters, where I paint a picture of our new and sexy law law land now and in the 'futuristic' robotic new world that we will all indeed face, supported by opinion, reports, forecasts, and data. I offered a number of insights into how we can bring some certainty into our world in these uncertain times and how you can be a real player in the imminent Age of Unlawyering.

With the plethora of challenges that lie ahead in a global marketplace where:

- Marketing is dead – Superseded by robot hits (marketing automation) and SocialHuman;
- Intimacy, service, branding, and reputation matter most; and
- The inevitable rise of the iCyborg lawyer and robot lawyer due to IBM's Watson-type AI technology and Ray Kurzweil's notion of the singularity.

Never has it been more important to 'get naked' and 'sound human' as we take on board the inevitable balancing act that is and will be required in embracing our humanness together with the technologies available in our drive to make our working, family, and leisure lives more comfortable and successful. All this while being cognisant of the dangers in the potential 'run-away' intelligence of the machines and its effect on society, law, and order.

The time is now to ask the question 'are we heading toward utopia or travelling along a dangerous road leading straight to hell?' And for policy-makers and law-makers to take steps to do something about it, now. It is because of this 'technology < > human' dilemma and inter-play that I passionately believe we lawyers need to take more risks for 'a life without risk is like no life at all'.

It's okay to be fearful. Tough challenges necessitate fierce courage. And that's okay, for as Mark Twain said, 'Courage is resistance to fear, mastery of fear, not absence of fear.'

In order to be prepared for the new world and to succeed and grow in it, we need to embark on new (and in some ways sophisticated) methods of training aided by technology and smart software – the likes of gamification, resonance, vibe intelligence, and psycho-lawyernetics – to attain the skills that are, and will be required, in this Digital Age and the ensuing Robotic Age. This was the focus of Chapters 4 and 5.

This, in turn, requires the educational and training establishment – the school of law and the business of law – to adapt, change and reinvent how it prepares its tomorrow's naked lawyers for the period 2015–2045. Fortunately, this transition is occurring in parts throughout the world, pioneered by Miami School of Law, which is managing to indoctrinate its entrepreneurial business minded law students who are then infiltrating law law land and beginning to break down the old ivory towers and walls.

And, there a number of businesses of law that are experimenting with gamification and other methods and processes of learning (such as the ROAR behaviour model) to help their lawyers be more productive and SocialHuman smart (recall the case studies I shared with you in Chapter 5?).

But there is much more still to do and to be done as we endure the relentless march of industrialisation, wearable technology, accelerating machine intelligence, and robotics in law law land and 'social land', culminating in our questioning of what it now means to be 'human'.

Indeed, the concept of lawyers becoming entrepreneurial – which I kicked off back in 2008 with the personal brand 'The Entrepreneur Lawyer' followed by the company and website EntrepreneurLawyer Limited (in 2009) – has become a reality. It has taken hold and we are now experiencing a tsunami of entrepreneurial lawyers and intrapreneurial lawyers in law law land, evidenced by the many reports and the number of businesses of law that have embraced this notion along with the need to focus on marketing, networking, and using technology smartly. Consequently, these entrepreneurial businesses are experiencing superior growth in contrast to their competitors.

The message to become an entrepreneurial lawyer is now old-hat, IMHO. It's here now. So let's stretch the boundaries and innovate again. And so, my new message with regard to how you can be successful in your career, business, love, and life, is to be a SocialHuman Lawyer by:

- Embracing NewTech;
- Embracing NewHuman; and
- Pioneering in NewLaw.

Technological advancements are pushing the boundaries of our 'humanness', and I delight in posing some 'challenging and uncomfortable questions' in Chapter 6 (politely worded in Professor Mayson's Foreword, I say).

Okay, I admit… I dabble with some ideas that may seem 'dangerous' when debating the ethics of robot hooker, robot wife, porn law, and law on Mars. It may well be viewed by some of you as pushing the boundaries a wee bit far. But 'an idea that is not dangerous is unworthy of being called an idea at all', as Oscar Wilde once said.

Nevertheless, you get my point in relation to where AI and robotic development is likely headed, both positively and negatively, rightly or wrongly, ethically or unethically, in the workplace, home, and society, inevitably requiring the attention of policy-makers and law-makers globally, nationally, and (where applicable) state/region wide. We need to get a grip of existing laws and in some respect we need to create new laws that are fitting for the Digital, Robotic, and Interstellar Ages.

For in this Age of Magic and Miracles, nothing is certain, but anything is possible.

it's a miracle...

What is? LIFE! We're still trying to figure out how 'life' began and its meaning, particularly as we now have some of the technology which may in fact unlock the secret – well, perhaps 'how life began', that is, but the answer to why we really exist is yet to be determined.

I guess we lawyers could contemplate the same question. For Stephen Mayson is quite right to comment in his Foreword that I am indeed encouraging you to 'think about what it *really* means to be a lawyer (and what it will mean to be a *real* lawyer) in the 21st century'.

But let us not forget that in these uncertain times and our hyper-competitive, challenging, and transitioning legal ecosystem 'with all its sham, drudgery and broken dreams, it is still a beautiful world'.[1] Perhaps we need to remind ourselves to stand and stare sometimes. Reflect. And perhaps we may come to realise that self-discovery and building and enjoying relationships IS the meaning of LIFE and lawyering, in the present and future.

It's why I encourage you to ROAR! And if this is so, then with respect to every person you come into contact with, in either a professional or personal capacity, you should ask of yourself the following question: 'Have you come into my life for a reason, a season, or a lifetime'?

Those of you who read *the naked lawyer* may recall I shared this with you then. Why? Because I'm curious. I'm hungry to know. I desire to continually learn... and I want to grow as a human being.

I engage in relationships, not knowing the answer to the above question, but I go about developing the relationship trying to figure out whether it is for a reason, a season, or a lifetime. When I do figure out which one it is, I know what to do for each person, and realise what they have done for me... and for that, I am grateful. For those of you who are in my life, past and present, THANK YOU.

And for those of you who are about to enter my life, HELLO! I'm looking forward to ROARing with you and celebrating LIFE!!!

comfort from uncertainty

Uncertainty is a fabulous thing, I reckon. Uncertainty makes us feel alive! It is uncertainty that fires us up to take action and forces us to get AIG. It's what changes the status-quo, drives exploration, adventure, innovation, and invention, prods and pokes us to take risks in finding solutions to problems, to grow, and to dance. Prrrrrrrrrrrrrr.

Apparently, the level of certainty impacts the way we make decisions. We take fewer risks when there is ambiguity. Uncertainty decreases reward and increases the emotional activity in the limbic system. This results in a built-in bias toward uncertainty to avoid the sense of threat.

At times of change, such as these, there is often a reduction of certainty and an inability to predict what will happen. The brain looks for patterns. If the anticipated pattern is as expected, we feel a sense of reward and dopamine is released. If the pattern is not as expected, an error message is generated and discomfort is felt. This probably helps to explain why we grab on to certainties for comfort until the next uncertainty needs dealing with!

I hope you can draw some comfort from the certainties and patterns that I have shared with you throughout *tomorrow's naked lawyer.*

joy in contrast

Contrast is a perplexing thing, but it provides us with equilibrium in what would otherwise be an overwhelmingly topsy-turvy, imbalanced world. One of the greatest contrasts (and enigmas!) is man and woman, IMHO. Yes, we are different… very different. I doubt any of us would disagree or argue… And therein lies uncertainty, challenge, and joy for both genders in our professional and personal lives!

We know, of course, which is the dominant gender in law law land and the business world across the globe, rightly or wrongly, ethically or unethically… it is what it is. I still find it remarkable that we lady lawyers are paid less than our male counterparts for doing the exact same job here in the UK in some businesses of law, when we possess the same level of IC and EI (and sometimes superior) and are delivering the same output (and sometimes superior). I'm incredulous.

If one good thing comes from robot lawyering it is simply this… It will be a level robot playing field in law law land. No longer will gender bias remain for Robot Lawyer. Whether the robot lawyer is a malebot or fembot, it will be doing the same job/role, its IC and EI will be of the same processing power and intelligence, its outputs will be the same, and it will be paid the same – that is, zero.

Great news for the business of law – less internal sex/age/race/gender discrimination claims perhaps; and great news for the client/consumer – assuming the cost savings are passed onto the client.

But until such time, it remains a MAN's commercial world, in general, across all nations.

Until the time comes that men grow a uterus, have a mindset shift lobotomy in relation to gender equality in the workplace, within society and in the home, globally, it will probably continue to be what it will be.

THAT debate aside, for I'm a lover not a fighter, we ought to celebrate this human contrast in biology, psychology, EI, and subsequent behaviour. In particular, we naked lady lawyers ought to celebrate our womanly attributes, I reckon. We ought to be proud of our achievements in facing the constant challenges and uncertainties in law law land and beyond.

And speaking of celebrating, did you know that International Women's Day is held every year on March 8th? Each year those who get involved share interesting facts about women. Permit me to share some with you now:

- International Women's Day was first observed worldwide in 1909;
- According to an ancient Sumerian legend, the universe was created by a female, the goddess Tiamat. This role of a female creator is not unique, as the Australian Aboriginal creation myth also credits the creation of life to a woman;
- The biological sign for the female sex, a circle placed on top of a small cross, is also the symbol for the planet Venus. The symbol is believed to be a stylized representation of the Roman goddess Venus' hand mirror;

- While many stars and moons are christened with female names, Venus is the only planet in our solar system given the name of a female goddess;
- The probability of a woman giving birth to a baby girl instead of a baby boy increases significantly the nearer the mother lives to the equator. While the cause of this gender selection is unknown, scientists believe the constant sunlight hours and abundant food supply in tropical regions may favour female births;
- In almost every country worldwide, the life expectancy for women is higher than for men;
- The word 'woman' is believed to have derived from the Middle English term *wyfman*, meaning the wife (*wyf*) of man. In Old English, women were described simply as *wyf*, while the term *man* was used to describe a human person, regardless of gender;
- The English language originally differentiated between women in different stages of life with the terms 'maiden', 'mother', and 'crone'. A maiden referred to a young girl who was unmarried, a mother referred to a woman in her child-bearing years, and a crone described a post-menopausal woman;
- The English word 'girl' was initially used to describe a young person of either sex. It was not until the beginning of the sixteenth century that the term was used specifically to describe a female child;
- The first woman to run for US president was Victoria Woodhull, who campaigned for the office in 1872 under the National Woman's Suffrage Association. While women would not be granted the right to vote by a constitutional amendment for nearly 50 years, there were no laws prohibiting a woman from running for the chief executive position;
- The first country to grant women the right to vote in the modern era was New Zealand in 1893;
- The first woman to rule a country as an elected leader in the modern era was Sirimavo Bandaranaike of Sri Lanka (previously named Ceylon), who was elected as prime minister of the island nation in 1960 and later re-elected in 1970;
- The two highest IQ's ever recorded (on a standard test) both belong to women; and
- The world's first novel, *The Tale of Genji*, was published in Japan around A.D. 1000 by female author Murasaki Shikibu.

What does all this mean? We definitely live in and on a topsy-turvy Earth where women really are from Venus and men are from Mars. But that's okay ladies. It sounds like we'll be able to rocket launch all the men back there within the next eight years!

The gravestone of W.C. Fields reads: 'All things considered, I'd rather be in Philadelphia'.

Reflecting on all the good things women have done, and will continue to do for mankind, I reckon mine will read: 'All things considered, this naked lawyer was glad to be woman. See you on Mars!'

rising to a challenge

Moving on from the challenges that we lady lawyers – and ladies as a whole – face, but remaining with the theme, I'd like to share with you now a lesson in business, leisure, love, and life from an ambidextrous lady golfer. As we're all adults here, I'm sure you'll receive this in the good humour in which it is intended:

A group of guys lived and died for their Saturday morning round of golf. (Sound familiar?)
One transferred to another city. It wasn't the same without him.
A new woman joined their club. She overheard the guys talking about their golf round.
She said, 'You know, I used to play on my golf team in college and I was pretty good.
Would you mind if I joined you next week?'
The three guys looked at each other. Not one of them wanted to say 'yes', but she had them on the spot.
Finally, one man said it would be okay, but they would be starting early – at 6:30 a.m.
He figured the early tee-time would discourage her. (As if!)
The woman said this might be a problem, and asked if she could be up to 15 minutes late.
They rolled their eyes, but said okay.
She smiled and said, 'Good, I'll be there at 6:30 or 6:45.'
She showed up at 6:30 sharp, and beat all three of them with an eye-opening two-under-par round.
She was fun and a pleasant person, and the guys were impressed.
Back at the clubhouse, they congratulated her and invited her back the next week.
She smiled, and said, 'I'll be there at 6:30 or 6:45'.
The next week she again showed up at 6:30 sharp. Only this time she played left-handed.
The three guys were incredulous as she still beat them with an even par round, despite playing with her off-hand.
They were totally amazed. They couldn't figure her out.
She was again very pleasant and didn't seem to be purposely showing them up.
They invited her back again, but each man harboured a burning desire to beat her. (Really?)
The third week, the guys had their game faces on.
But this time she was 15 minutes late, which made the guys irritable.
This week the lady played right-handed, and narrowly beat all three of them.
The men mused that her late arrival was due to petty gamesmanship on her part. However, she was so gracious and so complimentary of their strong play, they couldn't hold a grudge.
Back in the clubhouse, all three guys were shaking their heads. This woman was a riddle no one could figure out.
They had a couple of beers, and finally, one of the men asked her point blank: 'How do you decide if you're going to golf right-handed or left-handed?'
The lady blushed, and grinned. 'That's easy', she said. 'When my Dad taught me to play golf, I learned I was ambidextrous. I like to switch back and forth. When I got married after college, I discovered my husband always sleeps in the nude. From then on, I developed a silly habit. Right before I left in the morning for golf practice, I would pull the covers off him. If his you-know-what was pointing to the right, I golfed right-handed; if it was pointed to the left, I golfed left-handed.'
The guys on the team thought this was hysterical.
Astonished at this bizarre information, one of the guys shot back,
'But what if it's pointing straight up?'
She said…
'Then, I'm fifteen minutes late.'

The lesson? BE PREPARED for any challenge that lies ahead and NEVER miss an OPPORTUNITY. When challenges arise you must be creative in your approach to business, leisure, love, life, sport, and law. When you do you're more likely to emerge a winner! For example:

- A good lawyer knows the law. A great lawyer knows the judge!
- A good lawyer knows the law. A better lawyer knows ways around it!

Just kidding, btw. Prrrrrrrrrrrrrrrrrrrr.

era of opportunity

I attended a legal conference hosted by Neil Rose of *Legal Futures* entitled 'era of the entrepreneur' a few weeks prior to this book being released wherein a number of entrepreneurs in a variety of businesses of law shared their views and insights as to what opportunities lie ahead in law law land. Here is a quick summary:

- 'The opportunity is for law firms to focus on the consumer rather than asking what the lawyers and law firm want.' (Eddie Ross, CEO, Quality Solicitors). A message conveyed at least five years ago by me and others – now old-hat.
- 'People focus too much on the technical in law firms. The technical delivery is taken for granted by the consumer. It's all the other bits that the legal industry has the opportunity to work on.' (Eddie Ross, CEO, Quality Solicitors.) Another message conveyed at least five years ago by me and others – now old-hat.
- The mindset of the entrepreneurial lawyer is that 'there is no opportunity that they're not able to go for.' (Jon Whittle, marketing development director, LexisNexis.) Yet another message conveyed at least five years ago – now old-hat.
- Similarly, the mindset of an investor is there is no opportunity that they are not able to go for now in law law land due to the LSA 2007, ABS, and the fact that it is now an 'interesting sector' which has the likes of Keystone Law with its 'investable business model, impressive track record, strong leadership and team' (Simon Philips, managing partner, Root Capital – investor in Keystone Law) and 'happy lawyers' (William Robins, partner, Keystone Law). Ah, at last – how refreshing!

This following comment by a sceptical investor who is more risk adverse sums up the opportunity nicely, IMHO, for investor companies such as Root Capital which recognise the potential reward ahead that comes with investing in Keystone Law (and other businesses of law perhaps):

'I look forward to you making the business case. Sceptical. In principle, I quite like the idea of revolutionising the legal market. But it's stodgy. And no growth. And I thought we were already over-lawyered in the UK and, if so, the revolution will be slow. But I am sure you will prove me wrong…'[3]

Indeed, if the concept of lawyers becoming entrepreneurial – and entrepreneurs operating within the industry within established law firms or new sexy businesses of law with new sexy models in new sexy markets – is now old-hat, for we are already in the Age of the Entrepreneurial Lawyer, IMHO, and private equity houses and private investors are now interested in investing in businesses of law, I put it to you that law law land now represents an 'era of opportunity' where magic and miracles truly will happen, can happen, and do happen!

magic in the courtroom

When I mentioned Google Glass earlier in the book many of you may no doubt have been wondering how this gizmo thingy could actually work in your favour, right now, in your daily lawyering role and activities?

Well, the answer to this lies partially in an article written by Mitch Jackson called 'How Trial Lawyers Will Use Google Glass to Select Juries and Win Cases!' Mitch has kindly agreed to share his article and insights with you here[4]:

'Your trial judge looks over to you sitting at the counsel table. "Counsel, would you like to begin your voir dire?"

You stand up, thank the court, and walk over to the lectern. On your way over you say the command, "jury on" and your Google Glass comes to life. Instantly in the top section of your screen, a diagram with each juror's name is displayed. On the bottom half is your voir dire outline. Only you can see what's being displayed.

While you make direct eye contact with your potential jurors, the video function of Google Glass goes live and your entire voir dire is captured for later review and analysis. At the same time, the live password protected video stream is sent via Wi-Fi back to your office for young associates to watch and learn how to pick a jury. At a separate location on the other side of the country, jury consultants are also watching and listening to each question and answer.

As you look at juror number 1 sitting in front of you to your left, you start the dialog by asking, Ms Jones, "Is anyone in your family a doctor?"

Almost immediately Ms. Jones' profile pops up on the small screen above your eye. In this case, you've activated a third party app that uses facial recognition to identify people you look at and to access a special trial lawyer database that depending on your subscription, accesses a system similar to Lexis or Westlaw.

Using your touchpad placed on top of the lectern, you select "social" to switch from the current database to "Glass Social Summary" that displays an easy to read summary of Ms. Jones latest social media and blog posts.

As you ask your questions, you are immediately made aware of the fact that this juror's cousin is a cardiologist at UCLA Medical Center. When Ms. Jones answers your original question with a "no", you then follow up with "how about extended family members?" Ms. Jones smiles and happily reports that her cousin is a doctor at UCLA. The questions and dialog continue.

A text notice pops up on your private Google Glass screen while you're talking to Ms. Jones. The jury consultant who is also watching the live video feed doesn't like what she's seeing or listening to. She sends you the term "bump" indicating you'll want to eventually get rid of this juror with a challenge.

Rather than looking down and tapping your touchpad, you simply say "switch" and your Google Glass accesses the new court authorized jury person database (CAJPD). As with everything else at the courthouse, the paper juror information lists are a thing of the past. Today, counsel has limited access to CAJPD. Home, work and prior jury service details instantly fill your confidential screen. Because of the information made available to you through this technology, you spend less time than you normally would with this particular juror and move on to the next.

During the process, your designated legal associate back at the office shares thoughts, feedback and even a few questions via your Google Glass screen. You use several of the suggestions to complete your voir dire.

Before sitting down, you voice activate the "final step" command and your Google Glass runs a final program that automatically initiates an almost instant "accuracy" search for each person you questioned during jury selection. During your voir dire, everything that's been discussed has been automatically recorded and indexed by the related Google Glass "index" service. In this case, you're looking for inaccuracies between what's been represented to you by a prospective juror and what your databases show.

Several blue and green hits come back. A third hit is marked bright red. Earlier Mr. Green, juror #11, indicated he had never been in trouble with the law. The red hit tells you his memory is, shall we say, a bit lacking today. When asked by the judge at the beginning of voir dire, this gentleman neglected to acknowledge any prior criminal convictions.

Your automatic Google Glass "index" conflict search reveals that in truth, Mr. Green has been arrested and convicted several times for driving under the influence. Once in California and once in Nevada. Another "bump" message pops up on your Google Glass screen from your consultant. You think to yourself: "Really. Didn't think I'd figure that one out on my own did you?"

You eventually sit back down at the counsel table with a much more thorough understanding of exactly who your potential jurors are. Back at the office, your new young associates now have a better idea about what good jury selection looks like. Your jury consultant on the other side of the United States also is in the process of sending "Glass Updates" (similar to email or text) to your Google Glass screen to help you make some final decisions after opposing counsel is finished with his voir dire.

You did all this while maintaining eye contact with your jurors and never once looking down at your notes. Because of what has become a standard pre-trial motion *in limine* to exclude the mention that either counsel is using Google Glass, your potential jurors were not aware that counsel was taking advantage of this technology.

The entire jury selection process took less time while providing a more meaningful dialog. All counsel, parties and the court now have a much better understanding of who is sitting in the jury box. And that's a good thing. After all, isn't that what jury selection is really all about?'

Whether your area of law is contentious or non-contentious in nature, I'm confident you now have a better understanding of how this wearable tech could benefit you and your business of law, greatly. This is just one example of NewTech in operation, where the coming together of 'technology and human' provides an opportunity for you to be more productive and successful, IF you embrace it. Imagine if you embrace it along with all the other NewTech, AI, and robotics as and when they become available in the open market-place.

change your world or change the world?

I attended a brilliant and stimulating futurist seminar one evening at the turn of the year in London. I remember sitting there and thinking about the opportunity mankind has for creating a better world if we as a civilisation could really get our act together collaboratively across the globe and not only RETHINK and REINVENT our systems (social, economic, political, subsistence, and legal) but actually DO IT… fast!

Mankind will have the technology, intelligence, and will have achieved the scientific breakthroughs required to solve all of our worldly problems in the next 30 years BUT…and it's a MEGA HUGE BUT… unless there is a fundamental shift in human nature and behaviour, for example, to spurn our proclivity for the seven deadly sins, I suspect that the acceleration toward singularity may in fact be a hellish burden rather than a heavenly blessing.

Accordingly, we need to appreciate our LIFE and address HOW we each live it, now, before it is no longer our choice and we are no longer masters of our own mutiny. The machine intelligence/robot may indeed create a cataclysmic mutiny of our own making – but this is for discussion in my next book, perhaps.

Your life is happening now, today – not tomorrow or some distant far off future. You have to learn to really live it, now, while at the same time preparing yourself for the likely future and how you want it to be for you by investing in yourself, now. If this requires re-inventing yourself and/or your career and/or your business, then so be it.

The phrase life is what happens to you while you're busy making other plans was penned in the 1950s. Most of us recognise the expression courtesy of John Lennon, who adopted and crafted it into the splendid song 'Beautiful Boy (Darling Boy)' from 1980, hence making it 'his'. There was magic to his genius.

But let's get back to another genius who is crafting things: YOU! You, as either a tomorrow's naked lawyer, an entrepreneurial founder of a new business of law, an intrapreneur within an existing business of law, an investor with a keen eye for spotting opportunity, or a buyer of legal services who indulges in a little 'self-lawyering'[5] demanding value for your hard-earned money and precious time.

You are so busy reacting and battling with the uncertainties and challenges in 2014/15 that you have lost touch with the genius, the beauty, the joy inside you and your raison d'être. You have no doubt lost touch with the meaning of life; that very thing that you are so busy creating, even if you don't realise it… YOU.

Self-discovery and self-actualisation cannot occur in a non-stop, chaotic, threatening, uncertain, challenging, constantly reactive, and accelerating environment where you are continually switched 'on'. It's time to STOP, flick the switch and smell the roses. I mean, really smell them…

Really ask yourself what it means to be a *real* lawyer/entrepreneur/etc., now and into your future. You might come to the realisation that you don't even know what the beauty and joy of it all is any more, so you will have to step back to re-define what it means to you: now, today.

You have it within yourself to change YOUR WORLD. Truly. Take a look again at *the naked lawyer*. It will help you with this process. And for some of you, you hold the key to change THE WORLD for the better, I have no doubt. You may achieve this in your role as a legal practitioner, a law-maker, legal futurist, investor, intrapreneur, or entrepreneur within the legal industry or beyond. It will no doubt necessitate a leap of brand, a leap of faith, and a leap of re-thinking what is important to you in your life, not unlike the journey I myself went through five years ago and the journey of Adam Herscher who left Microsoft to launch his own Seattle based tech start-up company called HasMetrics nine months ago.

As you are aware, you will find my story in *the naked lawyer*. But I will share a little of Adam's who posted his on LinkedIn recently. It's a highly entertaining, touching, and motivating read:

When Adam told a few of his co-workers at Microsoft that he had one foot out of the door (of his own choosing) the most common reaction was something he described as a cross between admiration and 'Are you insane? You're just *going to* walk away from the *pay check*? I could never do it.'

This resonates with me as I experienced the same reaction from my lawyer co-workers. No doubt it resonates with you too?

The blunt response by his closest friend during a long walk when he was reflecting on life said it all: 'I just really love the f***ing money.'

Though a bit cliché, changing the world was what originally sold Adam on creating products at Microsoft. Similarly, it was why I became a practising lawyer; I wanted to change the world for entrepreneurs buying legal services.

Over time though, Adam began to 'feel real differences between starting something on a team of hundreds… versus starting something where you personally pour your heart and soul into all that's required to earn the business and trust of your first customers… I'd had a small taste of the latter in past start-up life, and found myself craving the unique experience, challenge, and exponential learning curve that are intrinsic in it.'

Again, I empathise. Adam did indeed leave Microsoft. He's never looked back. Start-up life so far is what he expected and more:

'I feel appreciation toward all my friends and colleagues at Microsoft who gave me the opportunity to learn and grow, and to the company itself for the resources and opportunities it afforded me as well. This really can't be overstated. And at the same time, I know there are so many brilliant minds out there aspiring to start their own thing, change the world—who haven't yet found the courage or opportune time to do so—particularly in the Seattle area where larger companies play a major role in the tech & business ecosystem.'

Similarly, I shared the same appreciation for my colleagues in law law land back in 2009 and I am greatly aware of the many hugely talented lawyers with genius minds aspiring to do their own thing and change the world, but they haven't yet found the courage or opportune time to do so, particularly in the UK where entrepreneurism is supported in the business and legal ecosystem.

I left law law land as a practising lawyer for all the same reasons that most entrepreneurial types move on; as I say, my story is in the prequel to this book so you can read it there if you're interested. I also felt that if I couldn't change the world by working within a law firm, I was going to attempt to change it by getting out!

This book is also dedicated to you if you have thought about, or are currently thinking about, leaving your corporate lawyerly job for start-up land. If your situation is anything like mine was back in 2009, I'd highly encourage it. It's now been five years since I departed and I haven't looked back once.

In fact, what spurred me on was my mindset: 'I'd rather be a poor happy soul without you, than a wealthy tormented soul with you' in reference to the legal profession and all that is frustrating and wrong with it. Good news: by no means am I poor with regard to income, friendship, stimulating work, and fulfilment, as I sit here today, writing and dancing with you. Prrrrrrrrrrrrrrrrr.

Yes, starting up your own business is challenging. HUGELY. And the challenges never disappear, btw. Yes, you will be overwhelmed by the waves of uncertainty… in the beginning… but the number of waves ebb and flow, eventually subside, and the height of them reduces as the months and years progress.

But in contrast, founding your own company offers opportunities beyond your wildest imaginings… Ultimately, you create the opportunity to not only change your own world; you have it within your sole power and control to change the world.

I am often asked 'Chrissie, how do you remain motivated and inspired in your vision and in running your own business?' Being absolutely honest with you the answer is that during these challenging and uncertain times it's the mixed bag of appreciation, gratitude, and admiration I receive from clients/customers, colleagues, friends, family, and boyfriend (not necessarily in that order, but roughly so), and in particular the humorous comments from complete strangers I've never met, such as the one reported by my boyfriend at the dinner table recently: 'Tell that girlfriend of yours to just keep pedalling.'

I believe it is pertinent both literally and metaphorically!

after dark activity

Graham Green once said: 'Eventually we have to open the door and let the future in.' Are you ready?

In the Christian religion and calendar, Christmas is a time for the embracing of tradition, magic, and miracles. Just as children ask their friends the question 'do you believe in Santa?', perhaps you should quietly now muse… 'Do I believe?'

Not in Santa (no disrespect intended Santa if you do exist, I hasten to add) but in the possibility of magic and miracles pervading our homes, offices, relationships, and lives at any time of year. If tradition and magic can sit comfortably together in the celebration of Christmas, then it's perfectly feasible that tradition and magic can sit comfortably in law law land, do you reckon?

Traditional lawyering and law together with traditional technology and traditional methods of marketing and networking can blend and exist harmoniously with SocialHuman lawyering together with NewTech, NewHuman, and NewLaw as they evolve.

The rate of acceptance in this Digital Age in embracing technology, AI, and robotics and the transition toward an AI and Robotic Age may vary incrementally across jurisdictions, nations, and cultures but one thing shall remain constant: the human spirit. The world and law law land will remain human and social. Our human spirit will differentiate man from machine, in whatever guise.

And so, I shall leave you now to figure out your own reason, season, lifetime conundrum, and to ponder how life began and what its meaning is, for yourself personally, for mankind, and for law and order on planet Earth and beyond. That should keep you occupied until the next *naked lawyer* book hits the cosmos!

just do something!

Believe!
Keep pedalling!!
And keep dancing!!!

References

1. From Max Ehrmann's 1927 poem 'Desiderata'.
2. See Hills, J., Hanson, L., and North, S., *Brain-Savvy Leading: Neuroscience, Tips and Tools*, Head Heart + Brain, London 2014.
3. From a slide shared by Root Capital.
4. Quoting Mitch Jackson of Jackson Wilson Law Firm in his article for the firm website, 'How Trial Lawyers Will Use Google Glass to Select Juries and Win Cases!', 23 April 2013. See http://jacksonandwilson.com/google-glass/.
5. 'Self-lawyering' is the phrase used to describe people making their own way through the legal system and doing more for themselves. They are people/clients/consumers who are attempting to do an element of their legal work themselves to save time and money; elements which were once solely the domain of a lawyer; unbundling has become more commonplace where lawyers will do a part of the entire legal matter and the client will do the remainder.

afterword

what's next?

Meet the team...

I'd like to introduce you to the experts who work alongside me so please visit: www.entrepreneurlawyer.co.uk/about/experts-who

get in touch

If you enjoyed reading *tomorrow's naked lawyer* and, in particular, if you followed the 'just do something' advice throughout, I'd love to hear how you're getting along. Should you decide to sign up for the e-ntrepreneur bullet newsletter (found on the EntrepreneurLawyer website, www.entrepreneurlawyer.co.uk/) you will have the opportunity to enjoy 15 minutes of FREE consultation with me via skype in relation to *tomorrow's naked lawyer.* My skype handle: chrissie.lightfoot.

Please do feel moved to ping me...

I'd be delighted to have the opportunity to begin building an enduring professional relationship with you.

If you'd like to do likewise, then please contact, connect, link, join, follow, and get involved in one (or all) of the following ways:

- Email: chrissie@entrepreneurlawyer.co.uk
- Website: www.entrepreneurlawyer.co.uk
- Blog: www.entrepreneurlawyer.co.uk/blog
- LinkedIn: https://www.linkedin.com/in/chrissielightfoot
- Twitter: https://twitter.com/thenakedlawyer
- Facebook: www.facebook.com/EntrepreneurLawyer
- LinkedIn Group – The Entrepreneur Lawyer Relationship Sales Network: www.linkedin.com/groups/Entrepreneur-Lawyer-Relationship-Sales-Network-2874570

Feel free to let colleagues and/or friends know about *tomorrow's naked lawyer* if you believe it will be of interest, benefit, and/or value to them.

I also welcome you to link to the EntrepreneurLawyer website – www.entrepreneurlawyer.co.uk – if you find the information in *tomorrow's naked lawyer* valuable and believe your website and users would benefit from it.

get naked

tomorrow's naked lawyer and *the naked lawyer* are the sum total of my life's knowledge, experience, skills, and talent that I have shared unreservedly with those of you who wish to take control of your career, business, and life in a positive way.

I hope you found either (or both) of them enlightening and that the series brought and continues to bring you many hours and years of both professional and personal, development, success, and fun... Please do keep in touch with me on your travels and life journey... and remember... Be happy!

Warmest regards

Chrissie Lightfoot

The Entrepreneur Lawyer (of the naked kind)

glossary

ABS	alternative business structures
AI	artificial intelligence
AIG	ass in gear
BCI	brain computer interface
Bitcoins	cryptocurrency
Blawg	blog by a lawyer, usually with a legal angle
BTW	by the way
CRM	customer relationship management
CMS	content management system
DM	direct message
EI	emotional intelligence
EQ	emotional quotient
EY	Ernst & Young
FMSP	Formidable Me Strategy & Plan
GSOH	good sense of humour
IMHO	in my humble opinion
IC	intellectual capital
IQ	intelligence quotient
IFA	independent financial adviser
IP	intellectual property
Law Law Land	the legal world/profession/industry
LIC	lawyerly intellectual capital
LOL	laugh out loud
LSA	Legal Services Act 2007
Peeps	web term used to describe people
POD	points of difference
ROAR	acronym for 'reach out and relate'
Robodites	term used as reference to a human being who resists the robot movement and evolution
ROI	return on investment/involvement
ROTF	roll on the floor
RT	retweet
SCRM	social customer relationship management
Semantic web	semantic web is a group of methods and technologies to allow machines to understand the meaning – or 'semantics' – of information on the internet
SEO	search engine optimisation

SM	social media
SME	small/medium sized enterprise/company
SN	social networking
SMSN	social media and social networking
SocialHuman	term for a human being embracing SMSN and optimizing social capital and human capital throughout life in both work and leisure
SSO	social search optimisation
SWOT	strengths, weaknesses, opportunities, threats
USP	unique selling point

inspiration

books

Abramson, B., Digital Phoenix: *Why the Information Economy Collapsed and How It Will Rise Again*, MIT Press, Cambridge, Mass., 2005.

Anderson, C., *The Long Tail: How Endless Choice is Creating Unlimited Demand*, Random House, London, 2006.

Bakan, J., *The Corporation: The Pathological Pursuit of Profit and Power*, Constable, London, 2004.

Beaton, G., *NewLaw New Rules: A Conversation About the Future of the Legal Services Industry*, Beaton Capital, Australia, 2013.

Blanchard, K., *Whale Done! The Power Of Positive Relationships*, The Free Press, New York, 2002.

Bostrum, N., *Superintelligence: Paths, Dangers, Strategies*, OUP, Oxford, 2014.

Bounds, A., *The Jelly Effect: How To Make Communications Stick*, Capstone Publishing Ltd., Chichester, 2007.

Branson, R., *Like A Virgin: Secrets They Won't Teach You at Business School*, Virgin Books, London, 2012.

Brogan, C., *Social Media 101: Tactics and Tips to Develop Your Business Online*, John Wiley & Sons Inc., New Jersey, 2010.

Brown, R., *Defy Gravity: Propel Your Business to High-velocity Growth*, Greenleaf Book Group Press, Austin, Texas, 2010.

Bryan, L. et al, *Race For The World: Strategies To Build A Great Global Firm*, HBR Press, Boston, MA, 1999.

Burg, B., *Endless Referrals: Network Your Everyday Contacts Into Sales* (3rd edn.), McGraw-Hill Books, New York, 2006.

Burg, B. and Mann, J. D., *Go-Givers Sell More*, Penguin Books, London, 2010.

Cardell, C., and Jay, J., *1001 Ways To get More Customers*, NABO Uk Ltd, London, 2014.

Carr, N., *The Digital Enterprise: How To Reshape Your Business For a Connected World*, HBR Press, Boston, Mass., 1999.

Christensen, C., *The Innovator's Dilemma: When New Technologies Cause Great Firms to Fail*, HBR Press, Boston, Mass., 1997.

Christensen, C., and Raynor, M., *The Innovators Solution: Creating and Sustaining Successful Growth*, HBR Press, Boston, Mass., 2003.

Collins, J., *Good To Great: Why Some Companies Make the Leap... and Others Don't*, Random House Business Books, London, 2001.

Conley, C., *The Rebel Rules: Daring To Be Yourself In Business*, Simon & Schuster, New York, 2001.

Croslin, D., *Innovate The Future: A Radical Approach to IT Innovation*, Prentice Hall, New York, 2010.

Csikszentmihalyi, M., Flow – *The Psychology of Happiness*, Rider, London, 1992.

Csikszentmihalyi, M., *Beyond Boredom and Anxiety*, Jossey-Bass, San Francisco, 1975.

Dayton, A., and Knapp, A., *LinkedIn and Blogs For Lawyers: Building High Value Relationships in a Digital Age*, West LegalEdcenter, Eagen, MN, 2012.
Fagerberg, J. et al., *The Oxford Handbook Of Innovation*, OUP, Oxford, 2005.
Fisher, W., *Promises to Keep: Technology, Law, and the Future of Entertainment*, Stanford University Press, 2004.
Gates, B., *Business @ the Speed of Thought: Using A Digital Nervous System*, Penguin Books, London, 1999.
Gawer, A., and Cusumano, M., *Platform Leadership: How Intel, Microsoft and Cisco Drive Industry Innovation*, HBR Press, 2002.
Gladwell, M., *The Tipping Point: How Little Things Can Make a Big Difference*, Little, Brown & Company, New York, 2000.
Godin, S., *Meatball Sundae: How New Marketing is Transforming the Business World*, Piatkus Books, London, 2007.
Goleman, D., *Emotional Intelligence: Why It Can Matter More Than IQ*, Bloomsbury Publishing, London, 1996.
Grey, A. de, and Rae, M., *Ending Aging: the Rejuvenation Breakthroughs that Could Reverse Human Aging in Our Lifetime*, St Martin's Press, New York, 2007.
Hamel, G., *Leading The Revolution*, HBR Press, 2000.
Handy, C., *The Empty Raincoat: Making Sense of the Future*, Hutchinson, London, 1994.
Handy, C., *The Elephant and the Flea*, Hutchinson, London, 2001.
Harford, T., *Adapt: Why Success Always Starts with Failure*, Abacus, London, 2012.
Harvard Business Review, *Harvard Business Review on Innovation*, Harvard Business Review, New York, 2001.
Haserot, P., *The Rainmaking Machine: Marketing Planning, Strategies and Management for Law Firms*, Garland Law Publishing, New York, 1989.
Hughes, M., *Buzz Marketing: Get People to Talk About Your Stuff*, Penguin Books, London, 2005.
Kotler, P., et al., *Marketing Moves: A New Approach to Profits, Growth, and Renewal*, HBR Press, 2002.
Kowalski, M., *Avoiding Extinction: Reimagining Legal Services for the 21st Century*, ABA Publishing, Chicago, 2012.
Kurzweil, R., *The Age of Spiritual Machines: When Computers Exceed Human Intelligence*, Penguin Books, New York, 1999.
Kurzweil, R., *The Singularity is Near: When Humans Transcend Biology*, Penguin Books, London, 2005.
Kurzweil, R., *How To Create A Mind: The Secret of Human Thought Revealed*, Penguin Books, London, 2012.
Lessig, L., *The Future of Ideas: The Fate of the Commons in a Connected World*, Vintage Books, New York, 2002.
Lessig, L., *Free Culture: The Nature And Future of Creativity*, Penguin Books, New York, 2004.
Levinson, J., and Rubin, C., *Guerrilla Marketing on the Internet*, Piatkus, London, 1995.
Lightfoot, C., née Burak, *Relative Work, Relative Leisure: Women Entrepreneurs in the 1990s*, BA (Hons) Leisure Studies, Leeds Metropolitan University, 1996.
Lightfoot, C., *The Naked Lawyer*, Ark Group, London, 2010.
Locke, C., *Gonzo Marketing: Winning Through Worst Practices*, Capstone Publishing Ltd., Oxford, 2001.

Maltz, M., *Psycho-Cybernetics*, Prentice Hall, New Jersey, 1960.
Maslow, A. H., *Motivation And Personality*, Harper, New York, 1954.
McKenna, R., *Total Access: Giving Customers What They Want in an Anytime, Anywhere World*, HBR Press, 2002.
McKeown, M., *The Truth About Innovation: A Small Book About Big Ideas*, Pearson, Harlow, 2008.
Moss-Kanter, R., *The Change Masters: Corporate Entrepreneurs At Work*, Routledge, London, 1984.
Murray, W., *Brand Storm: A Tale of Passion, Betrayal, and Revenge*, Prentice Hall, London, 2000.
Peters, T., *The Brand You 50: Fifty Ways to Transform Yourself from an 'Employee' into a Brand that Shouts Distinction, Commitment, and Passion!*, Alfred A. Knopf, Inc., New York, 1999.
Peters, T., and Waterman, R., *In Search Of Excellence: Lessons from America's Best-Run Companies*, Harper & Row, New York, 1982.
Pink, D., *A Whole New Mind: How to Thrive in the New Conceptual Age*, Cyan Books, London, 2006.
Prahalad, C.K., and Krishnan, M.S., *The New Age of Innovation: Driving Co-Created Value Through Global Networks*, McGraw-Hill Books, New York, 2008.
Rath, T., *StrengthsFinder 2.0*, Gallup Press, New York, 2007.
Rath, T., and Clifton, D., *How Full Is Your bucket?* Gallup Press, New York, 2004.
Rath, T., and Conchie, B., *Strengths Based Leadership*, Gallup Press, New York, 2008.
Russell, G., *Big Rocks: Balancing Life and Work*, Lifestyle Press, Sausalito, CA., 2005.
Scoble, R., and Israel, S., *Naked Conversations: How Blogs are Changing the Way Businesses Talk with Customers*, John Wiley & Sons, Inc., New Jersey, 2006.
Semler, R., *Maverick!*, Random House Business Books, Sydney, 2001.
Semler, R., *The Seven-Day Weekend: A Better Way to Work in the 21st Century*, Random House Business Books, Sydney, 2003.
Steare, R., *Ethicability: How to Decide What's Right and Find the Courage to Do It* (3rd edn.) Roger Steare Consulting Ltd., York, 2009.
Stratten, S., *Unmarketing: Stop Marketing, Start Engaging*, John Wiley & Sons, Inc., New Jersey, 2010.
Susskind, R., *The Future of Law: Facing the Challenges of Information Technology*, Clarendon Press, Oxford, 1996.
Susskind, R., *The Future of Law: Transforming the Law – Essays on Technology, Justice and the Legal Marketplace*, OUP, 2000.
Susskind, R., *The End Of Lawyers? Rethinking the Nature of Legal Services*, OUP, 2008.
Susskind, R., *Tomorrow's Lawyer: An Introduction to Your Futures*, OUP, 2013.
Thompson, D., *The Concise Oxford Dictionary*, (9th edn.), OUP, 1995.
Tupman, S., *Why Lawyers Should Eat Bananas*, Simon Tupman Presentations Pty Ltd., Byron Bay, 2000.
Watkins, J., *An Insider's Guide on Hiring a Business Attorney: And How to Make the Relationship Work*, Ocelot Atlanta LLC., Atlanta, GA, 2010.
Welch, J. F., Jack: *Straight from the Gut*, Warner Books, Inc., New York, 2001.
Wright, J., *Blog Marketing: The Revolutionary New Way to Increase Sales, Build Your Brand and Get Exceptional Results*, McGraw-Hill Books, New York, 2006.
Zeng, M., and Williamson, P., *Dragons At Your Door: How Chinese Cost Innovation Is Disrupting Global Competition*, HBR Press, 2007.

articles, journals, and reports

Berners-Lee, T., 'The World Wide Web – Past, Present and Future', *Journal of Digital Information*, Article No. 1, Volume 1 Issue 1, 17 July 2006.

BlizzardInternet.com, 'The Internet Future is Closer Than You Think', 14 August 2006. See: http://newsletter.blizzardinternet.com/the-internet-future-is-closer-than-you-think/2006/08/14.

Boswell, W., 'A Short History of the Internet', part of The New York Times Company. See: http://websearch.about.com/od/whatistheinternet/a/historyinternet.htm.

Boswell, W., 'The World Wide Web and The Internet – Not The Same Thing', part of The New York Times Company. See: http://websearch.about.com/od/whatistheinternet/a/worldwideweb.htm.

Braithwaite, T, 'Companies learn value of blogging', *Financial Times*, 17 July 2006.

Carroll, J., '10 big trends for the legal profession', 14 December 2005. See: www.jimcarroll.com/weblog/archives/000712.html.

Cerf, V., 'The Future of the Internet', Interview by Jennifer Robinson, *Gallup Management Journal*, 13 April 2006. See: http://gmj.gallup.com/content/default.asp?ci=22348.

Content Wire.com, 'FRESH PICKS: Law Profession Gets to Grip with Knowledge', 21 Aug 2006. See: www.content-wire.com/FreshPicks/Index.cfm?ccs=86&cs=4253.

Daniel, D., 'Networks of the future' 21 August 2006. See: www.computerworld.com/action/article.do?command=viewArticleBasic&taxonomyId=16&articleId=9002591

'Talking Semantics', *Director Magazine*, September 2006, p66–68.

'Apple and NBC enter the digital video race', *Financial Times*, 13 September 2006.

Gartenberg, M., 'Technology now defines the business', 10 August 2006. See: www.computerworld.com.au/index.php/id;61559839;fp;4;fpid;1398720840.

Hornsby, W., 'Improving the Delivery of Affordable Legal Services Through the Internet: A Blueprint for the Shift to a Digital Paradigm', ABA Standing Committee on the Delivery of Legal Services. See: www.abanet.org/legalservices/delivery/deltech.html.

Keynote, 'The Legal Services Market: Executive Summary'. See: www.keynote.co.uk/kn2k1/13712_02//doc_4.htm?uni=1155561027.

Keynote, 'The Legal Services Market: The Future'. See: www.keynote.co.uk/kn2k1/13712_02//doc_4.htm?uni=1155560649

Lightfoot, C., 'Understanding and Exploiting Opportunities in relation to the Future of the Law in the Digital Age: research, ideation, business model and development concepts – proposals for consideration', Leeds, 2006.

Martin, J., 'Gurgle, gurgle ...Google', *The Sunday Times, News Review*, 24 September 2006.

Maslow, A. H., 'A Theory of Human Motivation', *Psychology Review*, 1943.

Miniwatts Marketing Group, 'Internet Growth And Stats: Today's road to eCommerce and global trade', *Miniwatts Marketing Group*, 10 April 2006. See: www.allaboutmarketresearch.com/internet.htm.

Miniwatts Marketing Group 'Internet Users By Language', *Miniwatts Marketing Group*, 2006. See www.internetworldstats.com/stats7.htm.

Miniwatts Marketing Group 'Internet Usage in European Union: Internet User Statistics & Population for the 25 European Union countries and regions', *Miniwatts Marketing Group*, 2006. See: www.internetworldstats.com/stats9.htm.

Nerds2.0.1 wiring the world , 'The Future of the Internet: A Bigger Pipe'. See: www.pbs.org/opb/nerds2.0.1/wiring_world/future.html

Peters, A., 'Lawyers Stop Bowing Before Billable Hour: Firms use advanced software to encourage alternative billing arrangements', *Fulton County Daily Report*, 8 September 2006. See: www.law.com/jsp/legaltechnology/pubArticleLT.jsp?id=1157629871529
Price Waterhouse Cooper, 'UK Economic Outlook July 2006', July 2006.
PRLeap.com, 24 September 2006. See: www.prleap.com/pr/49226.
PRweb.com, 'New PR Firm is First to Combine Traditional, Digital Methods for Boomer Marketing', PR Web. See: www.prweb.com/releases/2006/9/prweb440547.htm.
Roulac, S., 'Learning How To Break Away To Get Alpha Results', *Global CEO*, 2008.
SeoChat.com, 'The Future of Search', *SEOChat.com*. See: www.seochat.com/c/a/Search-Engine-News/The-Future-of-Search.
SiteProNews, 'Five Social Media Predictions for 2010, *SiteProNews*, 11 January 2010. See: www.sitepronews.com/2010/01/11/five-social-media-predictions-for-2010/?utm_source=feedburner&utm_medium=email&utm_campaign=Feed%3A+sitepronews%2FICnA+%28SiteProNews%29.
Sloan, P. and Kaihla, P., 'Blogging for big bucks', *Business 2.0 Magazine*, 22 August 2006. See: http://money.cnn.com/2006/08/21/technology/bloggingdollars0822.biz2.
Terrett, A. and Monaghan, I., 'The Internet – An Introduction for Lawyers' in Edwards, L. and Waelde, C., *Law and the Internet: A Framework for Electronic Commerce*, Hart Publishing, Portland, OR, 2002.
Thirdage Inc., 'Tech Terms: Cyberspace'. See: www.thirdage.com/cgi-bin/glosdb.cgi?glos_name=tech&action=view&term_name=Cyberspace.
Thirdage Inc., 'Tech Terms: Internet'. See: www.thirdage.com/cgi-bin/glosdb.cgi?glos_name=tech&action=view&term_name=Internet.
Thirdage Inc., 'Tech Terms: WWW' http://www.thirdage.com/cgi-bin/glosdb.cgi?glos_name=tech&action=view&term_name=WWW;
TimesUnion.com, 'Turn trends into business advantages', *TimesUnion.com*, 8 August 2006. See: http://timesunion.com/AspStories/story.asp?storyID=506509&category=BUSINESS&newsdate=8/8/2006
Webber, G., 'Put A Brand On Your Work', *Fast Company*, 2000.
Webopedia.com, 'The Difference between the Internet and the World Wide Web', Jupitermedia Corporation. See: www.webopedia.com/DidYouKnow/Internet/2002/Web_vs_Internet.asp.
WebProNews.com. See: www.webpronews.com/blogtalk/blogtalk/wpn-58–20060912ProfessionalBloggingEffectiveOutsourcing.html.
Wright, G., 'Building a Thriving Legal Market', *Yorkshire Today*, 19 September 2006. See: www.yorkshiretoday.co.uk/ViewArticle2.aspx?SectionID=1299&ArticleID=1775336.

websites and links

EntrepreneurLawyer and the naked lawyer stuff

- http://entrepreneurlawyer.co.uk
- www.youtube.com/TheNakedLawyer
- www.youtube.com/EntrepreneurLawyer
- www.linkedin.com/in/chrissielightfoot
- www.twitter.com/TheNakedLawyer
- www.twitter.com/EntrepreneurLaw
- www.facebook.com/EntrepreneurLawyer
- http://budurl.com/TNL1
- http://budurl.com/mutiny

http://budurl.com/SNzenLaw
http://budurl.com/ItsABoxOfFrogs

In general stuff

- http://en.wikipedia.org
- http://www.personalbrandingblog.com
- http://hootsuite.com
- http://budurl.com
- http://hashable.com
- http://twitter.com
- http://facebook.com
- http://linkedin.com
- http://youtube.com

Illustrations

www.ingramcontent.com/pod-product-compliance
Ingram Content Group UK Ltd.
Pitfield, Milton Keynes, MK11 3LW, UK
UKHW051931100926
8556IPUK00022B/1477

9 781783 581740